WITHDRAWN

**Psychology
in
Progress**

General editor: Peter Herriot

Issues in
Childhood Social
Development

Psychology in Progress

Already available
Aspects of Memory
edited by Michael M. Gruneberg and Peter Morris

Thinking in Perspective
Critical essays in the study of thought processes
edited by Andrew Burton and John Radford

Forthcoming
Philosophical Problems in Psychology
edited by Neil Bolton

The School Years: A Social Psychological Perspective
edited by John Coleman

Brain, Behaviour and Evolution
edited by David Oakley and Henry Plotkin

Issues in
Childhood Social
Development

edited by
HARRY McGURK

METHUEN

First published in 1978 by
Methuen & Co Ltd
11 New Fetter Lane London EC4P 4EE

This collection © Methuen & Co Ltd 1978
Individual chapters © the respective authors 1978

Printed in Great Britain at the
University Press, Cambridge

ISBN *(hardbound)* 0 416 70560 X
(paperback) 0 416 71500 1

Contents

Notes on the contributors

Anthony Ambrose is a developmental psychologist, whose research field has been the organization and development of social behaviour in early human infancy. With a wide orientation ranging from psychoanalysis to ethology, his recent publications concentrate on the theoretical problems of developmental psychology. Believing that its real foundations lie in evolutionary biology, he is now exploring the implications of this for research and social application. He is currently Director of Minster Lovell Mill, Oxford, which is a study centre for the review of research and policy in the sciences of human development.

Jeanne Brooks-Gunn is currently a research scientist in the Institute for Research in Human Development, Educational Testing Service, Princeton, New Jersey, and in the Department of Pediatrics, Roosevelt Hospital, New York City. She is also Associate Director of the Institute for the Study of Exceptional Children in Princeton, New Jersey. A developmental psychologist, she carried out her graduate work at Harvard University and the University of Pennsylvania. Her research is primarily on infant development, focusing on the nature of early social relationships, the development of self-concept, and the effects of handicaps and at-risk conditions on social and cognitive development. She is also conducting work on psychosocial aspects of reproduction.

Charles K. Crook carried out his doctoral research in the Department of Psychology at Cambridge University. He has been a Research Associate at the Brown University Child Study Center and currently holds a Research Fellowship at Strathclyde University. His published work includes studies of sensory development during infancy and the control of feeding in neonates. Current research interests concern the dynamics of interactions between mothers and their infants.

Hans G. Furth has been Professor of Psychology at the Catholic University of America since 1960. He is the author of *Thinking without Language* (Free Press, 1966), *Deafness and Learning* (Wadsworth, 1973), *Piaget and Knowledge* (Prentice-Hall, 1969), *Piaget for Teachers* (Prentice-Hall, 1970) and *Thinking Goes to School* (Oxford University Press, 1975). He is currently researching children's understanding of social institutions, about which he is preparing a book.

Willard W. Hartup is Professor of Child Psychology and Director of the Institute of Child Development, University of Minnesota. He has been interested for some time in the social development of children and his recent research concerns peer relations in childhood – their contributions to child development and the conditions that enhance them. He is an adviser to numerous professional organizations and governmental agencies, and is Editor of *Review of Child Development Research* (Volume 6) which will be devoted to syntheses of scientific work originating in the non-English speaking countries of the world.

Corinne Hutt is Reader in Psychology at the University of Keele and is involved in a current research project on play, exploration and learning for the Department of Education and Science. With her husband, John Hutt, she has written or edited the following books: *Direct Observation and the Measurement of Behaviour, Behaviour Studies in Psychiatry* and *Early Human Development* and in 1972 she published *Males and Females*. She is currently engaged in writing a monograph on play.

Michael Lewis is Director of the Institute for the Study of Handicapped Infants and senior scientist at Educational Testing Service, Princeton. He is also clinical professor of pediatric psychology at Columbia University Medical Center. His interests include the social, emotional and perceptual-cognitive development in early childhood. His most recent books include *The Development of Affect* and

Social Cognition and the Development of Self, both published by Plenum Press.

Harry McGurk is currently Senior Lecturer in the Department of Psychology, University of Surrey. He is the author of numerous research papers on perceptual and cognitive development during infancy and early childhood. In addition, he has written an introductory text on the study of child development and has edited a collection of papers on ecological factors in human development. His current research activity includes a longitudinal study of the influence of hospital care of newborn infants upon their subsequent social and affective development, particularly where any abnormality attends the birth process.

Colin Rogers is lecturer in the Department of Educational Research, University of Lancaster, where he has responsibility for courses on the social psychology of education. He has published jointly with Dr P. Warr on the area of person perception and has recently been awarded the degree of Ph.D. by the University of Leicester for his thesis on the development of person perception in middle childhood. His current research interests focus on an application of Attribution Theory to a child's developing understanding of aspects of schooling, for example judgements of success and failure.

H. Rudolph Schaffer is Professor of Psychology at the University of Strathclyde. He is the author of *Growth of Sociability* (Penguin) and *Mothering* (Open Books/Fontana and Harvard University Press), and editor of *Origins of Human Social Relations* and *Studies in Mother–Infant Interaction* (both Academic Press). His research interests primarily concern early human development, with particular reference to interpersonal relationships in infancy and socialization processes.

James Youniss is Professor of Psychology at the Boys Town Center for the Study of Youth Development. He has written over fifty journal articles, chapters and review papers. His research interests include children's knowledge of interpersonal relations, how knowledge is socialized yet individually constructed, and also operations by which images are generated and connected.

Editor's introduction

In every culture the human infant is born into a complex network of social relationships extending from the immediate family, however organized, to the community and society within which the family unit is embedded. Whether the goal of development is viewed from a biological perspective (i.e. the survival of the individual to reproductive maturity and his successful involvement in reproductive activity), or whether development is seen as having other more psychologically or socially orientated goals, it is clear that in order to adapt successfully to and function effectively in the social network into which he is born, the individual has to gain developmental mastery of an extensive array of personal and social skills. Social competence involves the recognition of self as one among others; the capacity to enter into relationships with others, both between-generational (caretaker/child) and within-generational (peer) relationships; the ability to go beyond the behaviour of others to the intentions and dispositions underlying that behaviour and to organize one's own behaviour in terms of the perceived expectancies of others. Beyond the immediate context of interpersonal behaviour, social competence requires some understanding, implicit or explicit, of the structure of the larger society of which the individual is a part; of the function of different roles which the individual may occupy or with which he may interact within that structure and of the mores standards and values which govern relationships between roles. From this perspective, the endowment of the newborn infant is meagre indeed, restricted as he is to a few quasi-reflexive, biologically adaptive behaviours such as sucking, grasping, looking, hearing and crying–vocalizing. Without the support of a nurturant environment he would not survive and, at least from this viewpoint, his relationship with caretakers is one of total physical dependency. Yet, from this improbable beginning there emerges through childhood and adolescence into adulthood an individual who can engage in enduring relationships with other individuals, who can function effectively in groups and who can interact successfully with the larger social order. Of course, there is a wide range of diversity in the expression of these abilities from one individual to another. Some make less successful adaptations than others while a few individuals become social innovators, leaving their own distinctive impress upon society. It is with the psychological processes which underlie these outcomes that the student of social development is concerned.

It is due in large part to the apparent impressive helplessness of the human infant that psychology relied for so long upon models of social development which assigned to the individual himself an entirely passive role in the developmental process. Historically, there have been two conflicting, equally unilateral interpretations of psychological development. On the one hand, there were those who, impressed by the apparent regularity and uniformity of development, albeit within a range of individual differences, argued that development was determined by the unfolding of a biologically programmed process of maturation. On this account, the individual is the passive victim of his biological inheritance and experience plays only a modulating role, providing the occasion for minor variation upon a universal theme. Here development is an inside-out process and, as with other aspects of behavioural development, social behaviours emerge in maturationally determined sequence, biologically adapted to the environment in which they are expressed.

In contrast to the above, there have been others who, more impressed by individual variability in developmental phenomena than by any underlying regularity have attributed to environmental factors the primary causal influence in determining developmental outcome. Here, learning theory is taken as the model and social development is viewed as a process of rendering social that which is initially asocial. On this account development is an outside-in process and, again, the individual is ascribed a passive role. The behaviour of the infant and young child is shaped by parental child rearing practices and by the modelling and other learning experiences to which he is exposed. The child is viewed as an empty vessel into which are poured societally approved patterns of interpersonal conduct which are subsequently expressed behaviourally for their reinforcement value.

Few contemporary psychologists of childhood would espouse either of these extreme models of social development. Biological structure and an environment in which to function are necessary prerequisites for the manifestation of behaviour. Without structure there could be no behaviour and an environment is necessary before the behavioural propensity of any structure can be expressed. Thus, the necessity to recognize the joint influence of biological and environmental factors upon development is now generally acknowledged and an interactionist perspective is reflected in most contemporary theorizing on social development. In their original formulations, however, interactionist accounts were relatively static and still ascribed to the individual only a passive role in the developmental process. In such an account of social development, the infant might be seen as beginning life with a set of behaviours which are adapted for development in a particular environment. However, the course of development is canalized by the particular kinds of environmental encounter experienced by the infant. If he is exposed to a benign, adaptive environment which is sensitively responsive to his crying, vocalizing and other behaviours then the developmental prognosis is good. On the other hand, if the environment responds indifferently to these early behaviours then development may be deflected into maladaptive pathways. Moreover, this kind of model holds that within a wide range of individual differences in biological/constitutional endowment, initial exposure to benign environments will result in satisfactory outcomes. At the same time, only biologically/constitutionally robust individuals will be resistant to developmental casualty in less supportive environments. Accordingly, the model is truly interactive but notice that from the viewpoint of the developing individual it is still a passive model. The major difference between this version of interaction and the earlier unilateral models is that now the individual is perceived as being impelled along his developmental course by two sets of forces instead of one.

More recently developmental psychologists have come to recognize the necessity to include a role for the child himself in shaping his own development. This newer thinking recognizes that social development has a biological basis and recognizes also that environment, in interaction with biological endowment has a significant part to play in influencing development outcome. But it recognizes in addition that there is a third force operating: the child himself. Thus, the biologically organized individual not only elicits responses from his social environment and responds to it but in responding alters his environment and, in turn is himself modified by the changes he has brought about. Hence, the interaction process is reciprocal and dynamic. Moreover, such dynamic reciprocity is evident from the infant's first encounters with the social world and continues throughout the developmental process. From this modified perspective the development of social behaviour is seen neither as determined solely by maturational processes nor as the outcome of environmentally determined behavioural shaping. Rather, social behaviour develops through the child's active participation in social encounters in the course of which he modifies the behaviour of others as well as being influenced by them. Similarly, the development of social knowledge and social understanding proceeds, on this account, not according to passive learning processes but in terms of the child's active construction of a social universe through his interaction with the social order.

Issues contributing to and arising from the evolvement of this modified perspective are the subject matter of the present volume. It comprises a collection of original essays by prominent British and American investigators actively engaged in researching the development of social behaviour and social understanding during infancy and childhood. The aim of the book is not to provide an exhaustive, definitive account of all aspects of childhood social development and, thus, from its contents are omitted some topics which commonly appear in a comprehensive textbook. Similarly, in preparing their chapters, authors were not expected, textbook style, merely to survey the research literature within their field of discourse. Rather, they were expected to develop their own distinctive viewpoint and contribution to the field in the service of presenting an account of research in action and debate in progress in this important area of psychological enquiry.

The opening chapter by Ambrose looks at the biological basis of human social development and considers social development in evolutionary perspective. In particular, Ambrose considers the phylogenetic and ontogenetic development of those genetically transmitted behaviour systems that have adaptive social significance for the human organism. Throughout the chapter the interactive relationship between genotype and environment and their joint influence upon ontogeny are themes which are repeatedly stressed.

Chapter 2, by Schaffer and Crook, relates how the biologically given, endogenously organized behaviours of the young infant are integrated into a social context in the course of infant–caretaker interaction. Particular attention is given to the role of the mother in attributing social significance to the infant's early behaviour. A recurrent theme is the extent to which maternal behaviour becomes entrained with that of the infant, during which processes the behaviour of both partners is reciprocally modified. The authors argue that these initial behavioural 'conversations' lay the foundation for the development of social communication.

In the third chapter Brooks-Gunn and Lewis discuss how, through interaction with the social world, the infant acquires knowledge of self, of others and of the relationships between self and others. It is argued that through the active deployment of his perceptual and cognitive capacities the human infant is engaged in constructing his own social reality from the earliest stages of development.

The chapter by Rogers, chapter 4, carries the discussion of social perception and social cognition into middle childhood. Perception of self and perception of others are major themes of this chapter also. Rogers describes how the child's perception and understanding of other people proceeds from a state where global impressions are dominated by consideration only of such concrete attributes as general identity, appearance, possessions and the like, towards an increasingly differentiated state where perception of other individuals is informed by inferences about unique, integrated, underlying psychological dispositions, motivations and intentions. Changes in the child's cognitive and information processing skills are held to underlie these developments.

There is a vast literature on social development which stresses the role of adults as the agents of socialization. Much less attention has been given to the influence of peers on the development of social behaviour and social knowledge. In this respect, chapter 5 by Hartup provides a timely overview of the work, much of it conducted under his own aegis, on this emergent topic. Hartup discusses the significance of peer relationships not only for their part in contributing to normal social development but also with respect to the potential role of peers as child 'therapists' in the modification of developmental social deviance.

The issue of sex differences in social development arises at different points throughout this volume. Sex-role differentiation in social development is the substantive topic of chapter 6 by Hutt. Like Ambrose, Hutt discusses the joint influence of biological and environmental factors on the child's developing awareness of sex role identity. Hutt offers an epigenetic account of genotype- environment interaction in the development of sex role diffentiation.

In chapter 7, Youniss argues for conceptual clarification of the role of cognition in social development. Rejecting the view of cognition as an intervening variable between environmental input and behavioural output, Youniss, from a Piagetean perspective, argues that social development involves the acquisition of social knowledge as conceptions of interpersonal relations. Knowledge of relations involves understanding them as rule systems for interaction so that, within the framework advanced by Youniss, there is an unseverable connection between the development of social knowledge and the development of social behaviour.

The final chapter, by Furth, is also written from a Piagetean standpoint. Furth considers children's understanding of society at large and presents findings from his own extensive investigations of the development of knowledge of how commerce, trade and industry, education and government function. Furth argues for a model of the development of societal understanding in which the stages postulated parallel those advanced by Piaget to account for the development of formal operational thinking.

My task in editing this volume was much facilitated by the cooperation I received from all of the contributors and by their tolerance in responding to my requests for clarification, modification and revision. The responsibility for the final form and contents of the book is, of course, my own but I would like to express my gratitude to the colleagues whose work is presented here. I am also indebted to Peter Herriot, the series editor, and to Vanessa Mitchell of Methuen for their patience, forebearance and support at all stages in the preparation of the volume. Finally, grateful thanks are due to Dawn Lewis for her assistance with indexing and in preparing the manuscript for publication.

HARRY MCGURK

1 Human social development: an evolutionary-biological perspective

Anthony Ambrose

Orientation

The approach to be described in this chapter, based on evolutionary theory, implies that the relevance of biology for understanding the development of human social behaviour and action is far wider and more fundamental than is generally accepted in psychology. The term 'biological', when used in theoretical discussions of human behaviour, is still commonly equated with concepts such as 'physiological', 'maturational', 'innate', and even 'animal-like'. Contrary to the limited view reflected by such uses of the term, it is argued that a biological approach has major implications for the whole manner of thinking about human social activity and developmental process. In particular, it provides an integrative conceptual framework within which the tremendous diversity and complexity of the phenomena can be ordered, it is a guide in the construction of models that underlie the formulation of research problems, and it indicates a variety of methodological approaches to different kinds of problem within the total framework. Along the way, furthermore, it points strongly towards a position that would view social development, not just as one aspect to be studied among several others such as the cognitive, perceptual, emotional and physiological aspects, but as an area that has profound theoretical significance for all aspects of human functioning.

2   Issues in childhood social development

Sources of resistance to a biological perspective

Before elaborating these themes it is as well to recognize that, historically, there has been intense bias against considering human social activity in any sort of biological terms. Since this bias continues at the present time, it is worth taking note of its various sources, each of which can now be seen to have taken a very partial, if not prejudiced, view of the social significance of biology. The common feature in all the objections that have been raised to 'biologizing' in this field is that they regard it as leading to conclusions that are socially unacceptable. The most extreme form of this was Spencer's (1900) Social Darwinism which attempted to justify the 'shoulderings aside of the weak by the strong, which leave so many in shallows and miseries' in terms of an evolutionary theory that explains the emergence of species as the survival of the fittest in an endless struggle between predators and victims. Despite the logical defects of Spencer's use of Darwin's theory (Sorokin, 1928), it effectively bolstered opposition to the values on which social reformist and liberal movements were being built. Further depressing implications were drawn from the instinct theories of Freud (1930), McDougall (1908), Lorenz (1966), and others, which attributed to man in-built drives of a socially disruptive nature. The ideas that there is an animal as well as a finer side to human nature, and that social conflict and war are inevitable seemed implicit in these theories.

The understandable objections to these positions drew support from those schools of anthropology and sociology which took the view that, for purposes of studying human society and social development, man is not to be regarded as a biological organism at all. According to this view the differences between man and animals are decisive: not being a creature governed by innate behaviour patterns and with a unique capacity to conceptualize, man has his own special means of adaptation, namely culture. The information pool he has come to rely on is not carried by genes but is transmitted culturally, and the variability and rapid changes that occur in his way of life are due, not to natural evolution, but to cultural or social evolution. Fully compatible with this view was the outlook in psychology. Modelling itself on physics, its prime objective was to arrive by experimental means at generalizations about behaviour that held over wide ranges of the animal kingdom. With the upsurge of learning theory, and in keeping with a mechanistic viewpoint, the central focus of interest became the modifiability of behaviour. While due recognition was given to the biological status of the anatomical and physiological substrate of learning, this was treated in learning models essentially as a constant. There are many psychologists still who take no interest in biological considerations on the grounds that they cannot be altered and that the main aim in psychology is to understand how changes in behaviour take place or can be brought about.

Another more justifiable, reason for a negative attitude towards biological interpretations of human affairs has been a tendency on the part of some writers to draw conclusions that go beyond what the evidence warrants. Many of the recent books that have attempted to popularize ethology, summarized by Reynolds (1976), have taken principles that apply to social behaviour in animals and freely extrapolated them to the human level with little or no regard to whether or not the mechanisms involved are the same.

Toward modern behavioural biology

In relation to the perspective on human social development to be described, all of the biases just outlined against biological thinking will be seen to be misconceived. The reasons for this are of two kinds. First, over the last thirty years behavioural biology has itself been undergoing major transformation. As a result of the growing interaction of the two 'classical' schools of animal behaviour study, ethology and biopsychology, now leading to their integration, conceptual clarifications have taken place with profound implications for both comparative and developmental perspectives. Emphasis on the differences between species, even closely related ones, has shown that the possibilities of arriving at cross-species generalizations about mechanisms of behaviour and development are much more limited than was previously believed. Exposure of the misleading classification of behaviour as either innate or learned, inherited or acquired, has led to new appreciation of the complexities of organism–environment interaction that determines the course of development of social behaviour. Progress in behaviour genetics has further undermined the foundations of extreme positions regarding the causation of development, whether environmentalist or nativist. Dependence of the modifiability of an individual's behaviour on genetically based potential and limitations which vary both across types of behaviour and across age is now recognized to be ubiquitous. These and other conceptual developments led to new assumptions which now underlie the modern biological outlook on behavioural development. Much of the negative bias towards it, especially in psychology, is based on assumptions that are now outdated.

A second kind of reason for misconceptions in psychology about the value of a biological approach has to do with failure to understand the scope of biology itself as a science. Concerned with all aspects of life in the animal and plant kingdoms from the simplest cellular forms to man and from molecular to ecological levels, it has a very large number of branches of study. Among the various traditional classifications of these, one of the most basic is into the fields of functional and evolutionary biology (Mayr, 1976). The questions asked in the former are of the kind 'how does the organism and its parts operate?'; those in the latter are of the kind 'how did it become like it is?' and 'what is this or that part for?' The fields therefore necessarily differ greatly in outlook, basic concepts and method. Because traditional psychology has been so preoccupied with the study of behaviour modifiability through learning, its interest in what biology might have to contribute has been limited almost entirely to functional biology and particularly to neurophysiology. Thus it has looked towards one side of biological science and almost completely ignored the other. It is here proposed that evolutionary biology, far from being irrelevant to psychology in general and to developmental psychology in particular, forms the foundation for a biological approach to the study of human social development that will provide both rationale and direction for its theoretical and methodological progress.

The theory on which evolutionary biology is now based is known as neo-Darwinism, or the modern synthetic theory of evolution. This is really classical Darwinian theory which, since the 1920s, has been refined in the light of findings from population genetics (e.g. Mettler and Gregg, 1969). Darwin's (1859) theory of the evolution of the form and function of the characters of any species explains it as the outcome of a process of natural selection acting on genetic variation. The outcome, however, is not uniform within a species. Within any population there is a considerable genetic variability. This is now understood as a necessary insurance such that if a major change in the environment were to take place, as has so often happened over geological time, at least some of the variations might be adaptive enough to the new selection pressures to ensure survival of the species.

Among the many branches of evolutionary biology are those that study social behaviour and social organization in animals, namely ethology, biopsychology and sociobiology. It has been demonstrated in these disciplines that characters of behaviour, like those of anatomy and physiology, are subject to the principles of neo-Darwinian theory.

Not only can species-typical behaviour be used as a classificatory or taxonomic character (Lorenz, 1950), but it is to be explained as part of an adaptive strategy that enables species members to survive and reproduce in the face of natural selection pressures characteristic of the environment in which the species evolved (Tinbergen, 1965; Hinde, 1970; Wilson, 1976).

Now the important thing to notice about this kind of explanation is that, in order fully to understand how the evolutionary process works out for any particular species, five related but different kinds of knowledge are needed. First, if the behavioural properties of the species have evolved, then they must have an evolutionary history which can, in principle, be described. Second, if they are adaptive, it should be possible to show how they are, that is, what functions they serve. Furthermore, explanation is needed of the unique arrangement of behavioural features that have evolved in the form of that species. For this, knowledge is required, thirdly, of the nature of the natural environment that exerts the selection pressures, and, fourthly, of the nature of the genotypes on which these pressures operate. The operation of these two kinds of factor takes place, of course, during the life-cycle of each individual member of the species. The biological criterion of the adaptive effectiveness of each individual genotype is the reproductive success of the individual, which is necessary in sufficient numbers to ensure continuity of the species. This adaptiveness is tested ultimately in the adulthood of each member. But it is also being tested at all points in ontogeny up to that stage in the ability of the individual to survive, to thrive and to develop towards reproductive success. Complete understanding of the behavioural phylogeny of a species therefore requires knowledge of a fifth kind, namely of how behavioural ontogeny occurs under the influence of both genotype and environment. As Lehrman (1970) points out, to know what is the adult functional arrangement of behaviour *towards* which development takes place gives no indication of how the development is brought about *from* the starting point of the previous reproductive success, that is the zygote.

Thus the study of behavioural development falls into place as an integral part of the study of how the life of the species is maintained. Its context is the evolutionary process, which gives it ultimate meaning. Furthermore, this context entails a conception of the forces that shape behaviour and cause its development as being *both* environmental and genetic. Individual development then becomes meaningful in terms of the natural environment in which it occurs and the genotype of the individual. In man, perhaps more than any other organism, both of these kinds of factor vary across individuals. And although his environment is now totally different from that in which he evolved, this makes no difference logically to its status in the study of development. Culture, as part of our species' adaptive strategy, may have changed that early environment out of all recognition; but its products still exert pressures of natural selection even though they also exert another kind of pressure as well, namely cultural selection.

This, then, is the framework for the biological approach to the study of human social development to be described in this chapter. It focusses attention on five related but different issues, namely, evolutionary history, adaptive function, the natural environment, genotype and developmental process. The methodological approach required to study them is quite different in each case. Space allows consideration only of the bare bones of each, and illustration of the kinds of findings and insights that result from their use will have to be highly selective.

Because the overall approach is in fact an amalgam of different approaches, appreciation of its nature requires a facility that is normally part of the training of biologists. This is a capacity to vary the perspectives or measuring scales of both time and space used in thinking about social development. The time scales range from geological periods through the life-cycle to the matter of seconds it takes to make an adaptive response. The space scales range from the whole world that now comprises the social ecology of man to the intra-uterine and organic environment in which the parts of the foetus emerge. In short, the perspectives needed go far beyond those that stem from the limitations of what it is possible to study in the laboratory. They are of a scope that reflects the real nature of man, from his species origins to his life as a biological and social individual of a very unique kind.

Evolutionary history

Problems and approach

Descriptive study of the evolutionary history of man's social behavioural development is producing information relevant to questions about the following kinds of issue: (i) the origins and precursors of many of its features; (ii) the nature and extent of its uniqueness; (iii) the kinds of changes and trends that have led to the particular evolutionary outcome seen in man and (iv) the nature of the environments, physical and social, in which these changes took place. The changes concern not just specifically social features, but also structures, capacities and processes on which these depend. Descriptions of these kinds enable man to be seen against an evolutionary background instead of in isolation. They are also an essential preliminary for study of the processes of natural selection by means of which the basic character of his social behaviour and development evolved, to be considered in the following section.

Questions about the above issues refer essentially to the non-human primates that were in direct line with man as his evolutionary ancestors. These, including all the forms of hominid and early man, are of course extinct. Their characteristics have to be inferred, therefore, from indirect evidence. Such evidence comes from sources of two kinds: those living primates that are offshoots from the direct line but whose origin is the same as that of man's ancestors, and palaeontological and archaeological finds of the fossils of hominids.

Hominid fossils, and the locations and geological levels at which they are found, reveal clear trends in the evolution of morphology and body function; and a surprising amount can also be inferred from this kind of data on broad evolutionary trends in behaviour and in social organization (Campbell, 1971). It is in the attempt to obtain a more detailed picture of these behavioural and social trends that the living primates are proving of such value. Their extensive study (e.g. DeVore, 1965) is now yielding indications of the nature of the ecological parameters within which man's primate ancestry evolved, first in an arboreal forest environment and later in an open savannah environment. Furthermore, those primates that show some significant resemblance to the hominids, such as the common baboon in respect of its savannah environment, and the chimpanzee in respect to its physical similarities, can be used as animal models for some aspects of the social behaviour and organization of early man (Reynolds, 1976). When modern man is looked at in this perspective various unique features stand out, but in a context of many evolutionary continuities.

The fruitfulness of this approach is heavily dependent upon the care with which the comparative method is applied. The different kinds of problem that arise depending on the subject matter for comparison have been reviewed, for body form and function by Campbell (1971), for behaviour by Hinde (1970), for developmental change by Ambrose (1976), and for social organization by Crook (1976). The validity of conclusions about evolutionary relationship between species, about trends of evolutionary change and their significance for social development in modern man rests on the correctness of evaluations of several kinds. These include assessment of the classificatory equivalence of the characters being compared, of the extent of their similarity and difference, and of whether characters that show similarity are homologous or analogous, all of which are discussed by von Cranach (1976) and Atz (1970). In comparisons of man with non-human primates, while most morphological characters are homologous, having common origin, behavioural and social organizational characters may be at most analogous, having similarity of adaptive function though not necessarily of causal mechanism. The logic and usefulness of analogical comparisons has been examined by Masters (1976).

Body form and function
Man is unique among the primates in respect to his complete bipedalism, the refinement of his apparatus for communication by vocal and facial expressive means, absence of an estrus sexual cycle, and the size and complexity of his brain, especially the cortex. These unique features all emerged during the twenty million years or so of evolution in an increasingly open savannah environment from the earliest hominid Ramapithecus, through Autralopithecus and Homo erectus, to Homo sapiens (Pfeiffer, 1969). Many other essential features of man had previously emerged along the primate ancestry in an arboreal forest environment, making possible the later transition to the savannahs. These include stereoscopic binocular colour vision, the opposable thumb and the power grip, erect posture, and increases in brain size (Campbell, 1971). Other features had appeared still earlier with the coming of the mammals: the capability to maintain an appropriate body temperature under varying conditions, teeth of different shapes suitable for tearing or grinding, and a new kind of reproductive system involving retention of the egg inside the mother and a dependent parental relationship. The overall trend of all of these evolutionary developments is in the direction of continually increasing flexibility of adaptiveness to environments, physical and social, that become more and more variable and complex. Hence early man was already unique in his capacity to exploit a wide range of food resources, in mobility with the hands free for carrying, in ability to manipulate objects and to appreciate them as objects and not just patterns, in the scope of his communication system, and perhaps most significant of all, in his capacities for exploration, learning, information storage and symbolic thinking. These capacities, associated with massive develop-

ment of the cerebral cortex, were decisive for the emergence of the most unique of all man's specializations, his capacity for culture. A question of particular interest, therefore, concerns the nature of the environment that precipitated these developments.

An important feature of the period of massive increase in brain size is that this was also the period that saw the rise of hunting (Pfeiffer, 1969). The deposits containing hominids with the largest increases in cranial capacity are also the ones that contain the biggest proportion of large mammals killed. The period was also one associated with improvement in tool-making, for example from crudely pointed pebbles to hand-axes carefully chipped on both sides. The causal implications of these associations are controversial. The long held idea that the great expansion and development of the human brain can be explained by the increasing use of tools has been challenged by recent evidence. It is now known, for example, that apes already have that capability (e.g. Goodall, 1965). Also, study of endocasts of Australopithecus indicates that although its brain was much smaller than that of Homo, the frontal lobes even at that stage had a typically human morphology (Pfeiffer, 1969). It appears, therefore, that the brain had already developed sufficiently to provide the essential preadaptation necessary for tool-use, symbolic functioning and conceptual awareness in Homo.

If development of the brain and symbolic functioning were not, then, a by-product of tool-use, how is their emergence to be explained? Reynolds's proposal (1976) works the other way: 'that conceptual thought needs to be considered as a primary datum causally underlying the development of the big brain in our genus, *Homo*'. He makes the far-reaching hypothesis that the demands of the environment which led to conceptual thinking were not technological (e.g. stone-making and use of fire) but sociological. 'The emergence of man was essentially a coming into self-awareness of what was already a highly complex social being, and I think that this coming into conceptual awareness was the crucial and fundamental adaptation that enabled man to master first the savannah and later the rest of the world ... This was man's key social adaptation to the open country: the conscious ordering of social relations by conceptualization of the self and of the group, its structure and roles.' That it was problems of social relations and organization that taxed the mind of early man most is, as we shall later see, supported by evidence from the comparative study of intellectual functioning.

The massive increase in the size of the human brain, and therefore of the head, had other consequences. The maximum size of the foetus's head at birth is limited by the size of the aperture in the mother's pelvis through which the birth canal passes. This aperture increased in size with primate evolution, in association with increase in body-size, especially in the female. Nevertheless, its size in relation to that of the human brain and head at maturity is small. This problem was overcome in two ways. First, the degree of brain development at the newborn stage was drastically limited. Second, the bones of the newborn's skull were not fused together, thus facilitating flexibility of the head during birth and allowing for its rapid expansion in size afterwards. This circumstance whereby man has to be born in such a state of immaturity is part of an overall adaptive strategy which furthered his evolution in a way that has fundamental implications for the course of his ontogeny, now to be considered.

Neoteny and behavioural development
In the course of evolution countless species, including the direct forbears of man, have become extinct. One of the reasons for this is overspecialization. That is to say, form and function in a given species may be so well adapted to a particular environment, that, when gross changes in this environment have occurred, the specializations were unable to cope. In general, highly specialized species may not survive environmental changes that less specialized species might survive. In the evolution of mammals and primates, including man, degree of specialization has varied considerably, for example some primates are more highly adapted to arboreal life than others. We have seen that man has important specializations but that these are of kinds that promote adaptability to a wide range of environments. Nevertheless the overall trend of primate evolution has been in the direction of despecialization of form. This has been brought about by a type of change that is quite a common evolutionary phenomenon (De Beer, 1958), that is, neoteny. This is a retardation in growth rate such that, by the time sexual maturity is reached, the adult retains characters which, in the evolutionary ancestors of the species, were present only at an immature or juvenile phase of development. By this means many characters present in the early stages of the development of primates have been retained in adult man as typically human characters. These include the limited body hair, the flatness of the face, the limited development of brow ridges, the small size of the canine teeth, the shape of the foot (Montagu, 1962). Such an outcome in man appears to

be the result of a neotenous trend that persists through primate evolution as a whole. According to Schultz (1956), rate of growth in the primates varies systematically: 'in regard to all parts of post-natal life one can recognize a clear trend towards prolongation (of immaturity), beginning in monkeys, as compared to lemurs, more pronounced in gibbons, still more in all three great apes and by far the most marked in man'.

It is now apparent, as De Beer (1958) originally suggested, that neoteny applies not only to physical structures but also to behaviour. It is not yet clear how general neoteny is as a feature of human behaviour. In reviewing the issue, Mason (1968) pointed to such attributes of adult man as playfulness, curiosity, inventiveness and the persistence of infantile attachments as possibly indicative of behavioural neoteny. His most convincing demonstration of it, however, is in the way motor patterns are organized at different primate levels. In this respect, throughout infancy, the human is a less finished product than the chimpanzee, just as the chimpanzee is a less finshed product than the monkey. For example, over that evolutionary series, if the newborn is placed flat on its back there is a clear decline in the strength and persistence of the reflexes available for self-righting. The same applies to the reflex grasping by which the infant can support itself.

Associated with this evolutionary trend is another trend with important implications for the motor patterns subserving human social behaviour. There is a progressive increase from monkey to man in the number and variety of discrete motor acts available in the behaviour repertoire, and in the tendency to combine such acts spontaneously into new and more elaborate patterns. This is apparent in the deprivation syndrome, in play activities involving objects, and in social response patterns (Mason, 1968). In the trial and error learning involved in social development there is an increasingly broad reserve of responses available for use in trials. Implications of this are that the achievement of social interaction patterns appropriate for adulthood takes longer, individual differences in these become more prominent, and vulnerability to restrictions on social experience becomes reduced.

From the general neotenous trend in primate evolution Mason (1968) draws a number of important conclusions about differences in the nature of early behavioural development in human compared with non-human primates. These have particular relevance for the study of human social development. First, the human infant's needs for social stimulation are less specific, the range of equivalent stimuli is wider, development is less dependent on particular features of stimulation, and the reactions to specific forms of stimulus deprivation are more variable and diffuse. Second, once a developmental sequence has been set in motion the human infant will show a greater tendency to elaborate on it, as for example in vocalization and in play. Third, because of the retardation of growth rates and the 'loosening' of behavioural organization, developmental stages are less sharply delimited. Sensitive periods are more difficult to establish, there is less likelihood that the withholding of any specific experience will result in developmental arrest, and there is a much stronger tendency for behaviour to reflect a blending of developmental stages, different response patterns and different motivational systems.

The evolutionary achievement of such plasticity of behaviour in man is, of course, basic for the development of his complex intellectual functioning. Indeed Kuttner (1960) proposed a general explanation of this too in terms of neoteny, namely that the evolution of intelligence is a consequence of the retention in higher species of a trait of behavioural plasticity that is characteristic of more primitive organisms only during immature stages. The complementary aspect of this process is the progressive recession, or perhaps reorganization, not just of reflexive but of instinctual behaviour as a whole. As Mason (1968) points out, 'of all the primates, man has gone farthest in an evolutionary venture in which the reliability and efficiency of instinctive patterns have been sacrificed to achieve the behavioral plasticity and the liberation of psychic energies that are so much a part of the human condition'.

The reciprocal of the human evolutionary outcomes discussed so far is, of course, a long period of dependence on parental care. Parental care, especially in the earlier phases, provides the vulnerable infant with protection, with food, and the initial information and emotional security required for learning about the world and for gaining social competence. The basic plan of the infant–mother relationship which provides these requirements is very much the same in man as it is in apes and monkeys. The newborns of all have rooting, sucking, grasping and many other reflexes in common. All give distress cries, and all are comforted when properly held. Furthermore, the social response patterns of all occur at first to a range of stimuli and then gradually become limited to rather specific stimuli emanating from the mother. And in each case a mutual attachment develops, and infants of all types possess responses for maintaining close proximity. Also in common are the qualitative changes that occur in the infant–mother relationship as it develops through the three stages described by Harlow et al. (1963): those of attachment and protection, of ambivalence and of separation. With progress through these stages goes another development in common: a massive expansion in the infant's exploration and play activities, first directed at the mother, then away from her but with the mother acting as a secure base, and finally independently of her and more in relation with siblings, the father, and non-parents living in the same group.

Such similarities in the broad features of early social development in primates, which extend also to mammals of certain other kinds, form a context for looking at the differences. These differences are of course associated with diversity between species in behaviour repertoire, in learning and cognitive capacity, in natural environment and in the social organization of the group in which the young are reared. Among the most distinctive differences are the quality and extent of the social bonds formed in the course of early development.

The early human mother–child relationship is characterized by a degree of intimacy, of face-to-face communication, of mutual play, and by a range, flexibility and frequency of mutual interactions not seen at non-human levels. From an evolutionary perspective such features appear as the outcome, not only of a progressive reduction in the amount of reflex-like behaviour in the infant, but also of an increase in the amount of initiative and maternal care required from the mother to sustain the relationship. The human infant, for example, cannot cling for long and even if it could the mother does not possess body hair that would make this possible. It is up to the mother, in the last analysis, to maintain proximity, and she is well equipped to do this through her bipedalism that enables her to carry her infant around, and her responsiveness to his signals. Beyond this, however, the logistics of the feeding situation and of most other maternal activities promote eye-to-eye contact, and mutual communication is further facilitated by the uniquely human smiling response and vocalization possibilities.

Other features of this social bond are also notable. There is a marked variability of behaviour in both infant and mother, both within and across age, due mostly to the rapidity of developmental change in the infant's response patterns and cognitive abilities. Hence differences between infants in their social behaviour are not highly stable from one time to another, and predictability of degree of social attachment from one age to another is notoriously unreliable. Another feature of this bond is its lack of exclusivity, that is, it does not prevent the development of bonds with other people, whether additionally or alternatively. Once the stranger reaction is overcome an infant will develop relationships with other persons besides the mother, and if the mother has to be replaced by an adoptive mother the necessary adjustment in making a new bond is usually eventually achieved. In other words there is a remarkable degree of flexibility in the infant's social behaviour that readily allows for the creation of a multiplicity of social bonds.

It is of interest in the present context that Cairns (1976) concluded that the properties of high variability and flexibility of early human social behaviour are probably neotenous. In other species, including many primates, where there is a strong mother–infant bond it is primarily in the neonatal period that the greatest instability and flexibility are shown. Lest there be any tendency to conclude, however, that the form of all human social development can be explained in terms of neoteny, he points out a number of features that do not fit the neoteny hypothesis. In particular, 'the child's capabilities for multiple relationships seem to be accelerated relative to those of "more primitive" species. Along with the acceleration . . . are correlated capabilities for symbolic communication and classification of persons, objects, and places. Hence, in the child one finds superimposed on a relatively immature physical structure an advanced development of communi- cation–discrimination processes.' The possession of such advanced capacities is fully in keeping with the nature of the social environment in which human young have to develop.

The social environment
The social environment of the developing human being is more intrusive, all-embracing and complex than that of any other primate. From the moment of birth onward the infant has to begin to adapt to two lifelong features of his environment, namely living in groups and cultural selection. The groups within which he forms social relation- ships, from the family onward, become increasingly diverse and extensive, and they form the settings for two major developmental tasks which every individual must face. One is to take up the information which the prevailing culture tries to transmit to him as a means of maintaining intergenerational continuity. The other is to survive the processes of cultural selection, namely the sanctions against deviation from the norms of the groups in which he lives. These cultural processes

and the group–living to which they are related are themselves the outcome of evolutionary process, however, and the changes that led to such an outcome need to be understood.

The emergence of culture as a fundamental adaptational strategy of man involved a new mechanism which, though still based on variation and selection, vastly increased both the rate of change and the variability of his social behaviour. Instead of being dependent on the slow processes of random genetic variation and stabilization of adaptive outcome by natural selection, such change and variability resulted from the entirely new order of cognitive and behavioural flexibility in man. The new source of variation was human imagination and inventiveness; the new means of selecting and stabilizing adaptive outcomes were institutions; and intergenerational transmission of knowledge and sanctions was subserved not by genes but by imitation and learning.

Current thinking on how these cultural processes could have emerged in the course of evolution, too extensive for review here, is directed toward three kinds of phenomena on which they ultimately depend. First is the use of language and other features of human communication: language is the basis of the symbolic thinking necessary to generate new knowledge, of the storage of this knowledge, and of the communication necessary for its transmission. Second is the way learning operates during ontogeny to provide both the continuity of culture across generations, and innovations in it. Third are the basic parameters of group structure and social organization which both affect and are affected by the social interactions of the individuals that constitute groups.

Adaptive function

Problems and approaches
Behavioural biology now takes full account of an important distinction made by Tinbergen (1951) in the kinds of meaning that can be given to the question of why a particular animal behaves in a particular way. The different meanings are: 'what caused it to happen?' (immediate causation); 'how did the animal develop the capacity to do it?' (developmental antecedents); 'what is the point of, or the part played by, the behaviour in the life of the animal?' (adaptive function); and 'how did the species as a whole become able to behave in this way?' (evolutionary antecedents).

Having looked at human social behaviour and development in terms of the last of these questions we now turn to the question of adaptive function. In psychology this type of question has for long been confused with questions of the first two kinds. Unlike causal and developmental questions, however, questions about function refer to the effects and consequences of behaviour. The occurrence of a particular type of behaviour, such as infant crying, has ramifications of many kinds that range from immediate effects on the mother which have further effects back on the infant's state, to long-term effects on the infant's emotional condition depending on the nature of the usual immediate effects (Ainsworth and Bell, 1969). Functional questions about one or another kind of social behaviour thus direct attention, first to the part played by it within sequences of social interaction as a whole, and second to the consequences of its typical occurrence for subsequent development.

This way of understanding the significance of social behaviour is the outcome of a biological approach which, strictly speaking, seeks to explain the occurrence of a given behavioural character in the repertoire of a species in terms of its adaptive value for the survival of that species. This approach therefore focusses on a very specific kind of behavioural consequence namely effects on the organism's subsequent reproductive success. This is the study of biological function in the strict sense. It is a subject that has been open to misunderstanding of various kinds. Hinde (1975) has recently brought characteristic clarity to the concept, and three points must be mentioned here. First, not all of the consequences of a behavioural character are beneficial for reproductive success: some may be neutral and others harmful. In the example above, crying is obviously conducive to infant survival, but it can activate aggression in the mother even to the point of baby-battering. Such a character is said to be biologically adaptive if its beneficial consequences outweigh the harmful ones. Second, not all of a species' characters have biological functions. For example, some characters of group size or structure may be by-products of the behaviour of individuals that is biologically adaptive through other consequences; and some items of behaviour such as certain reflexes in the newborn may be relics of formerly adaptive characters. Third, Hinde distinguishes between weak and strong meanings of the concept of function. A weak meaning answers the question 'what is it good for?' without necessarily indicating precisely how the character in question contributes to reproductive success. A strong meaning attempts to answer the question 'through what consequences does natural selection act to maintain this character?' In both cases a comparison is implied with a hypothetical organism similar in every respect except that it lacks the character in question.

In the case of human behaviour such an approach has, at first sight, very much the flavour of an armchair theoretical exercise. In modern man cultural selection has largely replaced natural selection and absence of a particular behavioural character is usually adequately compensated for by special training; for such reasons characters that probably had major survival value in the evolution of early man can no longer be demonstrated to have it. In practice, however, the functional biological perspective outlined has led to two approaches, inductive and deductive, to the study of human social behaviour. These are yielding new insight into the adaptive significance of some of its developmental features.

Inductive study of function
A good example of the inductive approach, and of the kinds of problems it poses, is Bowlby's (1969) study of the function(s) of attachment behaviour. This is inductive in that functional inferences are made from empirical observation of the circumstances, effects and consequences of the occurrence of the behaviour. Bowlby (1958) originally proposed that an infant's attachment to his mother is subserved by a number of species-characteristic behaviour systems, namely crying, smiling, sucking, following and clinging. These systems emerge at different times and are relatively independent of each other at first. But as they become organized the principal feature of the environment by which they are controlled becomes the mother. The immediate effects of their occurrence in the infant's interactions with her, that is, their function in the weak sense, is that they bring the two into close proximity and contact with each other. Because for a time they are directed almost solely to the mother and indicate a strong preference for her which continues even as they gradually become extended to other people as well, Bowlby classed them together as attachment behaviours. Their effects are brought about partly by the infant's own initiatives in signalling to the mother, partly by his responsiveness to her when present, and partly by his eliciting and motivating maternal responsiveness in her.

Before Bowlby's work no explicit functional analysis of the child's tie to his mother had been made, function being hopelessly confused with causation. Because the tie was conceived essentially in terms of secondary drive theory, the implication was either that the tie derives from hunger and serves to keep the infant close to his food supply (Freud, 1940) or that it derives from excessive stimulation due to unsatisfied physiological needs and serves to dispose of the excess (Freud, 1925). Bowlby (1969) squarely faced the issue of biological function in the strong sense and directed attention to the consequence which, in the course of evolution, led attachment behaviour to become incorporated into the biological equipment of the species. He asked 'precisely what advantage does the behaviour . . . confer on individuals endowed with ability to develop it that leads them to achieve greater breeding success than is achieved by those who are deficient in the ability?' His proposal was that the function of attachment behaviour is protection from predators. Admitting that there is too little evidence for anyone to be sure about this, he considered an alternative hypothesis that the behaviour affords opportunity for the infant to learn from the mother various activities necessary for survival. He regarded this as implied by a statement of Murphy (1964) that the mother not only meets nutritional and other bodily needs but supports the development of the specific ego functions. While recognizing that learning is an important consequence of the child's tie to his mother, Bowlby did not accept this as the crucial biological advantage in question for two reasons. It does not account for the facts, first that attachment behaviour persists into adult life long after learning from the mother is complete, and second that it is elicited at high intensity under conditions of alarm.

While Bowlby's proposal has itself served a useful function in directing attention to a basic issue, there are a number of reasons why it would be premature to accept it. First, attachment behaviour is a composite of several different response systems and it is not necessarily the case that all emerged as a result of the same selection pressures. For example, although crying may have been selected under alarm conditions it does not follow that smiling was. Second, it is an oversimplification to look for *the* consequence that is biologically adaptive because a character may be selected for more than one consequence (Mayr, 1976). The biological adaptiveness of a response that occurs in infancy may therefore lie not just, or not at all, in its immediate effects but in its longer-term consequences. In the case of infant smiling, for instance, it has immediate effects both in establishing a mutuality of relationship with the mother and in facilitating exploration of the environment (Ambrose, 1969). Both of these are of fundamental importance for the further development of the infant in numerous respects, especially through enabling the infant to learn the rules that govern changes in his complex environment (Bruner, 1969). Even in the environment in which the evolution of the smiling response took place, the early learning of these rules could have been at least as vital for later reproductive success as defence against predators.

Can such inductive arguments ever be more than speculative? In respect of the consequences on which selection pressures actually operated during evolution, probably not. The significance of raising such questions, however, is twofold. At a theoretical level, insofar as it is claimed that a social behaviour pattern, such as crying or smiling, is a direct outcome of evolution (Ambrose, 1960), it is necessary to try to arrive at a view about the nature of its adaptiveness. At a practical research level, in the assessment of what is the importance for later social development of one or another kind of behaviour or experience in infancy or childhood, such questions have the potential of stimulating new thinking about consequences, including non-biological ones, for further study. Furthermore, even for those concerned primarily with study of behaviour causation, preliminary functional analysis has value in giving more precise definition to the context, or causal frame of reference, in which the behaviour naturally occurs.

Deductive study of function
The hypothetico-deductive approach, concerned with the strong meaning of 'function', studies the implications of natural selection for social behaviour. It starts from a few given facts about an animal and, by deducing the implications of natural selection, then makes predictions about many other features of the animal which must have adaptive value, these being testable by observation. Such features may be kinds of behaviour, causal mechanisms, or types of developmental change.

This approach arose in the attempt to solve the puzzle of how evolutionary theory could be applied in explaining the existence of altruistic behaviour, which appears at first sight to reduce the reproductive fitness of the altruist. For example, warning calls in animals under conditions of predation increase the chances of survival of group members while endangering the life of the caller; and parental behaviour, while beneficial for the reproductive success of the young, may reduce the rate at which the parents can produce further offspring. Because many species possess behaviour patterns that seem to facilitate the survival of the group at the expense of the individual, Wynne-

Edwards (1962) proposed that natural selection operates at the group level in addition to the individual level. There is, however, a major theoretical difficulty in this idea. Insofar as the group contains some individuals that are more selfish than others, selection operating between individuals in the group will lead to the elimination of those with altruistic traits. Such a result, in respect of group survival, will be evolutionarily unstable (Maynard Smith, 1964). Many biologists, following the theoretical work of Hamilton (1964, 1970), now believe that all behavioural traits previously regarded as instances of group selection can be adequately explained as the product of selection operating not just on individuals but on the genes carried by individuals (Dawkins, 1976a). To appreciate the power of this position it is necessary to take account of a number of basic concepts.

The whole point, biologically speaking, of reproductive success is that all of the genes that make up the gene pool of a population or species get carried forward from one generation to the next. While some genes, or gene complexes, are common to all members of the species, others are carried by only some of the members. Now some combinations of genes that determine the characteristics of bodily and behavioural make-up of individuals will be more conducive to individual reproductive success than others. Whether or not a given combination of genes succeeds in getting replicated in the next generation depends upon a compromise. Most bodily or behavioural characters under some degree of gene control have some consequences that are beneficial for reproductive success and others that are disadvantageous; for example, conspicuous plumage in a bird may greatly facilitate courtship but also be attractive to predators. The form and function of any given character is thus the result of a compromise, worked out over a long period of evolution, between selection pressures of different kinds. So also is the total combination of the characters that make up an individual. The outcome that is characteristic of a species is assumed to be optimal, the 'best possible', with respect to the particular constellation of circumstances in which the species lives. A general feature of optimization is that it results from a 'trade-off' process, in which costs and benefits of different aspects of the process are counterbalanced (McFarland, 1976). In animals this balancing of costs and benefits is done by natural selection. Analysis of the trade-off process for behavioural characters takes account both of 'time–energy budgeting' with regard to the frequency and conditions of their occurrence, and also individual differences, that is, the extent to which a given character is present and operative among members of the species.

Many examples of such analyses are given by Clutton-Brock and Harvey (1976). For instance, in attempting to explain why, in many species, intra-species aggression is at such low key, the benefits of vicious or mortal attacks in competition for sexual partners or dominance positions are balanced against the costs to both contestants such as the danger of violent counter-attack by the loser or the time and energy needed to kill the rival. Analyses on these lines that are of special relevance for human developmental psychology are those of Trivers (1971, 1972, 1974) on the evolution of reciprocal altruism, of parental investment and of parent–offspring conflict.

Two other concepts that are important for this approach must be mentioned. One is 'the evolutionarily stable strategy' (Maynard Smith, 1964). Wherever there is a particular conflict of interest between members of a population (i.e. in virtually all aspects of social life), with each individual trying to maximize his own reproductive success, the behavioural strategy that persists is one which, once evolved, cannot be bettered by any deviant individual. The genes underlying different kinds of behaviour are selected, not as 'good' in isolation, but as good at working for reproductive success against the background of the other genes in the gene pool. Genes that give rise to altruistic behaviour have to exist with others that give rise to selfish behaviour. The ratio of the two kinds of genes in a stable gene pool will be such that any individual whose gene composition deviates from this, e.g. leading to excessively selfish or altruistic behaviour, will be penalized by selection.

Another concept, pivotal in Hamilton's model, is 'inclusive fitness'. This concept rests on the assumption that what really matters in evolution is the survival and replication of genes rather than of the particular individual who carries them. A proportion of the genes carried by an individual will be the same in the siblings of that individual; and its immediate offspring will carry 50 per cent of the same genes. Thus the individual's genes are passed on both via its own young and via the young of its relatives. Genes which cause their carrier individuals to produce more replicas of themselves increase in frequency in the population as a whole: they are selected for. Consequently one would expect selection for genes which cause relatives to be given favoured treatment. But favouring relatives may reduce the individual's own future reproductive potential. The genes selected for, therefore, would be expected to be those which cause altruistic favours to be distributed most to closely related relatives, such as own offspring, and to a decreasing extent to more distant relatives. Inclusive fitness for reproductive success refers to the fitness not just of the individual but also to all of its kind that contain the same genes. Thus the evolution of individual altruism may be regarded as based on kin selection. This is not a form of group selection but a consequence of the essentially selfish nature of the gene, which gives rise to a readiness to assist replicas of itself that are carried by other individuals (Dawkins, 1976a).

It is instructive to see how Mason (1975) applies a cost-benefit analysis to understanding the adaptive significance of a long period of parental dependence, which is a consequence of progressively slower developmental rates in primate evolution. On theoretical grounds strong selection pressures *against* the prolongation of immaturity are to be expected: the late-maturing organism will be delayed in making its first contribution to the gene pool, and extended infantile dependence adds to the parental investment in each offspring with the consequence of reducing the total number of offspring that will be produced. The common functional explanation for prolonged immaturity, that it provides more time for learning to occur, is unsatisfactory: 'more learning' is not necessarily beneficial, and in any case the immature primate is generally a less efficient learner than the adult. An alternative possibility is that it is the parent that is the primary beneficiary: the parent gains from being able to enlist the older, but still dependent offspring, in assisting with the care of younger siblings. Such a trade-off, however, does not seem profitable. A further possibility is that both parent and young benefit: each may act as an ally to the other in competitive interactions with a non-relative. In none of these cases, however, is it necessary to extend the period of infantile dependence in order to create such benefits. Mason then considers the relevance of the primate trend towards prolongation of such dependence as a major source of evolutionary innovation: that is, it could be a means for bringing about new structures, functions and organizational possibilities. On this view neither parent nor young need profit directly during the period of dependence, the benefits occurring in the form of basic changes in the way of behaviour is organized throughout the life cycle. The principal adaptive significance of this kind of innovation would be in an increase in behavioural plasticity accomplished by creating 'openness' in major functional schemas. Such an evolutionary conse-quence of increasingly prolonged dependence in the primate would require adjustments in parent and young. We see these particularly clearly in man. The parents act not just as providers and protectors but as purveyors of information, values and skills: they actively engage in the deliberate education and socialization of the child. Complementary adjustments in the child take the form of 'trust', 'identification', interest in what the parent does. Phylogenetically, such a reorganization results in relaxation of direct environmental control over behaviour. Onto-genetically, the organism's dependence on information about the environment is greatly increased. Such a strategy entails risks of at least two kinds. One is that the parent may neglect its socializing and educative functions so that, as the deprivation studies show, the child is likely to become functionally inadequate. Here the strategy relies heavily on the strong and enduring emotional ties between parent and child, especially in man. Another risk is that the parent will perform its functions so thoroughly that the child becomes a behavioural replica of the parent, which would reduce the child's chances of coping with a changing environment. This risk is reduced by the occurrence of a developmental period, of so-called adolescent rebellion, when norms established in childhood are tested and updated and used as a point of departure for the development of new approaches.

Along with the primate evolution of behavioural plasticity and of the open programming of behaviour has gone the evolution of even more superior intellectual abilities. Humphrey (1976) has used the cost-benefit approach to support his important suggestion that the high-level creative intelligence seen in anthropoid apes and man is the result primarily of social selection pressures. He starts by asking why the higher primates need to be as clever as they are, and how clever must they be before the returns on superior intellect become vanishingly small. He maintains that intellectual capacity in higher primates is far higher than is required by the practical technical problems of everyday living. The evidence from field studies of chimpanzees all points to the fact that subsistence techniques are hardly, if ever, the product of premeditated invention; they are arrived at instead by trial-and-error learning or by imitation of others. The remarkable creative reasoning of which such animals are capable in laboratory situations seems to have no parallels in the same animals in their natural environment. The assumption on which Humphrey bases his answer is that the life of the higher primates depends critically on the possession of wide factual knowledge of practical technique and of the nature of the habitat. Such knowledge can only be acquired in the context of a *social* community:

this provides both a medium for the cultural transmission of information and a protective environment in which individual learning can occur. His proposal is that the chief role of creative intellect is to hold society together. 'Social primates are required by the very nature of the system they create and maintain to be calculating beings; they must be able to calculate the consequences of their own behaviour, to calculate the likely behaviour of others, to calculate the balance of advantage and loss – and all this in a context where the evidence on which their calculations are based is ephemeral, ambiguous and liable to change, not least as a consequence of their own actions. In such a situation, "social skill" goes hand in hand with intellect, and here at last the intellectual faculties required are of the highest order. The game of social plot and counter-plot cannot be played merely on the basis of accumulated knowledge, any more than can a game of chess.'

The above examples show that the theory of natural selection can make good sense of basic features of human social behaviour and development that are usually taken for granted by developmental psychologists. More important, they show how the theory can provide a frame of reference for social developmental theory: as Hamilton (1975) points out, no general theory of human social behaviour can be incompatible with the implications of natural selection.

Ecology

Problems and approaches

In behavioural biology knowledge about the ecology of a species is of fundamental importance for understanding both the functions and the causation of social behaviour. The natural environment is the source of the selection pressures against which the adaptiveness of behaviour is tested, and it is the only context in which biologically relevant variables can be chosen for study of causation. The natural environment of most organisms, however, is not static, but a continually changing phenomenon. Every organism is in constant interchange with it and it is by means of this that its development can occur. The environmental factors that causally affect its behaviour and development, furthermore, are not confined just to the immediate setting: they may extend to variables as diverse as group structure, natural resources and climate. It is because of both the scope and the dynamic nature of these factors that a perspective which comprehends them is more appropriately called ecological, rather than environmental.

Psychology, historically speaking, has tended to ignore an ecological perspective in its headlong plunge into experimental work (Ambrose, 1977). Consequently the quip by Bronfenbrenner (1977) that developmental psychology is, in many respects, 'the science of the strange behaviour of a child in a strange situation with a strange adult' contains more than a grain of truth. One serious outcome of this position is that, faced with major questions of social policy on issues ranging from child-rearing techniques and educational planning to population density and urban planning, this science still has too little to contribute by way of relevant factual information. If this is true, it is a measure of the failure of developmental theory to embrace, or even adequately to conceptualize, the relevant variables. The question to be addressed in the present section therefore is as follows: What are the essentials of the biological conception of ecology, and what are its implications for the way we conceive both of the environment in which human social development takes place and of the relations of the developing individual to it? The biological approach to be considered next is, in fact, influencing two areas of human study concerned with these problems. One is ecological anthropology, which shows promise of bringing the diversities and complexities of culture within the ambit of ethology (reviewed by Blurton Jones, 1975, 1976). The other, of more immediate relevance and therefore to be included below, is ecological psychology.

The biological approach
In ethology and sociobiology the perspective on an animal's relations with its environment is fundamentally an ecological one. It is the ecology of an animal, as distinct from its environment, that forms the conceptual context for studies of natural selection and biological function, of social organization, and of the causation of behaviour. It is because the ecology of an animal is a highly complex, multivariate phenomenon that naturalistic observation is accepted as an essential part of any such studies, at least in the early stages.

Ecology as a biological science has its roots in natural history. Its central concept, the ecosystem, has a huge connotation. It refers to a community of all the living organisms in a given natural environment interacting with each other and with the non-living components of that environment (Ricklefs, 1973). The concept comprehends both structural and functional aspects that can only be handled with a variable-focus perspective. Its scope ranges from many different species living together, through populations of any given species, social groups of individuals within a population, to individuals interacting within a social group. It also includes the environment of any of these units, conceived variously as habitat, territory or resources. These structural features are functionally related by dynamic interactions and relationships of many kinds such as the cyclical exchange of materials or energy between the living and non-living parts of the system, the food-chain, predator–prey relationships, competition and co-operation.

The key to conceptualizing the content of this vast ecological arena lies in a systems approach. Structurally the total system is seen as constituted of interdependent subsystems. These subsystems exist at many different levels of organization. Within the ecosystem as a whole Odum (1971) distinguishes subsystems of populations, organisms, organs, cells and genes. Subsystems at each level of organization operate according to principles that are different from those underlying other levels; for example the principles of population dynamics are entirely different from those of physiology. Each subsystem functions in relation to others of the same level, and the meaning of each is to be found in the functional whole within which they exist, that is in a subsystem of the next higher level.

A system in ecology is viewed as a living whole. Four aspects of this holistic concept must be emphasized. First, the parts of the whole are seen, under normal conditions, as in regular and consistent interaction with one another according to specifiable rules. The whole is an organized network of interacting parts as, for example, the individuals in a social group. Second, each system is open, not closed: it has inputs and outputs in relation to other systems of the same level. The social behaviour of an organism, for instance, is both dependent on the organism's perception of others and also has effects on those others. Third, a system has continuity. A population, for instance, extends over time that is longer than the lives of individual members: it is dependent on the continual replacement of its component parts as they go through their life-cycle. Fourth, depending on the mutual adjustment of its parts, a system is in a state of equilibrium or disequilibrium. The capacity to regulate its own state is a general property of any biological system: they are cybernetic, that is they depend on negative feedback to ensure regulation within set limits. If conditions force variation to exceed these limits then positive feedback usually results in the system running out of control.

Under normal conditions any given subsystem fits with others into a functional whole. By virtue of the ways it interacts with others it makes some contribution to the effectiveness of the whole, so that without it the whole would be different. The place into which it fits in this way is its 'ecological niche'. This term seems to be used in biology in a number of different ways, but in relation to a species, population or individual it usually refers either to its way of life or to the precise requirements for its survival. Whereas 'habitat' is a structural term referring to the *environment*, 'niche' is a functional term referring to *interaction* with the environment, within the context of the ecosystem.

The approach of ecological psychology

In relation to the human species the biologist's approach to ecology has burgeoned into a major applied science that aims to understand and control the effects of man's behaviour on the environment, the emphasis being on such features as pollution, overcrowding, threats to resources of food and raw materials, damage to wildlife, etc. Less known is the use of this approach by psychologists both to reveal the nature and scope of the natural environment that causally affects human behaviour and development, and to reach towards a conception of person–environment relations that is more 'realistic' than that of traditional psychological theories. 'Ecological validity' has now become an issue for psychological research, especially in the area of human social development. While the meaning of the term in this context is rooted in its use by biologists, psychologists are now becoming quite sophisticated in adapting it for this new application.

Overton and Reese (1977) make the important point that an ecological perspective on human behaviour is distinguished not by the use of such concepts as 'ecological niche', 'enduring environment', 'molar behaviour' but by the way these concepts are understood and used. What is crucial, according to them, is not the scope of the environment or of behaviour that is taken into account but the nature of the relations between man and his environment. There are two views of these relations, long held in philosophy and psychology, that are not compatible with ecological thinking. One is the empiricist view that all thought and action is a function of the environment, which is the basic material reality. According to this, complex variant processes of behaviour are reducible to invariant elementary pieces called responses, and development is a shaping process with the environment as the sole shaping agent. The other is the idealist, phenomenal view that the environment is really a construction of man. Our knowledge of it is no more than a reflection of man's own nature. The ecological view is something of a synthesis of these two extreme positions in that it sees man and environment as continually changing each other. It is, however, more than just a synthesis. It is a 'systems' view, whether of man and environment each as interdependent systems, or of the two as representing one whole system: the relations between man and environment are of the nature of reciprocal and cumulative interaction. Analyses of these relations must therefore be two-way, not just of the effects of the environment, and all part-analyses are given meaning only by the context of the whole.

In viewing human development from this perspective, two features require emphasis. One is the concept of an 'active' organism. This is fully compatible with the facts of human social interaction from the earliest phases onwards. Even the neonatal infant does not just react to external stimuli, he shows endogenous behaviour that has effects on other people (Korner, 1974). Studies of the neonate's spontaneous activity (Prechtl et al., 1968; Escalona, 1969), sensori-motor schemas (Piaget, 1953) and visual pattern preferences (Fantz, 1967) all reveal endogenous structures functioning in certain directions rather than others. All are readily modifiable by the environment but this is different from saying that they are caused by the environment. Indeed the very assumption of spontaneous activity entails denial of a complete causal determinism and rejection of the ideal of complete prediction and control (Overton and Reese, 1973).

The other feature is the conceptualization of developmental change as qualitative as well as quantitative. The active organism model represents man as a system in which any change in a part alters the configuration of the whole. Development is seen as the emergence of new properties, new configurations of parts giving rise to new structures. These are not reducible to lower levels and therefore qualitatively different from them. Piaget's (1953) whole theory of cognitive development is of course based on this perspective: man as an active system assimilating and accommodating to other active systems in the environment, transformations continually taking place in both as a result. Development is thus a shaping process on the basis that man both actively shapes the environment and, due to the process of active interaction with the environment, undergoes transformation as well.

As for the implications of an ecological perspective for research on human social development it may be said with truth that it has not so far led to any new developments whether by way of generating propositional theory, of making natural observation techniques more fruitful, or of yielding substantive discoveries. What it has done, nevertheless, has been to point to new ways of looking at old problems and to expand greatly the horizon of areas for scientific enquiry. Such implications have been highlighted by Bronfenbrenner (1977) against the contrasting background of the conventional research model. He has spelt out a number of ways in which an emerging ecological model would differ from this. In summarizing these the present author has selected examples of research which conform to one or another aspect of such a model.

In the classical research model there were usually two parties, an experimenter E and a subject S, usually a child. The process under study was unidirectional, E presenting the stimulus and S giving a response. Correspondingly, in a field situation such as a home, a parent's behaviour would be viewed as stimulus and the child's behaviour as response. A first step towards an ecological model would be to see the process as bidirectional. Developmental studies for instance would be designed to show not only the influence of the parent on the child but also that of the child on the parent. This approach presupposes a dyadic model of interaction as in the studies of Lewis and Lee-Painter (1974) and Brazelton et al. (1974). A further step would be extension of a two-person model to a three or N-person one on lines indicated by Parsons et al. (1955) and Bales (1968). Little employed in practice, such a model has the potential for revealing not only first-order effects such as those of a mother or father on their child, but second-order effects as well, such as the effects of the father on the mother's interactions with the child.

Turning to the research setting, the model would extend this from a single setting to a multiple one, for example home, school and peer group. This not only introduces a comparative perspective but also recognizes joint effects, and interactions between settings. Events in a peer group, for instance, may change a child's pattern of interactions with his parents with consequent effects on the course of his development. This approach was pioneered by Barker and Wright (1955) and continued by Schoggen and Barker (1977). A further development would be in the way settings are conceptualized. While categorizing settings as 'home' or 'school' may throw into relief major type-differences, it does not allow for differentiation of the nature of the child-setting interactions. The way in which development is affected by interaction in a given setting requires study of the properties of that setting as well as of the interactions in it. This approach has been used, for instance, in showing how home and institutional settings differentially affect the social development of the child (Cochran, 1975). The course of social development is, of course, influenced not only by a child's immediate settings but also by the nature of encompassing systems, described by Brim (1975) as macro-environments. These include the neighbourhood, the requirements of the parents' work, transport facilities, child care and welfare arrangements and national, social and economic policies that bear upon family life. These too must be included in any attempt at a comprehensive ecological perspective. Furthermore, the subsystems that constitute any human ecological situation are always associated with an ideology that endows meaning to social networks, institutions and roles. Since different people tend to attach somewhat different meanings to a given situation, full understanding of the variance in their interactions is likely to come only if the research includes a phenomenological approach which taps perceptions and attitudes, in addition to objective observation (e.g. Ugurel-Semin, 1974).

Finally, in taking account of the dynamic nature of any ecological system Bronfenbrenner points out the importance of studying processes of change. It is not only the child that changes during its development; the micro-systems in which it lives also change, as also in the modern world do the macro-systems. Changes in population size and density, in the proportion of mothers who go out to work, in sexual norms, in educational techniques: each of these will affect the total system in which the child develops. Study of such change effects, whether change be natural or induced by the investigator, are of interest not only in their own right but also as revealing the nature of systems in action. Action research of various kinds, exemplified by Rice and Trist (1952) and Emery (1967) and by many other studies, shows the delicate balance between the individual as he develops through one or another phase of life and the systems of which he is a part.

Consideration of concepts and approaches needed to study all of these aspects of human behavioural ecology leads inevitably to sociology and anthropology. A review of the kinds of concepts and variables studied in those disciplines that are of relevance for understanding the social ecology of human development has been made by Ambrose (1965).

Genetics

Problems and approaches
Although it is now widely accepted that the development of social behaviour, in man as well as animals, is dependent on genetic as well as on environmental factors, in practice research in developmental psychology as a whole remains heavily biased towards the exclusive role of the environment. As one behaviour geneticist puts it, 'The nature–nurture controversy has not really died or even faded away; with a sprinkling of a few pleasant words about heredity for modern flavour, the nurture side of the argument thrives in quiet complacency ... Lacking is an appreciation of the enormous amount of genetic variability existing in human and animal populations ... In short, the very essence of the gene-environment interaction concept has been missed' (Erlenmeyer-Kimling, 1972). Although this concept is absolutely basic in biological thinking about behavioural development, the study of genetic influences on specifically social behaviour and development in man has not yet advanced very far. The situation is not helped, furthermore, by its status as a political hot potato. Nevertheless genetics has yielded many fundamental facts and indications (Fuller and Thompson, 1960; McClearn, 1970; Ehrman et al., 1972) that can help us to size up the problems in this area and approach them with theoretical insight.

The basic principles of genetics have emerged from fundamental research on plants and animals. While the objection has sometimes been raised that animal models give an incomplete representation of the human situation, the fact remains that simplification can often be a useful precondition for understanding complex phenomena. The advantages of some animals such as Drosophila, mice and rats for behaviour genetics research are that they have large numbers of progeny, have short generation intervals and, most important of all, allow strict control both of mating and of the environment. The principal techniques employed include study of inbred strains whether in similar or in different environments, study of hybrids of inbred strains, study of correlations among relatives, and study of the effects of single genes on a variety of structures. Types of behaviour investigated include activity, hoarding, sexual behaviour, social dominance, aggression, emotionality and learning performance. The main aim of such studies is to assess the relative importance of genotype, environment, and genotype-environment interaction, in accounting for variance in any given phenotype. Since most phenotypes studied, particularly behavioural ones, are quantitative, continuously distributed traits, the methods and techniques of biometrical analysis are employed.

The extent to which a phenotype is under genetic control is revealed by an estimate of heritability (DeFries, 1972). Although heritability, broadly speaking, is an attribute of the population studied rather than of particular individuals in it, its value is as an indicator for further study at the levels of the individual and of physiological and biochemical mechanisms. As Jensen (1972) puts it, the heritability estimate may be regarded as a 'Geiger counter with which one scans the territory in order to find the spot one can most profitably begin to dig for ore.' In respect of the heritability in animals of the types of behaviour mentioned above, two preliminary points can be emphasized. There has been consistent success in demonstrating a hereditary basis for them. Furthermore, the domain of behavioural phenotypes is not particularly unique, and no rules of inheritance other than the Mendelian rules employed for non-behavioural characters need be invoked to account for their genetic transmission.

In the case of man heritability estimates are more difficult to obtain. Not only are population environments difficult to define adequately, but genotypes cannot be controlled because of the inability to carry out selective breeding. Both because of these difficulties and because concern is much more with questions about individual variation, most analytic tools used in animal research are inappropriate to the objectives of human behaviour genetics. Nevertheless, since the late fifties a good deal of methodological progress has been made; this has been summarized by Thompson (1972).

Although virtually all the behavioural traits of interest in man are under polygenic as well as environmental control, much can be learned from study of the effects of single locus and chromosome anomalies (e.g. Beck and Rosenblith, 1972) with respect both to the range of their physiological and behavioural effects and to their inheritance down through family pedigrees. As regards normal behaviour, the most convincing studies of the contributions of heredity and environment to complex characters are the comparisons of identical and non-identical twins, of identical twins in different environments, of adopted and natural children in similar environments, and of correlations between relatives (von Bracken, 1972).

The animal and human genetic studies, taken as a whole, have profound implications for the conceptualization and study of human social development. Those to be discussed concern the mode of action of genes on behaviour and development, the significance for social behaviour of genetically based differences between individuals and between populations, and the nature and extent of gene–environment interaction in social development.

Behaviour heritability and development
It is still commonly believed in the social sciences that the role of genetic factors in human behavioural development is limited to effects on the biological substrate of behaviour, various visible characteristics such as height, eye and hair colour, and certain well-known types of defective behaviour. The complex behaviour used in normal everyday life, which is so much subserved by cognitive functioning and so heavily controlled by learning, is held to be so far removed from genes and metabolic processes that, for all practical purposes, genetic factors can be ignored. There are two quite basic flaws in this conclusion. One is that some characters that are very largely under genetic control, such as the morphological characteristics that determine appearance, can have far-reaching consequences for the nature of a person's social interactions due to issues of social acceptability or disadvantage. The other, of more profound significance, is that such a position totally conflicts with the consistent findings of human behaviour genetics that many aspects or components of behaviour and physiology, to which social behaviour is related, are in part heritable. This is not to imply that any human social behaviour is directly under the control of specific genes in the way that certain movements are in Drosophila or in honeybees. Most geneticists now see the relationship as one of non-congruence: single genes characteristically affect many forms of behaviour, and single psychological traits have variance ascribable to many genes. The impact of genotype on social behaviour in man appears to be primarily on the parameters that reflect its adaptability or effectiveness and its mode of expression, namely intelligence, and temperament. The literature in these areas, reviewed respectively by Fuller and Thompson (1960) and Vandenberg (1967), even after taking account of methodological limitations, gives consistent evidence of a hereditary component underlying them. IQ correlations in most parent–child, sib and twin studies range from 0·40 to 0·70, and higher still for identical twins (Erlenmeyer-Kimling and Jarvick, 1963). It is also clear that various special abilities involved in general intelligence

such as verbal ability and ability to visualize spatial relations are related to genotype. In studies of human traits of personality and temperament the hereditary component is, in some cases, as high as that for intelligence. Vandenberg (1967), for instance, found this to be true for various clusters of traits described as extraversion–introversion, dominance, assertion, self-confidence, activity, vigour, need for achievement, depression and neuroticism among others.

Nervous system function has been implicated in numerous studies. For example, identical twins share identical EEG patterns (Omenn and Motulsky, 1972) and the highly heritable nature of extraversion–introversion in humans has been related to the functioning of inhibitory systems (Eysenck, 1956). Hormone production and the reactivity of target organs, which particularly affect the emotional components of social behaviour, are also under strong genetic influence (Hamburg, 1967).

While all the traits mentioned so far have a close bearing on social behaviour and interaction, there have been rather few studies directed to specifically social variables. However, in addition to extraversion which may be taken as an indicator of sociability, substantial heritability has been found for person orientation (Gottesman, 1963) and for sociableness (Vandenberg, 1967); and twin studies show a heredity factor in infant smiling, social interest and stranger fears (Freedman, 1965).

A feature of some heritability studies with important developmental implications is that heritability correlations for behavioural variables may vary at different age-levels (Thompson, 1968). The presumption is that this is because gene expression is continually affected by developmental variables. Insofar as many components of a final phenotype that are absent initially may emerge only gradually with age, a trait at different stages may represent the expression of different components of the genotype.

Precisely how genes affect normal behavioural development via the metabolic processes that they initiate remains largely unknown. On the basis of the embryological model of morphogenesis discussed by King (1968) it seems probable that gene action has effects on the time of onset of behaviour patterns, on rates of maturation which may differ for different behaviour patterns, on critical periods, and on the way behaviour is affected by the environmental medium in which they occur.

Perhaps the most significant of all the advances in modern behaviour genetics are the findings that demonstrate gene–environment interaction in development. Before considering these, it is necessary to be clear about the scope of genetically based individual differences.

Genetic variability and individual uniqueness
It is a basic tenet of neo-Darwinist evolutionary theory that any species or smaller population of a given type of organism will show genetic variability. It is a biological necessity because without it natural selection could not occur. It is ensured by a number of mechanisms such as Mendelian inheritance and by sexual and other types of selection (Wilson, 1976). Empirical work in human population genetics fully confirms this position. Genetic variability shows most obviously in physiological and morphological characters, but all human attributes including intelligence and behaviour are implicated. Naturally the nearer one gets to social behavioural characters that are most subject to cultural influence the more difficult it becomes to *demonstrate* a genetic basis for differences. Furthermore, in discussing this emotionally charged area it is important to distinguish whether the discourse concerns within-population or between-population differences.

The main human polymorphisms are apparent within all populations. The one with greatest social developmental implications is, of course, sexual dimorphism (Hutt, this volume). Some idea of the possible extent of genetic variation that is not sex-dependent can be gained from the figures for certain blood types. For instance in typical European populations the frequencies of the A, B, AB and O blood types are 41 per cent, 10 per cent, 4 per cent, and 45 per cent respectively (Bodmer, 1977). As regards the overall variability of individuals, studies of the protein products of different genes in many species including man have enabled geneticists to agree that the proportion of our genes that are likely to vary significantly within any population is of the incredible order of magnitude of 30 per cent (Harris, 1969; Lewontin and Hubby, 1966).

The implications of such a figure for variability in dimensions related to social behaviour and development are at present quite unknown. At the present stage of research it is not possible to make any firm statements about the genetic basis of the many individual differences in specific aspects of normal behaviour in newborn and young infants such as sensory thresholds, activity level, distress reactivity (Escalona, 1969), because prenatal and perinatal variables confound the issue. The problems are greater still for specific differences in older children

(Thomas et al., 1964) because of the influence of experience. Some indications come, however, from studies of between-population differences.

Interpretation of interpopulation, especially racial, differences requires the very greatest caution. Genetic variability in morphological and anthropometric characters (Dobzhansky, 1970) is of course fully acknowledged, as also is that in certain physiological traits such as lactose tolerance which makes possible the digestion of milk (Gottesman and Heston, 1972). Socially relevant behavioural traits, however, are a source of the hottest controversy. Jensen's genetic interpretation, for instance, of the well-known fact that black children reared by their own families have IQ scores which, on average, are about fifteen points below whites has shown up all the problems. These include test validity, the role of environmental factors, and the fact that within-population variability in IQ is not related by any simple function to between-population variability (Jensen et al., 1971). Similar uproar (Wade, 1976) has met Wilson (1976) for even entertaining the possibility that cultural differences between populations might possibly have at least some genetic basis. With regard to simple sensory traits, however, Spuhler and Lindzey (1967) have documented a number of racial differences in visual, auditory, olfactory and tactile discrimination. The supposition of racial differences in temperament gains support from a study by Freedman (1972). While matched Chinese-American and European-American newborns had similar scores of sensory and motor development, CNS maturity and interest in the social environment, the Chinese-Americans were strikingly less perturbable and more readily consolable.

Clearly the whole question of the extent to which individual *social behavioural* variability in humans has a genetic basis will be very difficult to sort out. The continuing progress of biochemical genetics (Omenn and Motulsky, 1972) is certainly worth watching in this respect. In the meantime, in the light of the whole direction of findings in behaviour genetics as a whole, two points stand out. First, social policies that ignore genetic factors in social development can only lead to pathology or suffering, as for instance the attempt in Italy and in some Arab countries to convert left lateral dominants to use of the right side (Young, 1977), and attempts in some immigrant schools to enforce milk-drinking. Second, theories of human social development that place exclusive emphasis on the environment as the basis of all normal individual differences will have to be regarded as highly questionable.

This is particularly so in view of the extensive research that clearly demonstrates the importance of gene–environment interaction in development.

Gene–environment interaction

The ubiquity of gene–environment interaction in the development of behavioural phenotypes appears to be fully agreed among geneticists (Erlenmeyer-Kimling, 1972). Three aspects of this concept will be emphasized here as of utmost relevance for understanding human social development.

The first is that different genotypes will respond differently to the same environmental conditions. In animals this has been amply demonstrated by study of strain differences in the effects of early experience. Among mouse strains, for instance, early treatments are far from universal in their effects (Erlenmeyer-Kimling, 1972). Whereas the C57BL strain responds to all types of treatments more frequently than others, the BALB strain shows generally low responsiveness. Whereas critical treatments for the former strain are the more traumatic ones such as handling, shock or noxious noise, for the latter they are changes in general background variables such as isolation, environmental enrichment or cage illumination. The behavioural measures showing maximal responsiveness to early treatments also vary: C57BL shows it in all except defecation scores, DBA shows it mainly in maze learning ability. Some genotypes, furthermore, show effects that are quite the reverse of others. In dogs, for instance, experimental deprivation effects on locomotor activity and on intensity of social interaction can be in opposite directions in different breeds (Fuller, 1967). Animal findings such as these make it imperative that studies of environmental effects on humans should allow for variability due to genetic factors, as did Bowlby (1973) in examining the effects of maternal separation on human infants.

One of the difficulties of demonstrating gene–environment interaction at the human level is to be seen in the relations between intelligence and socio-economic status. While it is possible that members of low socio-economic classes possess low intelligence by virtue of interaction with a poor environment, one cannot rule out the other possibility that natural selection engenders downward mobility for those possessing low innate ability (Thompson, 1972). Perhaps the most convincing interactional studies are those on the effects of nutrition on growth, reviewed by Riciutti (1977). Height differences in genetically equivalent populations varying in the quality of their pre- and post-natal environments are in fact regarded by Gottesman and Heston (1972) as a good model for traits which, like behavioural ones, are under both genetic and environmental control. According to this, each genotype has its own reaction range: that is, over the range of a relevant environmental parameter it will give rise to a range of phenotypes. Genotype A in restricted and enriched environments will show a range of heights; genotype B under similar conditions will show a different range that may or may not overlap: hence the conclusion that different genotypes may have the same phenotype and different phenotypes may have the same genotype.

This leads to a second aspect of the gene–environment interaction concept. Different genotypes have different susceptibility to environmental influence, that is they are differentially buffered, and this buffering may vary at different periods of development (Thompson, 1968). The large extent of this susceptibility at the human level is clearly the culmination of a long evolutionary trend in which the ability of a genotype to react to the environment became increasingly selected as advantageous. It is to be expected that suspectibility will be more advantageous at certain periods of development than others. In animals the most striking examples of this are the critical periods in birds, for imprinting and mating-choice, and song learning (Hinde, 1970). These instances also reflect another aspect of the same phenomena, namely a predisposition or facility to learn certain kinds of things rather than others. This and many of the constraints on learning discussed by Hinde and Stevenson-Hinde (1973) are conceivable as outcomes of genetic buffering. In human young, language learning is an example of a readiness to learn in a certain direction that is not so marked outside a limited age-period. Because human adaptation depends so heavily on maximal flexibility, however, it is hardly surprising that brief, fixed critical periods have not been found. Instead there is a prolonged period when learning can occur relatively unconstrained through observation, imitation, instruction and play (Bruner, 1972). Although the infancy literature contains indications that such learning is to some extent directional, relatively little has been done yet to study either this kind of problem or that of age-differences in readiness to learn in particular directions.

However wide the range of learning possibilities may be, there is always some genetic limitation on phenotypic variability. This, the third aspect of the concept under discussion, relates to canalization which is the predisposition for an organism to develop along a genetically determined growth path, called by Waddington (1971) a creode. This is an embryological concept that reflects the 'self-righting' tendencies of foetal growth processes and the difficulty of deflecting an organism from its growth path. The best-known example in children is the 'catch-up' phenomenon following a change of environment from growth-retarding to growth-promoting conditions (Tanner, 1970). Much of the resilience and recovery following early social deprivation, documented by Clarke and Clarke (1976), becomes more meaningful when seen in this context. Scarr (1975) has mustered strong evidence in support of her view that intelligence development in the sensorimotor period is well canalized.

Developmental process

Problems and approaches

The four related perspectives described in the preceding sections form the framework within which biologists view the ontogeny of behaviour. It is necessary at this point to emphasize that, in relation to the study of ontogeny, these perspectives yield no more than a framework. As Beer (1971) has pointed out, argument from facts pertinent to questions about the evolution and adaptiveness of behaviour to conclusions about individual behavioural development is weak. Facts about heredity and about the nature of the environment carry no precise entailments about processes of development. What the framework does do, however, is to affect fundamentally the way biologists and biological psychologists conceptualize development. This in turn has major consequences for research strategy and for the kinds of data that are sought in attempting to answer developmental questions. These consequences have emerged most clearly in the direction taken by ethology and biopsychology over the last thirty years. The conceptual and methodological advances there have, however, been percolating into developmental psychology, exposing the weaknesses of some of its long-held assumptions.

Ethologists have maintained clear distinctions between different types of developmental question: what changes take place as the individual develops? (descriptive); what are the factors that influence the course of development and what kinds of effect do they have? (causal); how do these influences produce their effects? (process or mechanism). These types of question are, of course, in no way different from those asked in traditional child psychology. The sorts of answer to be expected, however, have been quite different in the two fields. In psychology the emphasis in description was on the measurement of changes in capacity and performance in standard situations. In causal study the only factors considered relevant in the shaping of behaviour were environmental. The only type of process by which these could take effect was considered to be learning, the main debates being over the nature of the learning mechanisms involved. In ethology, by contrast, the central interest in descriptive work has been in those aspects of behaviour that are functionally adaptive in the natural environment, usually in a social context, and how changes in them seem to be related to causal factors both within the individual and in the others with whom it interacts. Causal study has been based on recognition that both internal and external factors can affect the individual in multiple ways, not just through learning, and that development results from the continual interaction of individual and environment. Accepting that the causal determination of behaviour, both moment to moment and developmental, is usually a matter of the utmost complexity, process studies have come to be concerned with constructing models that do justice to this without necessarily being of wide generality. This approach has led to many conceptual advances, schematized in the rest of this section. These advances are gradually freeing the study of human social development from the cramping conceptual restrictions inherent in the behaviourist view of its complete dependence on environmental shaping according to models of learning theory.

Classification and developmental issues

It is a great help in understanding the approach of biologists to complex problems, such as those of development, to bear in mind that the subject matter of their science, the whole of the animal and plant kingdom, is hallmarked by diversity. The way towards finding order in such diversity in terms of principles that accept and do not deny its ubiquity was, of course, shown by Darwin (1859) in his historic demonstration that each species is functionally adapted to a particular way of life, the differences being explicable in terms of evolution by natural selection. Such a demonstration that diversity among organisms is not random could not, however, have been achieved without a vital preceding step. This was the ordering of phenomena by means of classification, which culminated in the Linnean taxonomic system. It is not surprising, therefore, that the advances made by biologists over the last thirty years in conceptualizing development have been due in no small way to the attention paid to classifying, not only diverse behaviour itself, but also the diverse kinds of problem involved in studying its organization and development. Much of this work has been done by Hinde (e.g. 1959, 1971) who, aware that any classification has limits to its usefulness, has helped to expose classifications that have been misleading.

Diversity in behaviour was of central interest to the 'founders' of both ethology and biopsychology. The studies of Lorenz (1958) and Tinbergen (1951) on the adaptive functions of behaviour showed that a similar function in different species could be served by quite different types of behaviour. Schneirla (1952), in his studies of the processes at work in organism–environment interaction, placed great emphasis on the fact that similar types of behaviour in different species could be subserved by different mechanisms. Thus the two schools of thought shared a common attitude towards comparative study. Contrary to the behaviourist view which looked only for similarities across species for the purpose of establishing the wide generality of principles of learning, they regarded the differences as just as revealing, if not more so, than the similarities.

There were, however, major theoretical differences between the two schools about the ways in which behaviour and development could be affected by inherited and environmental factors. It was the consequent interplay between ethologists and biopsychologists that was largely responsible for the first major conceptual advance: exposure of the logical inadequacy of the traditional dichotomous classification of behaviour into the categories of innate and learned. The detailed analyses of instinctive behaviour patterns in animals by Lorenz (1950) and Tinbergen (1951), and the discovery of imprinting, had already pointed to serious limitations to the generality of conventional learning theories. Then the conception that all change in behaviour due to environmental influence could be attributed to learning was challenged by Schneirla's (1957) exposition of the role of 'experience' in development. He showed that this concept refers to a wide range of processes, of which learning is only a relatively small part. Lorenz (1965), however, continued to uphold the dichotomy in his view that fully developed, functionally adaptive, behaviour patterns consist of an intercalation of elements that are either innate or learned, the source of information leading to their adaptiveness being, respectively, either the genes or the environment, never both. Lehrman's attacks (1953,

1970) on this position reflected Schneirla's much more developmental orientation, development being conceived as a continual process of interaction between organism and environment, the multiple effects of external and internal stimulation depending intimately on the changing nature of the organism at successive phases of development. This view links naturally with that of the behaviour geneticists on gene-environment interaction described in the previous section. The resulting clarification was decisive. As pin-pointed by Bateson and Hinde (1976), classification of behaviour in terms of its sources or origins is neither the same as saying that behaviour is either innate or learned, nor does it have implications for the processes by which it develops. Such a classification is of use only in referring to differences between species or individuals. Once these have been identified as either genetic or environmental in origin, further analysis is necessary to understand how such factors produce their effects. As emphasized by Hebb (1953), the development of behaviour is fully dependent on both genes and environment, like the area of a rectangle is on its length and breadth. How the two interact in the development of an individual can only be determined by empirical analysis.

Classification of the kinds of factor to be taken into account in such analysis has played a large part in recent theoretical work in ethology. The fruitfulness of this work has been due in no small way to its freedom from limitation by either a learning theory or an innate behaviour frame of reference; also to its recognition that learning is only one of many kinds of developmental process. Correspondingly, it has led to formulation of the fact that learning in the natural environment is subject to constraints of many kinds. Comparative and developmental research brought together by Hinde and Stevenson-Hinde (1973) has produced a large array of examples of the fact that each species has its own particular limitations and predispositions in learning, and attempts are being made to classify these. They are by no means just a matter of capacity. Stimulus selection, reinforcement effects varying from one response to another, interference by other responses in the learning situation, homeostatic conditions, condition of the nervous system, sex differences: these and other types of factor all affect the nature and extent of the learning that can occur in a particular situation. Furthermore such constraints are not constant throughout ontogeny, as is well known from the study of critical periods. At the human level considerations such as these are, of course, of the utmost theoretical and social significance. But it is only through becoming aware of the possibilities here that investigators will start to enquire about the limitations of learning in social development.

In developmental research an initial problem is always the specification of variables, whether dependent, independent or multiple, that are both biologically relevant and susceptible to analytical procedures. The difficulty has always been greatest in the case of 'social' variables. Here again consideration of the way these are classified has led to important distinctions that can affect research strategy. For instance, decisions about how far the behavioural units to be studied should be molar or molecular can be affected by whether the classification used is a functional or a causal one. Whereas a causal category is one which groups activities according to a common causal factor (e.g. maternal behaviour in relation to a child), a functional one groups them according to a common adaptive consequence (e.g. reproductive behaviour) (Hinde, 1970). While the two sorts of classification often correspond and the functional may be a good guide to the causal, this is not always the case. In reproductive behaviour, for example, sexual behaviour and parental behaviour depend on different causal factors; and even a single motor pattern, such as smiling, may have different functions in different causal situations (Ambrose, 1960). Many discussions of human development referring to types of behaviour that are functionally defined, such as aggression, get into difficulties through assuming that its causation is uniform in all situations (e.g. Montagu, 1976).

Another type of conceptual distinction concerns the effects of causal factors in development. In terms of duration these may range from momentary to the whole span of an individual's development (Bateson, 1976). At the same time the scope of the effects may be considered and a distinction made between those that are specific and those that are general (Bateson, 1976). Although findings about one type of effect in no way imply the others, the temptation to go beyond the evidence is not always resisted. For instance, the research on the deleterious short-term effects of mother–infant separation has sometimes been taken unjustifiably to imply similar long-term effects as well. That the prevailing interest in the developmental significance of the early mother–infant relationship needs to take account of distinctions such as these is already apparent from the evidence for self-righting tendencies in early human development (Dunn, 1976), and for the effects of early social interaction on later cognitive development (Honzik, 1972).

Systems and development

Implicit in the way biologists approach the study of development is the assumption that they are dealing with systems. The fully functioning organism is viewed as a system that is built up of subsystems at different levels of organization. Enduring structures of acids and proteins constitute cells, structures of cells of various types constitute organs, and structures of organs constitute organisms. There is a tendency for such a systems view to be extended beyond the individual organism. Individuals in enduring relationships with one another are the parts that constitute groups, and groups related to each other in particular ways constitute social organizations. The problems of understanding structure and function at each level may be equally complex, but the concepts and principles used at each level are of a different order, such as those of biochemistry, neurophysiology, psychology, anthropology and sociology. Just as the whole is more than the sum of its parts, so the properties of one level of organization cannot be predicted from those at lower levels. Analysis at lower levels may, however, help in explaining them. But because analysis always involves abstraction of certain parts of a system in order to study relations between them, alone it is not enough. As emphasized by Hinde (1971), its usefulness depends on the possibility of resynthesis: description and explanation of relations between components must be seen to fit consistently into the functioning of the system as a whole. The steady retreat from learning theory analyses of the complexities of human behaviour is due in no small part to failure in this respect.

A constantly recurring problem in the study of social development concerns the level of analysis to be used. Behaviour, a concept at the level of the individual organism, is organized and controlled by factors at other levels of conceptualization, such as hormones (biochemical and physiological) and disapproval (psychological and cultural). The level of organization chosen for analysis will depend both upon the type of behaviour and the type of causal factor in which the investigator is interested. This may depend in turn on the ontogenetic, and phylogenetic status of the organism. With respect to behaviour subserving social interaction, for instance, Tavolga (1970) has classified several different levels of communicative interaction in the animal kingdom such as the tonic, signal, symbolic and language levels. These link with the broader classification into biosocial (organic) and psychosocial (involving learning in a social situation) levels. In human development the emphasis on different levels of analysis will vary with age according to the kinds of controlling factor to which behaviour is susceptible. Furthermore, the nature of social influences can themselves be usefully treated in terms of levels. Hinde and Stevenson-Hinde (1976) have distinguished between social interactions (moment to moment), social relationships (series of social interactions occurring regularly between the same individuals) and social structure (a set of social relationships between different individuals).

It is sometimes thought that the only really satisfactory analyses of how behaviour occurs and develops will be in terms of structure and function at the level of the nervous system. Ethologists do not, however, believe this. Understanding of how different computers perform according to a given programme does not come from studying their complete wiring diagrams: they may be constructed in quite different ways and still produce the same result. Dawkins (1976b) points out that the useful answer to how they work is in terms not of the hardware but of the software. He suggests that just as the major principles of genetics were all inferred from external evidence long before the internal molecular structure of the gene was thought about, so understanding of behaviour will come from distillation of principles at a higher level. Such a view implies that real progress in understanding behaviour and its development is dependent upon the construction of adequate models.

In seeking to conceptualize behavioural developmental processes, ethologists and biopsychologists at the present time are not aiming for some all-embracing theory as did Werner (Langer, 1970), because the state of our empirical knowledge makes this totally premature. Rather are they feeling towards concepts and models that help to bring order into relatively limited ranges of diverse data, both across species and across ontogeny. The models are basically of two kinds: first, those concerned with what it is that changes during development, namely the structure and processes underlying functional behaviour occurring at any given time, and, second, those concerned with how these change, that is, the processes underlying developmental change.

Among the earlier attempts to formulate how behaviour is organized were Lorenz's energy model of motivation (discussed by Hinde, 1960), Tinbergen's (1951) hierarchical organization of behaviour and its causal stimuli, and Schneirla's (1959) biphasic approach–withdrawal process. While these models, based on the study of lower vertebrates and insects, made important contributions to research at the time, this research eventually showed their limitations especially in explaining behaviour at mammalian levels (Hinde, 1970). Central problems in understanding complex behaviour are how to analyse its sequential occurrence and how to conceive of the tremendous amount of information by which it must be regulated. In approaching these problems two concepts that are fundamental in the treatment of systems in biology have dominated the scene, namely hierarchy and regulation by negative feedback, or homeostasis. The combination of the two in the TOTE system of Miller et al. (1960) greatly influenced subsequent thinking, and the potential power of the hierarchy concept in ordering behaviour has been pointed out by Dawkins (1976b). Other models that have been applied to the problems, reviewed by Vowles (1970), include control systems that operate by continual monitoring of the mismatch between actual and required states, and finite systems which handle transitions between a limited number of possible states. Vowles has also explored the use of grammatical models such as phrase structure and transformational grammars, because of their ability both to economize on methods of storing prodigious amounts of information and to reduce the number of rules governing transition probabilities. The usefulness of optimality theory which treats successive decision-making in terms of the analysis of costs and benefits is being studied by McFarland (1976).

In attempts to conceptualize how behavioural development occurs embryology has been a major guide in the formation of models. From the zygote onwards cells multiply and differentiate into many different types under the control of genes on the one hand and the environmental medium on the other. As different structures appear new levels of integration become possible, some structures serving body maintenance and physiological homeostasis, others taking forms that are preparatory for later behavioural functions. While the process is one of continual interaction between structure and environment it is also self-stabilizing. The course followed in the development of structures and their relations to each other is resistant to modification, or canalized: there are mechanisms that regulate the direction of change along developmental pathways, and Waddington (1971) modelled these as a ball running down an epigenetic landscape.

While the interactional model of the development of all behaviour, including social, is now generally accepted in ethology (Hinde, 1971), thought is currently directed to the question of internal regulating mechanisms. The relevance both of the developmental pathway concept and of the systems theory concept of the convergence of different routes on the same steady state, or equifinality, has been examined by Bateson (1976). He suggests a model for behaviour whereby its development is guided by internal rules, but reciprocity between individual and environment gives these rules greater flexibility and definition.

The influence of these and other biological models on theory and research in human social development appears to be on the increase. Reference to discussions of canalization and self-righting tendencies in infant development has already been made. Many features of the models discussed will be recognized in biologically orientated human developmental theories of cognition (Piaget, 1953) and of attachment (Bowlby, 1969). They are also evident in theoretical studies by psychologists of the basic requirements for constructing developmental models (e.g. Freedle, 1976; Witz, 1976).

Conclusion

The scope of the biological approach to human social development that has been proposed in this chapter is determined by neo-Darwinian evolutionary theory. According to this theory, the social behaviour, and its mode of development, that is characteristic of the human species including the operation of culture, verbal language and other unique features, is part of an adaptive strategy that has evolved under pressures of natural selection. The place of ontogeny within the theory is as the means whereby genes that subserve this strategy get tested for their adaptive consequences and then replicated, thus enabling the continuation and perhaps further evolution of the species. In this context, study of the development of human social behaviour becomes biologically meaningful only when conceived against the background of (1) its evolutionary history, (2) its adaptive functions, (3) the ecology of the individual, (4) the genotype of the individual and (5) the interactional nature of developmental process.

References

Ainsworth, M. D. S. and Bell, S. M. V. (1969) Some contemporary patterns of mother–infant interaction in the feeding situation. In A. Ambrose (ed.) *Stimulation in Early Infancy*. London: Academic Press.

Ambrose, A. (1969) Discussion in A. Ambrose (ed.) *Stimulation in Early Infancy*. London: Academic Press.

Ambrose, A. (1976) Methodological and conceptual problems in the

48   Issues in childhood social development

comparison of developmental findings across species. In M. von Cranach (ed.) *Methods of Inference from Animal to Human Behaviour.* Paris: Mouton.

Ambrose, A. (1977) The ecological perspective in developmental psychology. In H. McGurk (ed.) *Ecological Factors in Human Development.* Amsterdam: North-Holland.

Ambrose, J. A. (1960) *The Smiling Response in Early Infancy.* London University: Ph.D. Thesis.

Ambrose, J. A. (1965) The study of human social organization: a review of current concepts and approaches. *Symposia Zoological Society of London 14*: 301–14.

Atz, J. W. (1970) The application of the idea of homology to behavior. In L. R. Aronson, E. Tobach, D. S. Lehrman and J. S. Rosenblatt (eds) *Development and Evolution of Behavior.* San Francisco: W. H. Freeman.

Bales, R. F. (1968) Interaction process analysis. In D. L. Sills (ed.) *International Encyclopaedia of the Social Sciences,* Vol. 7. New York: Crowell Collier and Macmillan.

Bales, R. F. (1976) Interaction process analysis. In E. P. Hollander and R. G. Hunt (eds) *Current Perspectives in Social Psychology.* Oxford: Oxford University Press.

Barker, R. G. and Wright, H. F. (1955) *Midwest and its Children.* New York: Harper and Row. (Reprinted by Archan Books, Hamden, Connecticut, 1971.)

Bateson, P. P. G. (1976) Specificity and the origins of behaviour. In J. S. Rosenblatt, R. A. Hinde, E. Shaw and C. Beer. *Advances in the Study of Behavior,* Vol. 6. New York: Academic Press.

Bateson, P. P. G. and Hinde, R. A. (eds) (1976) *Growing Points in Ethology,* Editorial 6. Cambridge: Cambridge University Press.

Beck, S. L. and Rosenblith, J. F. (1972) Constitutional factors in behavior. In J. F. Rosenblith, W. Allinsmith and J. P. Williams (eds) *The Causes of Behavior.* Boston: Allyn and Bacon.

Beer, C. G. (1971) Diversity in the study of the development of social behavior. In E. Tobach, L. R. Aronson and E. Shaw (eds) *The Biopsychology of Development.* New York: Academic Press.

Blurton Jones, N. (1975) Ethology, anthropology and childhood. In R. Fox (ed.) *Biosocial Anthropology.* London: Malaby.

Blurton Jones, N. (1976) Growing points in human ethology: another link between ethology and the social sciences? In P. P. G. Bateson and R. A. Hinde (eds) *Growing Points in Ethology.* Cambridge: Cambridge University Press.

Bodmer, W. F. (1977) Social concern and biological advances. *Journal of the Royal Society of Arts,* March: 180–91.

Bowlby, J. (1958) The nature of the child's tie to his mother. *International Journal of Psycho-Analysis 39*: 350–73.

Bowlby, J. (1969) *Attachment and Loss, Vol. 1: Attachment.* London: Hogarth Press.

Bowlby, J. (1973) *Attachment and Loss, Separation Anxiety and Anger, Vol. 2:* London: Hogarth Press.

Bracken, H. von (1972) Development in psychological twin research. In F. J.

An evolutionary-biological perspective 49

Mönks, W. W. Hartup and J. de Wit (eds) *Determinants of Behavioral Development.* New York: Academic Press.

Brazelton, T. B., Koslowski, B. and Main, M. (1974) The origins of reciprocity: the early mother–infant interaction. In M. Lewis and L. A. Rosenblum (eds) *The Effect of the Infant on its Caregiver.* New York: Wiley.

Brim, O. G. (1975) Macro-structural influences on child development and the need for childhood social indicators. *American Journal of Orthopsychiatry 45*: 516–24.

Bronfenbrenner, U. (1977) Ecological factors in human development in retrospect and prospect. In H. McGurk (ed.) *Ecological Factors in Human Development.* Amsterdam: North-Holland.

Bruner, J. S. (1969) Discussion in A. Ambrose (ed.) *Stimulation in Early Infancy.* London: Academic Press.

Bruner, J. S. (1972) The nature and uses of immaturity. *American Psychologist 27*: 687.

Cairns, R. B. (1976) The ontogeny and phylogeny of social interactions. In M. E. Hahn and E. C. Simmel (eds) *Communicative Behavior and Evolution.* New York: Academic Press.

Campbell, B. (1971) *Human Evolution.* London: Heinemann.

Clarke, A. M. and Clarke, A. D. B. (1976) *Early Experience: Myth and Evidence.* London: Open Books.

Clutton-Brock, T. H. and Harvey, P. H. (1976) Evolutionary rules and primate societies. In P. P. G. and R. A. Hinde (eds) *Growing Points in Ethology.* Cambridge: Cambridge University Press.

Cochran, M. M. (1975) The Swedish child rearing study: an example of the ecological approach to the study of human development. Paper read at the Third Biennial Conference of the International Society for the Study of Behavioural Development. University of Surrey, Guildford.

Crook, J. H. (1976) Problems of inference in the comparison of animal and human social organizations. In M. von Cranach (ed.) *Methods of Inference From Animal to Human Behaviour.* Paris: Mouton.

Darwin, C. (1859) *On the Origin of Species.* London: John Murray.

Dawkins, R. (1976a) *The Selfish Gene.* Oxford: Oxford University Press.

Dawkins, R. (1976b) Hierarchical organization: a candidate principle for ethology. In P. P. G. Bateson and R. A. Hinde (eds) *Growing Points in Ethology.* Cambridge: Cambridge University Press.

De Beer, G. (1958) *Embryos and Ancestors.* London: Oxford University Press.

DeFries, J. C. (1972) Quantitative aspects of genetics and environment in the determination of behavior. In L. Ehrman, G. S. Omenn and E. Caspari (eds) *Genetics, Environment and Behavior.* New York: Academic Press.

DeVore, L. (1965) *Primate Behavior.* New York: Holt, Rinehart and Winston.

Dobzhansky, T. (1970) *Genetics of the Evolutionary Process.* New York: Columbia University Press.

Dunn, J. (1976) How far do early differences in mother–child relations affect later development? In P. P. G. Bateson and R. A. Hinde (eds) *Growing Points in Ethology.* Cambridge: Cambridge University Press.

Ehrman, L., Omenn, G. S. and Caspari, E. (eds) (1972) *Genetics, Environment and Behavior.* New York: Academic Press.

Emery, F. E. (1967) The next thirty years: concepts, methods and anticipation. *Human Relations 20*: 199–237.

Erlenmeyer-Kimling, L. and Jarvick, L. F. (1963) Genetics and intelligence: a review. *Science 142*: 1,477.

Erlenmeyer-Kimling, L. (1972). Gene–environment interactions and the variability of behavior. In L. Ehrman, G. S. Omenn and E. Caspari (eds) *Genetics, Environment and Behavior*. New York: Academic Press.

Escalona, S. K. (1969) *The Roots of Individuality*. London: Tavistock.

Eysenck, H. J. (1956) The inheritance of extraversion–introversion. *Acta Psychologica 12*: 95–110.

Fantz, R. L. (1967) Visual perception and experience in early infancy. In H. W. Stevenson, E. H. Hess and H. L. Rheingold (eds) *Early Behavior: Comparative and Developmental Approaches*. New York: Wiley.

Freedle, R. O. (1976) Some ingredients for constructing developmental models. In K. F. Riegel and J. A. Meacham (eds) *The Developing Individual in a Changing World, Vol. 1*. Paris: Mouton.

Freedman, D. G. (1965) An ethological approach to the genetical study of human behavior. In S. G. Vandenberg (ed.) *Methods and Goals in Human Behavior Genetics*. New York: Academic Press.

Freedman, D. G. (1972) Genetic variations on the hominid theme: individual sex and ethnic differences. In F. J. Mönks, W. W. Hartup and J. de Wit (eds) *Determinants of Behavioral Development*. New York: Academic Press.

Freud, S. (1925) *An Autobiographical Study*. Standard Edition, *20*. London: Hogarth Press.

Freud, S. (1930) *Civilization and its Discontents*. Standard Edition, *21*. London: Hogarth Press.

Freud, S. (1940) *An Outline of Psycho-analysis*. Standard Edition, *23*. London: Hogarth Press.

Fuller, J. L. (1967) Experiential deprivation and later behavior. *Science 158*: 1645–52.

Fuller, J. L. and Thompson, W. R. (1960) *Behavior Genetics*. New York: Wiley.

Goodall, J. (van Lawick-) (1965) Chimpanzees of the Gombe Stream Reserve. In I. DeVore (ed.) *Primate Behavior*. New York: Holt.

Gottesman, I. (1963) Heritability of personality: a demonstration. *Psychological Monographs 77*: (Whole No. 572).

Gottesman, I. and Heston, L. L. (1972) Human behavioral adaptations: speculations on their genesis. In L. Ehrman, G. S. Omenn and E. Caspari (eds) *Genetics, Environment and Behavior*. New York: Academic Press.

Hamburg, D. A. (1967) Genetics of adrenocortical hormone metabolism in relation to psychological stress. In J. Hirsch (ed.) *Behavior-Genetic Analysis*. New York: McGraw-Hill.

Hamilton, W. D. (1964) The genetical theory of social behavior (I and II). *Journal of Theoretical Biology 7*: 1–16, 17–32.

Hamilton, W. D. (1970) Selfish and spiteful behaviour in an evolutionary model. *Nature 228*: 1218–20.

Hamilton, W. D. (1975) Innate social aptitudes of man: an approach from evolutionary genetics. In R. Fox (ed.) *ASA Studies – Bisocial Anthropology*. London: Dent.

Harlow, H. F., Harlow, M. K. and Hansen, E. W. (1963) The maternal affectional system of rhesus monkeys. In H. L. Rheingold (ed.) *Maternal Behavior in Mammals.* New York: Wiley.

Harris, H. (1969). Enzyme and protein polymorphism in human populations. *British Medical Bulletin 25* : 5–13.

Hebb, D. O. (1953) Heredity and environment in animal behaviour. *British Journal of Animal Behaviour 1* : 43–7.

Hinde, R. A. (1959) Some recent trends in ethology. In S. Koch (ed.) *Psychology, a Study of a Science.* New York: McGraw-Hill.

Hinde, R. A. (1960) Energy models of motivation. *Symp. Soc. exp. Biol. 14* : 199–213.

Hinde, R. A. (1970) *Animal Behaviour: A Synthesis of Ethology and Comparative Psychology.* New York: McGraw-Hill.

Hinde, R. A. (1971) Some problems in the study of the development of social behavior. In E. Tobach, L. R. Aranson and E. Shaw (eds) *The Biopsychology of Development.* New York: Academic Press.

Hinde, R. A. (1975) The concept of function. In G. Baerends, C. Beer and A. Manning (eds) *Function and Evolution in Behaviour.* Oxford: Clarendon Press.

Hinde, R. A. and Stevenson-Hinde, J. (1973) *Constraints on Learning.* London: Academic Press.

Hinde, R. A. and Stevenson-Hinde, J. (1976) Toward understanding relationships: dynamic stability. In P. P. G. Bateson and R. A. Hinde (eds) *Growing Points in Ethology.* Cambridge: Cambridge University Press.

Honzik, M. P. (1972) Intellectual abilities at age of 40 years in relation to the early family environment. In F. J. Mönks, W. W. Hartup and J. de Wit (eds) *Determinants of Behavioral Development.* New York: Academic Press.

Humphrey, N. K. (1976) The social function of intellect. In P. P. G. Bateson and R. A. Hinde (eds) *Growing Points in Ethology.* Cambridge: Cambridge University Press.

Jensen, A. R. (1972) Discussion in L. Ehrman, G. S. Omenn and E. Caspari (eds) *Genetics, Environment and Behavior.* New York: Academic Press.

Jensen, A. R., Hirsch, J., Hudson, L., Rose, S. P. R. and Richards, M. P. M. (1971) Race, intelligence and IQ: a debate. In N. Chalmers, R. Crawley and S. P. R. Rose (eds) *The Biological Bases of Behaviour.* London: Harper and Row.

King, J. A. (1968) Species specificity and early experience. In G. Newton and S. Levine (eds) *Early Experience and Behavior.* Springfield: Thomas.

Korner, A. F. (1974) The effect of the infant's state, level of arousal, sex and ontogenetic stage on the caregiver. In M. Lewis and L. A. Rosenblum (eds) *The Effect of the Infant on its Caregiver.* New York: Wiley.

Kuttner, R. (1960). An hypothesis on the evolution of intelligence. *Psychological Reports 6* : 238–89.

Langer, J. (1970) Werner's theory of development. In P. Mussen (ed.) *Carmichael's Manual of Child Psychology.* Third edition. New York: Wiley.

Lehrman, D. S. (1953) A critique of Konrad Lorenz's theory of instinctive behavior. *Quarterly Review of Biology 28* : 337–63.

52   Issues in childhood social development

Lehrman, D. S. (1970) Semantic and conceptual issues in the nature–nurture problem. In L. R. Aranson, E. Tobach, D. S. Lehrman and J. S. Rosenblatt (eds) *Development and Evolution of Behavior*. San Francisco: W. H. Freeman.

Lewis, M. and Lee-Painter, S. (1974) An interactional approach to the mother–infant dyad. In M. Lewis and L. A. Rosenblum (eds) *The Effect of the Infant on its Caregiver*. New York: Wiley.

Lewontin, R. C. and Hubby, J. L. (1966) A molecular approach to the study of genic heterozygosity in natural populations. *Genetics 54*: 595–609.

Lorenz, K. (1950) The comparative method in studying innate behaviour patterns. *Symp. Soc. exp. Biol. 4*: 221–68.

Lorenz, K. (1958) The evolution of behavior. *Scientific American 199*: 67–78.

Lorenz, K. (1965) *Evolution and Modification of Behavior*. Chicago: University of Antiago Press.

Lorenz, K. (1966) *On Aggression*. London: Methuen.

Mason, W. A. (1968) Early social deprivation in the nonhuman primates: implications for human behavior. In D. C. Glass (ed.) *Environmental Influences*. New York: Russell Sage.

Mason, W. A. (1975) The adaptive significance of developmental rates. Paper read at Third Biennial Conference of the International Society for the Study of Behavioural Development, University of Surrey, Guildford.

Masters, R. D. (1976) Functional approaches to analogical comparison between species. In M. von Cranach (ed.) *Methods of Inference from Animal to Human Behaviour*. Paris: Mouton.

Maynard Smith, J. (1964) Group selection and kin selection. *Nature 201*: 1145–7.

Mayr, E. (1976) *Evolution and the Diversity of Life*. Cambridge: Belknap Press.

McClearn, G. E. (1970) Genetic influences on behavior and development. In P. H. Mussen (ed.) *Carmichael's Manual of Child Psychology, Vol. 1*, Third edition. New York: Wiley.

McDougall, W. (1908) *An Introduction to Social Psychology*. London: Methuen.

McFarland, D. J. (1976) Form and function in the temporal organization of behaviour. In P. P. G. Bateson and R. A. Hinde (eds) *Growing Points in Ethology*. Cambridge: Cambridge University Press.

Mettler, L. E. and Gregg, T. G. (1969) *Population Genetics and Evolution*. Englewood Cliffs: Prentice-Hall.

Miller, G. A., Galanter, E. and Pribram, K. H. (1960) *Plans and the Structure of Behavior*. New York: Holt, Rinehart and Winston.

Montagu, A. (1976) *The Nature of Human Aggression*. Oxford: Oxford University Press.

Montagu, M. F. A. (1962) Time, morphology and neoteny in the evolution of man. In M. F. A. Montagu (ed.) *Culture and the Evolution of Man*. New York: Oxford University Press.

Murphy, L. B. (1964) Some aspects of the first relationship. *International Journal of analysis 45*: 31–43.

Odum, E. P. (1971) *Fundamentals of Ecology*. Philadelphia: Saunders.

Omenn, G. S. and Motulsky, A. G. (1972) Biochemical genetics and the evolution of human behavior. In L. Ehrman, G. S. Omenn and E. Caspari (eds) *Genetics, Environment and Behavior*. New York: Academic Press.

An evolutionary-biological perspective   53

Overton, W. F. and Reese, H. W. (1973) Models of development: methodological implications. In J. R. Nesselroade and H. W. Reese (eds) *Life-Span Developmental Psychology: Methodological Issues.* New York: Academic Press.

Overton, W. F. and Reese, H. W. (1977) General models for man–environment relations. In H. McGurk (ed.) *Ecological Factors in Human Development.* Amsterdam: North-Holland.

Parsons, T., Bales, R. et al. (1955) *Family, Socialization and Interaction Process.* New York: Free Press.

Pfeiffer, J. E. (1969) *The Emergence of Man.* New York: Harper and Row.

Piaget, J. (1953) *The Origin of Intelligence in the Child.* London: Routledge and Kegan Paul.

Prechtl, H. F. R., Akiyama, Y., Zinkin, P. and Grant, D. K. (1968) Polygraphic studies of the full-term newborn: I. Technical aspects and quantitative analysis. In M. Bax and R. C. MacKeith (eds) *Studies in Infancy: Clinics in Developmental Medicine.* London: Heinemann.

Reynolds, V. (1976) *The Biology of Human Action.* Reading: W. H. Freeman.

Rice, A. K. and Trist, E. L. (1952) Institutional and sub-institutional determinants of change in labour turnover. *Human Relations* 5: 347–71.

Riciutti, H. (1977) Adverse social and biological influences in early development. In H. McGurk (ed.) *Ecological Factors in Human Development.* Amsterdam: North-Holland.

Ricklefs, R. E. (1973) *Ecology.* London: Nelson.

Scarr, S. (1975) An evolutionary perspective on infant intelligence: species patterns and individual variations. In F. D. Horowitz (ed.) *Review of General Development Research,* Volume 4. Chicago: University of Chicago Press.

Schneirla, T. C. (1952) A consideration of some conceptual trends in comparative psychology. *Psychological Bulletin* 49: 559–97.

Schneirla, T. C. (1957) The concept of development in comparative psychology. In D. B. Harris (ed.) *The Concept of Development,* Minneapolis: University of Minnesota Press.

Schneirla, T. C. (1959) An evolutionary and developmental theory of biphasic processes underlying approach and withdrawal. In M. R. Jones (ed.) *Current Theory and Research in Motivation.* Lincoln: University of Nebraska Press.

Schoggen, P. and Barker, R. G. (1977) Ecological factors in development in an American and an English small town. In H. McGurk (ed.) *Ecological Factors in Human Development.* Amsterdam: North-Holland.

Schultz, A. H. (1956) Post-embryonic age-changes. *Primatologia* 1: 887–964.

Sorokin, P. (1928) *Contemporary Sociological Theories.* New York: Harper and Row.

Spencer, H. (1900) *Principles of Sociology.* New York.

Spuhler, J. N. and Lindzey, G. (1967) Racial differences in behavior. In J. Hirsch (ed.) *Behavior-Genetic Analysis.* New York: McGraw-Hill.

Tanner, J. M. (1970) Physical growth. In P. H. Mussen (ed.) *Carmichael's Manual of Child Psychology.* New York: Wiley.

Tavolga, W. N. (1970) Levels of interaction in animal communication. In L. R. Aranson, E. Tobach, D. S. Lehrman and J. S. Rosenblatt (eds) *Development and Evolution of Behavior.* San Francisco: Freeman.

Thomas, A., Chess, S., Birch, H. G., Hertzig, M. E. and Korn, S. (1964) *Behavioral Individuality in Early Childhood.* London: London University Press.
Thompson, W. R. (1968) Genetics and social behavior. In D. C. Glass (ed.) *Genetics.* Biology and Behavior Series. New York: Rockefeller University Press.
Thompson, W. R. (1972) Discussion in L. Ehrman, G. S. Omenn and E. Caspari (eds) *Genetics, Environment and Behavior.* New York: Academic Press.
Tinbergen, N. (1951) *The Study of Instinct.* Oxford: Clarendon Press.
Tinbergen, N. (1965) Behavior and natural selection. In J. A. Moore (ed.) *Ideas in Modern Biology,* Proceedings XVI International Zoology Congress, Washington: 521–42.
Tinbergen, N., Broekhuysen, G. J., Feekes, F., Houghton, J. C. W., Kruuk, H. and Szulc, E. (1962) Egg shell removal by the black-headed gull. Larus ridibundus, L. *Behaviour 19* : 74–117.
Trivers, R. L. (1971) The evolution of reciprocal altruism. *Quarterly Review of Biology 46* : 35–57.
Trivers, R. L. (1972) Parental investment and sexual selection. In B. Campbell (ed.) *Sexual Selection and the Descent of Man 1871–1971.* London: Heinemann.
Trivers, R. L. (1974) Parent–offspring conflict. *American Zoologist 14* : 249–64.
Ugurel-Semin, R. (1974) Ecology of attitudes in adolescents in a rural part of Turkey. In H, Thomae and T. Endo (eds) *The Adolescent and his Environment.* Basel: S. Karger.
Vandenberg, S. G. (1967) Hereditary factors in normal personality traits. In J. Wortis (ed.) *Recent Advances in Biological Psychiatry,* Vol. 9. New York: Plenum Press.
Von Cranach, M. (1976). Inference from animal to human behaviour. In M. von Cranach (ed.) *Methods of Inference from Animal to Human Behaviour.* Paris: Mouton.
Vowles, D. M. (1970) Neuroethology, evolution and grammar. In L. R. Aranson, E. Tobach, D. S. Lehrman and J. S. Rosenblatt (eds) *Development and Evolution of Behavior.* San Francisco: Freeman.
Waddington, C. H. (1971) Concepts of development. In E. Tobach, L. R. Aranson and E. Shaw (eds) *The Biopsychology of Development.* New York: Academic Press.
Wade, N. (1976) Sociobiology: troubled birth of a new discipline. *Science 191* : 1151–5.
Wilson, E. O. (1976) *Sociobiology.* Cambridge: Belknap Press.
Witz, K. (1976) Conceptualizing behavioural development. In K. F. Riegel and J. A. Meacham (eds) *The Developing Individual in a Changing World, Vol. 1.* Paris: Mouton.
Wynne-Edwards, V. C. (1962) *Animal Dispersion in Relation to Social Behaviour.* Edinburgh: Oliver and Boyd.
Young, H. B. (1977) Social pressures and biological expressions. Paper read at the Fourth International Conference of the International Organization for the Study of Human Development, Paris.

2 The role of the mother in early social development

H. Rudolph Schaffer
and Charles K. Crook

Introduction

The child's transformation from a biological to a social being in the space of just the first year or two of life is surely the most important aspect by far of early development. How it occurs is a matter of fascination to both the student of human nature and the practitioner wanting to improve the conditions under which children are reared.

That the particular society in which children are brought up has powerful effects on the course of their development cannot be doubted. Anthropological evidence in particular can highlight the sharply contrasting effects on personality development that different child-rearing patterns may have. Take some of Margaret Mead's (1935) descriptions of socialization practices and their outcome in different cultures: the angry rejection by the Mundugumour mother of her child from the moment of pregnancy onward and the pattern of hostility which pervades all adult behaviour; the pathological teasing that Balinese children continually experience from their mothers and the emotional bluntness that becomes the outstanding characteristic of individuals in that society; the reversal of sex-role appropriate behaviour in comparison with Western norms that Tchambuli upbringing of boys and girls induces, and so on. The same point emerges from intra-societal comparisons, albeit in a less dramatic form: the influence of social class on language acquisition and subsequent intellectual performance is one such instance.

Yet it is easy to concentrate on differences and neglect the similarities underlying the diversity. The very nature of mother and child imposes constraints that ensure a basic similarity underlying the social behaviour of all. Thus all infants are born motorically helpless and dependent and signal their needs by such species-specific responses as crying and smiling, and the manner of responding to these signals on the part of their caretakers shows remarkable similarities too – see, for example, the universal usage of adults' baby language when addressing young children (Fergusson, 1964). An account of social development ought therefore not to confine itself to explaining differences alone: it should also consider similarities.

The society that impinges on a child is, of course, not an abstract entity; it functions through particular agents. Two questions arise, namely who these agents are and how they function. Our concern in this chapter is with the latter problem; before we turn to its examination, however, let us also acknowledge the importance of the former. The identity of socialization agents varies to some extent from one culture to another: older siblings, the maternal uncle, and unrelated women have all been found to play roles in other societies that they do not play in our own. Yet in our society too there is nothing absolute about the identity of socialization agents, particularly in view of the rapid changes overtaking such institutions as the nuclear family. The increasing recognition given to the influence of the father (Lamb, 1976) and of peers (Bronfenbrenner, 1971; Hartup, 1970) is ample testimony of this fact, as is the virtual disappearance of the wet-nurse and the nanny who in former times played such important parts in certain social circles.

Nevertheless, in the first year or two of life (the period of concern to us in the present chapter) the child's care in most cases tends to be the primary responsibility of one person. That person – whether the child's biological parent or not, even whether male or female – we shall refer to as 'mother'. It is by analysing the child's interactions with that individual that we can learn how the first steps in the socialization process are taken. This chapter will therefore examine the events that take place in these interactions, with particular reference to the part played by the mother in determining their structure.

Approaches to socialization

Socialization is an umbrella term that refers to a wide range of topics frequently bound together in only the most tenuous manner. The very diversity of definitions given to the term is an indication of this confusion. LeVine (1969), for example, distinguishes three views of the process, namely socialization as enculturation, as the acquisition of impulse control, and as role training. The three views are said to correspond roughly to the orientations of cultural anthropology, psychology and sociology respectively.

Yet even within any one of these disciplines, with particular reference to psychology, there is by no means unanimity. To a large extent this is a reflection of the particular theory of child development that happens to be prevalent at the time. For example, as long as learning theory was the predominant point of view, the child was seen as an essentially passive organism, shaped by whatever forces he happened to encounter in his environment. Socialization was thus seen as a kind of clay-moulding process: the child, that is, arrives in the world as a formless lump of clay and society, as represented by mothers, fathers, teachers and other authority figures, proceeds to mould him into whatever shape it desires. The end product would thus be wholly explicable in terms of the external forces which the child encountered, and if by chance this product turned out to be undesirable it could be regarded as entirely the responsibility of the socializing agents. It follows that all attempts to understand how socialization comes about must involve an analysis of the behaviour of the adults with whom the child comes into contact: the child's own part was confined simply to observing, learning, retaining, imitating and reproducing whatever occurred in front of him.

The advent of Piagetian theory put an end to this one-sided view – though only to substitute another equally one-sided account. From birth on, Piaget maintained, the child's behaviour shows form and organization. Far from being a *tabula rasa* the neonate is already equipped with certain behavioural structures by means of which he acts on the environment and which enable him to influence others as well as be influenced by them. Far from being a passive being, the infant interacts spontaneously with his surroundings; far from responding to every stimulus to which the environment happens to expose him he carefully selects those aspects of his surroundings that fit in with his predilections. A considerable body of empirical research on infant behaviour has now spelled out the details of psychological competence in the early months and years of life and demonstrated the many avenues open to the infant to make contact with others. The child-rearing literature echoed this change of orientation: from a concern with the socializing adult's action it switched to a concern with the socialized child's action, and a primarily child-centred approach thus came into being – one which focused solely on the child and took the environment for granted, neglecting its variations and treating it simply as a constant. We thus see a swing from one exteme to the other, from a preoccupation with environmental forces to a preoccupation with the individual child without any reference to that environment. In each case a uni-directional view is taken which neglects one half of the picture.

It is only more recently that a *dyadic* view has emerged. Socialization, thus conceived, is based on interaction and its function is to smooth the conduct of such interaction. It always involves two (or more) participants, each already equipped with his own set of predispositions, aims, intentions and predilections, and any interaction between them must therefore inevitably involve a negotiating process, as a result of which progressive modification in the behaviour of both participants takes place. Zigler and Child (1973) bring us nearest to this point of view with their characterization of socialization as 'the whole process by which an individual develops, *through transactions with other people*, his specific patterns of socially relevant behaviour and experience' (italics ours). To understand the socialization process means therefore that these transactions must be examined in detail, for by attending to the behaviour of *both* parties we can learn how the child becomes gradually transformed into an increasingly acculturated being.

This also means, however, that our concern is no longer solely with long-term effects – with just the final product that eventually emerges in maturity. Much of previous research involved efforts to link early experience in child-rearing situations to personality characteristics in maturity – efforts that (as reviews by Orlansky, 1949, and Caldwell, 1964, have shown) have resulted in ambiguous and often negative results. It is now apparent that the attempt to forge such links over time is too fraught with methodological and conceptual difficulties to make simple antecedent–consequent statements possible (Clarke and Clarke, 1976). Instead, consideration needs to be given to all the intermediate steps, i.e. to the here-and-now effects that indicate how the child and his adult caretakers progressively modify each other.

That children's behaviour is changed as a result of interacting with socializing agents, and that this change occurs in particular directions which reflect the values of the society in which they live, is, of course, not in question. How the change is brought about, however, is still open to debate. In the past socialization has generally been treated as though a model of 'potty training' were applicable to it all: as though, that is, it is solely concerned with preventing the child from doing what is natural and forcing him to comply with some quite arbitrary requests by powerful adults for new and unnatural behaviour. Such a view sees the child as being in fundamental opposition to society, and conceives of socializing techniques as those forces (often punitive) that push the child into compliance. Many such techniques have been suggested in the past (Hoffman, 1970), power assertion and withdrawal of love being perhaps the most common. Thus much of the socialization literature is concerned with sanctions and with the way in which socially desirable behaviour is reinforced and undesirable behaviour punished.

There are a number of criticisms of this view that one can make: the slippery nature of the concept of reinforcement and the consequent difficulty of ever proving or disproving it; the fact that the techniques suggested are rarely derived from observing what parents actually do; the highly constrained model of the rewarding or punishing parent which laboratory studies of social reinforcement generally assume, and so on. But more important, it neglects the basic mutuality between mother and child that recent studies have so strongly emphasized and that forms the framework within which any attempt to understand the socialization process must be placed.

Mother–child mutuality

Much of the literature concerned with the child's earliest stages of social development has centred on the concept of attachment (see Ainsworth, 1974; Bowlby, 1969; Schaffer, 1971). A considerable body of research has now accumulated around this topic; most of this, however, treats attachment as an essentially individual-based characteristic, i.e. as though it were the property of individual children which they must acquire in the course of development and which from then on forms part of their personality. The questions asked by investigators have accordingly concerned such topics as the age when attachments first become evident, the behaviour patterns whereby they are expressed, the variations in intensity of both an intra- and an inter-individual nature, the persons to whom they are directed, and so on. The focus of study, in other words, is on the child *per se*, with relatively little attention being paid to his social partners and the interaction with them.

It is only recently that a new direction has been taken in the way in which early social development is approached, with emphasis given to the interactive quality of social behaviour (Schaffer, 1977a). The mother–child relationship is seen, in other words, as a total dyadic system in which both partners play a part in achieving mutual synchrony. Accordingly, the questions now asked by investigators are different: they concern the nature of these early dyadic systems, their characteristics at different developmental stages, and the respective contributions which mother and child make to the interaction.

Some early social interactions

Let us first acknowledge the fact that from birth onwards an infant participates in interpersonal behaviour sequences of many types, of varying degrees of sophistication and intricacy, and involving different channels of communication (visual, vocal, tactual, and so on), but all already bearing some of the hallmarks that characterize interpersonal dialogues. Some examples, though drawn from very different situations, show the communality that exists among these early dialogues.

The sucking response is the first means whereby an infant comes into close contact with another being. A great body of work (reviewed by Kessen et al., 1970) testifies to the intricacy of this response; in particular, we have learned a great deal in recent years about the innately based temporal organization underlying sucking. This normally takes the form of a burst–pause pattern, i.e. sucks tend to occur in a series of bursts, with pauses interspersed. We are thus confronted with a high-frequency micro-rhythm – an apparently simple motor activity that is in fact organized in complex time sequences regulated by an endogenous mechanism in the brain (Wolff, 1967). It is perhaps ironic that a highly social response such as sucking has, until recently, usually been abstracted from the interpersonal context in which it generally occurs and studied in isolation. Yet, as the work of Kaye (1977) indicates, by adopting a wider focus of study and including the mother's as well as the baby's behaviour during feeding, sucking emerges as just one part of an interpersonal dialogue that takes place in this situation. In particular, Kaye has shown that mothers tend to interact with their babies in precise synchrony with the burst–pause pattern of sucking. During bursts they are generally quiet and inactive; during pauses, on the other hand, they jiggle, stroke and talk to the baby, thereby setting in motion an alternating pattern in which first one and then the other is principal actor while the other remains passive. This is primarily brought about, however, because the mother allows herself to be paced by the infant's spontaneous behaviour: she fits in with his natural sucking pattern, responds to his ceasing to suck as though it were a signal to her, and in this way sets up a dialogue between them.

This example provides us with a prototype for a great deal of early interaction. In particular, it emphasizes that the interpersonal synchrony generally observed between mother and infant is based on the integration of the two participants' responses *over time*, and that it is accomplished on the basis of two main factors: first, the baby's spontaneously occurring behaviour, temporally organized according to endogenous mechanisms, and, second, the mother's sensitivity to such periodicity and her willingness to fit in with this pattern. The precision and smoothness which generally characterize the interaction is thus the resultant of these two factors.

A second example concerns vocal interchange. One common way of ensuring the smoothness of many forms of interaction is by means of an alternating pattern of dialogue. This is especially evident in adults' verbal conversations, where an intricate set of rules for turn taking and the smooth exchange of speaker- and listener-roles can be discerned (Duncan, 1973). A study by Schaffer et al. (1977) has shown, however, that formal characteristics of verbal interchange such as turn taking antedate the appearance of language: the vocal exchanges of pre-verbal infants with their mothers in a free play situation were just as much characterized by an alternating pattern as those of older, verbal children. Moreover, among the former the exchanges of speaker- and listener-roles were just as easily handled, with the same kind of split-second timing, as was found in the older group.

Among adults the turn-taking pattern is, of course, usually brought about by the *joint* action of the two participants: they both know the rules and both attend to the signals on which these rules are based. It seems highly unlikely that this applies to infants too; instead, a much more likely explanation is that the responsibility is almost wholly assumed by the mother. The infant's vocalizations, that is, occur in bouts and, by carefully attending, the mother is then able to fill in the pauses between the bouts. Thus – as with sucking – we find that the interaction starts with the infant's spontaneous behaviour and that the mother, by virtue of her sensitivity to the temporal patterning of her baby's responses, then incorporates these into a mutual exchange in which she acts *as if* his behaviour had truly communicational significance.

One further example comes from a study by Collis and Schaffer (1975) on the way in which mothers and infants establish mutual attention to features of the environment. Observations in a novel environment containing a number of attention-compelling foci (large, brightly coloured toys placed at a distance from the pair) highlighted two findings. First, it was noted that there was a strong tendency for both partners to be attending to the same object at the same time (a phenomenon termed 'visual co-orientation'), and, second, when one examines how such mutual attention is brought about it emerges that almost invariably it was the baby that led and the mother that followed. The baby, that is, showed spontaneous interest in the various toys, the mother closely monitored his behaviour almost continuously and then, as if allowing herself to be led by him, she looked in that direction too. Visual co-orientation means that the couple share a topic of interest and it thus may become the first step in a whole series of further interactions involving this topic (talking about it, manipulating it, and so forth). More important to our present concern is that once again we have an illustration of a type of interaction that is initiated by the infant but converted by the mother into a dyadic experience.

Social interactions, even those involving young infants, generally give the impression of 'smoothness'. Somehow the various participants manage to enmesh their individual responses into a synchronous dyadic flow with all the appearance of dialogue. Yet these early interactions are really 'pseudo-dialogues', for the two partners do not play an equal role. In each of the examples we have examined the infant sets the pace and the mother allows herself to be phased by his behaviour. Reciprocity, in the sense of both partners taking equal responsibility for maintaining the interaction by assuming interlocking and exchangeable roles, is not yet evident.

The infant's contribution

It is apparent that the 'smoothness' of these early interactions is due to contributions from both mother and infant. As to the infant, it has been pointed out elsewhere (Schaffer, 1978) that his behaviour has all the hallmarks of being socially pre-adapted, i.e. that by virtue of its endogenous characteristics it is from the beginning specifically suited to social interaction. Two aspects of social pre-adaptation may be distinguished, namely *structural* and *functional* aspects. The former refer to those bodily structures which serve to bring the infant into contact with other people, such as the oral apparatus that is precisely adapted to cope with the nipple and food that the mother will provide, his visual structures that are highly sensitive to those aspects of stimulation that tend to emanate from other people's faces, and his auditory equipment that is selectively attuned to the human voice. Functional aspects refer to the way in which these structures are used, and may be seen in particular in the fact that from the first weeks of life the different behaviour patterns of the child (sucking, smiling, crying, and so on) are organized according to specific temporal sequences. Thus the biological rhythms that underlie such responses as sucking have a regularity which make it possible for the mother to anticipate the infant's behaviour, and it may well be that the split-second timing that characterizes so much of interactive behaviour is the result of such anticipation. And furthermore, the on–off nature of so much of sensori-motor activity (seen, for example, in the bout structure of vocalization) provides the pauses that enable the other person to take turns with the infant and in this way to set up the pseudo-dialogues so characteristic of the infant's early social life.

A basic compatibility between the infant and his caretakers is thus ensured. In due course, through repeated participation in interactive sequences, the infant's primitive temporal patterns become transformed into vastly more complex and flexible structures. Pseudo-dialogues become dialogues, in that *both* partners take a share in sustaining them and playing mutually integrative and exchangeable roles (speaker and listener, actor and spectator, giver and taker, and so forth). For this to come about, however, the child's social partners must be willing to afford the necessary opportunities for interaction through involvement in dialogue-like exchanges.

The mother's contribution

It is apparent that a considerable onus lies with the mother to ensure that the infant's social experience is appropriately structured. How does she play this part and, for that matter, how may one best study what she does?

In the past the examination of the mother's relationship with her child has been based to a considerable extent on the use of interviews and questionnaires, in which the individuals involved reported on their own behaviour. The advantage of such global techniques lies, of course, in their economy: within the space of a few minutes a mother can make generalized statements about her behaviour within the last twenty-four hours, the last week or the last few years. She has, moreover, access to parts of the family's daily life that outsiders would not normally penetrate, and in addition she can endow events with an emotional significance that might well be missed by an impartial observer.

Yet the disadvantages of such an approach have gradually come to outweigh the advantages. In part this arises from increasing doubts about the reliability of data so obtained: for instance, in an unfortunately only too rare attempt at replication Yarrow et al. (1968) completely failed to confirm the classical study of Sears et al. (1957), in which reports from the mothers of 379 five-year-old children had been obtained regarding the rearing practices they had adopted at various phases of the child's life. Using the same techniques and measures of Sears et al. in order to examine the child-rearing antecedents of dependence, aggression and conscience formation, Yarrow and her colleagues were unable to find the patterns of relationships previously obtained, and were thus forced to conclude that the assumed link between maternal influence and child behaviour has as yet no roots in solid data and that its verification thus remains a subject for future research.

Equally compelling, however, was the gradual disillusionment with the kinds of concepts that were used for elucidating parental behaviour – concepts like warmth, rejection, authoritarianism, and so forth. Adopted originally because of their wide-ranging nature, it gradually became clear that they were far too global and arbitrary for explanatory purposes. As summary variables they average out parental characteristics over time and situation and as a result not only neglect some of the most meaningful nuances of the relationship but also fail to act as predictors of child behaviour. Concepts need to arise out of the behavioural data to which they refer rather than be imposed on them.

Accordingly, a much more observationally based approach to the study of the mother–child relationship has now been adopted – impelled to a considerable extent by the growth of human ethology (Blurton Jones, 1972). It has also become apparent that when this approach is employed at a highly detailed, micro-analytic level of description, a great many new phenomena may be uncovered which throw light on the way in which mother and child establish mutuality (Schaffer, 1977a). In particular, it is now becoming possible to specify much more precisely just what dyadic techniques a mother employs in interacting with children at various ages (see Schaffer, 1977b, for further discussion).

That mothers carefully and continuously adjust the type of stimulation offered to an infant throughout the course of an interactive episode and that they most sensitively, though generally quite unconsciously, adjust their behaviour towards him in the light of their perception of his capacities, has been documented by a number of writers. For example, analyses of speech addressed by mothers to their children show that linguistic complexity varies quite systematically with the child's age: the younger the child, the simpler the verbal input which the mother provides (Snow, 1972; Phillips, 1973). Similarly, as Stern et al. (1977) have described, the behaviour of a mother talking to a three-months-old infant is characterized by the highly repetitive nature of her vocal and gestural acts, the grossly exaggerated form of her facial expressions, and the slowing down of her vocalizations. Not only the content but also the form of her behaviour is adjusted to the infant – as though she were aware of his limited capacity for information processing and hence wanted to ensure that she would not lose his interest. Stimulation is thus offered in such a way that it matches the infant's ability to assimilate it.

These are illustrations of the sensitivity that mothers – indeed most adults – quite naturally display in their interactions with young children. That same sensitivity was also highlighted in our previous discussion of visual co-orientation, vocal interchange and feeding, for in all of these cases we see the extent to which mothers are aware of the often very rapid sequential patterning of the infant's behaviour and are able to enmesh their own responses with his into one continuing flow. The dialogue thus produced may be a one-sided one in its dependence on the mother's willingness to sustain it, but it is already one of exquisite precision of timing and patterning.

Sensitivity is surely the single most salient general quality which one can discern in maternal behaviour. Whether it can be treated as a unitary entity that remains relatively constant across time and situation is an open issue that need not occupy us here any further; suffice it that this is the quality that makes possible the very prompt response to and anticipation of the infant's behaviour that we find repeatedly in dyadic situations. The conditions that give rise to it in the mother's history, the reasons for its absence in some pathological cases, and the extent to which it can be improved through training and experience are all further issues to which we have as yet no answer. What is clear is that sensitivity involves a close monitoring of the child's actions, the ability to respond appropriately and to monitor in turn the effects on him of the mother's own behaviour, and the willingness subsequently to change that behaviour in the light of these effects. It represents a basic condition for the occurrence and development of mother–infant dialogues.

The infant's active role in determining the course and content of social interactions clearly deserves emphasis. Let us, however, also note that most of the recent work in this area has been based on situations specifically set up to bring out this fact, i.e. they have maximized the possibility for the infant to take the intitiative, confining the mother to following his lead and adapting to his particular requirements. However, in acknowledging the reality of this phenomenon there is a danger that we may swing from one extreme to another: from seeing mother as a dictator (albeit benevolent) to seeing her as a nonentity (albeit an alert one). In other words we would no longer be acknowledging the obvious fact that mothers do have to take the initiative from time to time, that they do have purposes and goals and needs of their own which they wish to convey to their children and with which the children have to fit in. The more assertive aspects of maternal behaviour must thus also be accounted for if we are to do justice to the total range of mother–child interaction: accordingly we shall turn to an examination of maternal control techniques in the next section.

Maternal controls

Given the new approach to the study of mother–child interaction, with its emphasis on the dyadic nature of the relationship and the use of micro-analytic techniques to examine its structure in detail, it is time to return to an old problem with a fresh look and ask the question that lies at the heart of the socialization issue, namely *what do mothers in fact do when they wish to direct their children's behaviour into particular channels* ?

This problem arises in its most acute form in the second year of life. It has been suggested that 'obedience' cannot be expected until the end of the first year (Stayton et al., 1971); in any case, the onset of independent mobility around this time means that there is now a pressing need for controlling tactics that are rapidly administered and effective. Fortunately at this time too the child begins to reveal a rudimentary comprehension of spoken language, and the need to control behaviour from a distance is thus partly met. Whereas in the first year the mother's control techniques are likely to assume a primarily non-verbal form (i.e. through physical manipulation of the child and his environment), the development of language comprehension and the greater understanding of gestures on the part of the child offer a vastly increased scope for methods of influencing the course of his behaviour. The nature of these methods and their functioning need describing.

We have recently been studying maternal control techniques in two groups of mother–infant dyads, involving children aged fifteen and twenty-four months respectively. Each mother–child pair is observed under free play conditions for a period of eight minutes. There is a large number of toys in the room in which the observations are made, and to ensure that she takes an active role in the interactions the mother is instructed to encourage the child to play with as many toys as possible and not to have him spend all the time with one or two toys. The entire procedure is video-recorded from behind a one-way screen and it is the fine-grain analysis of the records of these social encounters that provides the basis for our discussion on control techniques.

The nature of control techniques

It is important to emphasize that control techniques, as the term is used here, should not be understood in a purely negative fashion, denoting force, inhibition, punishment, and so on. Rather, *control techniques are all those methods employed by the adult with the aim of changing the course of the child's behaviour.* Such methods may take many diverse forms, by no means all of a negative nature. In each case, however, the adult has some particular end-result in mind that he wants the child to achieve, and it is his task therefore to communicate his purpose in such a way that the child will come to share this purpose. How such a relatively assertive role is played – didactically, bolt-out-of-the-blue fashion, or by preserving the same mutuality that the study of other aspects of mother–infant interaction has highlighted, is an empirical problem to which we need to give attention.

Sociologists (e.g. Bernstein, 1971) see control techniques as stemming from some specific policy designed to evoke a particular moral, cognitive and affective awareness in the child as part of his acculturation. Our concern here, however, is far less with the socialization policy that underlies a parent's behaviour and the values it expresses, and far more with the behaviour patterns themselves that are used to bring about control, i.e. that are intended to result in the child's compliance with the adult's wishes. We are also not concerned with the long-term effects on the child, i.e. with the internalization of the social values conveyed to him. The primary need at present is to examine control techniques in terms of their here-and-now impact.

The range and variety of control techniques

Any attempt at detailed description of how mothers set out to influence their children's ongoing behaviour must do justice to the extraordinarily wide range of techniques employed by them. However, analysis of the play sessions observed by us suggested a way of organizing these techniques within one global taxonomic scheme, which is illustrated diagrammatically in Figures 2.1 and 2.2. A discussion of the distinctions drawn within this scheme may serve to convey some flavour of the variety of control techniques applied to children in the second year of life.

Verbal controls.   A fundamental distinction is that between controls administered through the medium of language and those manifest in other, non-verbal, aspects of the mother's behaviour. As to the former,

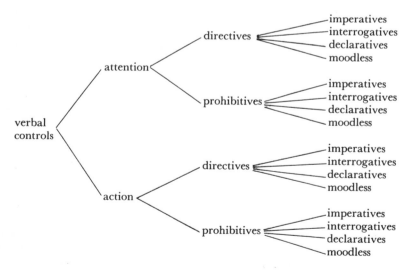

Fig. 2.1   Classification of verbal control techniques

approximately half of all maternal utterances in both the age groups observed by us were judged to be verbal control utterances. It would be a mistake, however, to analyse these simply in terms of the categories commonly applied to directive speech found in adult social encounters (e.g. Ervin-Tripp, 1976), for such a procedure would not respect the special features of speech addressed to young children. In particular, one salient difference to which an examination of the latter points is that between utterances pertaining to the *control of attention* and those pertaining to the *control of action*.

Action controls aim to modify the course of the child's behaviour by specifying some activity that he is expected to perform. Thus they involve verbs such as 'push', 'fetch', 'kick', etc., designed to initiate some response that the child is not at the time engaged in. However, action controls may also be intended to modify an activity that is already underway; the action verb may then be implicit, e.g. 'Do that again over here!' By these means the child's behaviour is constrained or channelled in some respect; the degree of constraint, however, may vary considerably according to the nature of the utterance and the extent to which it permits a variety of 'appropriate' responses. Thus, at one extreme, a mother is highly explicit in what is expected from the child: 'Push the car to me!', specifying action, object and location; at the other extreme a statement such as 'Play with the car!', while also a command, is far less specific as to what the child is to do and leaves a wide range of choices open to him. There may well be an important dimension of maternal differences in this respect that deserves to be explored; a mother's controls can be viewed in terms of the range of options they provide for compliance, and the question of consistent individual differences can thus be raised.

Attention controls attempt to focus the child's visual or auditory attention ('Look at that lovely ball!'; 'Listen to the noise it makes!') and thus serve to introduce an object (or a locality) into the sphere of play. The child is thereby expected to identify or locate something, generally as a prelude for the performance of some action related to that object. That action is, however, left unspecified: a remark such as 'Look, there's teddy!', made to a child pushing an empty pram, is more like a 'gentle hint' and thus displays a kind of subtlety that is actually quite commonplace.

Influencing the course of a child's behaviour involves not only initiating activities but also terminating or preventing activities. This distinction is made with the terms *directives* and *prohibitives*. While directives control behaviour by guiding it into specified channels, prohibitives control it by blocking channels, the child being told *not* to act or *not* to attend.

However, the aim of preventing or terminating an activity is not exclusively served by prohibitives. Consider a mother coping with a child who has put a toy in his mouth: she may, it is true, issue a straightforward prohibitive, 'Don't eat teddy!'; on the other hand, she may attempt to achieve the same aim with 'Take teddy out of your mouth!' or even 'Put teddy in the pram!' These more subtle ways of preventing some action deemed undesirable by the mother are especially characteristic of attention controls for which prohibitives, although possible, occur only infrequently. The task of shifting a child's attention away from something is usually achieved by distraction, i.e. by providing an alternative and, ideally, more interesting focus – thus, to the child who has seen an electric socket: 'Look [instead] at this lovely spinning top!' Speech containing many prohibitives is usually regarded as authoritarian, and it may well be important to distinguish maternal strategies that are highly reliant on the use of prohibitives. It is clear, however, that a mother may be just as restrictive but achieve her end in more positive ways, i.e. by the skilful and timely use of directives.

The examples of verbal controls with which we have illustrated the discussion so far, and the widespread view that speech addressed to young children tends to be highly simplified (e.g. Snow, 1972), might suggest that control utterances are always delivered in the simple grammatical form appropriate to commands, i.e. the *imperative*. This, however, is by no means so; action and attention can also be manipulated by *interrogatives*, *declaratives* and by *moodless* utterances (i.e. those lacking a verb, c.f. Sinclair and Coulthard, 1975).

The imperative category does, of course, provide the most unambiguous examples of verbal control: 'Throw me the ball!', 'Look at those bricks!' Interrogatives tend to be much more varied, and to an adult different interrogative constructions can provide questions with subtle variations in meaning (Ervin-Tripp, 1976). Consider, for example, 'Shall we sit teddy over there?', 'Can you sit teddy over there?', 'Will teddy sit over there?', 'Why not sit teddy over there?' It seems unlikely that very young children can discriminate the shades of meaning that distinguish these utterances, and available evidence (Shatz, 1978) suggests that children in the second year react to such questions much as they would to imperatives. One way of viewing these interrogative utterances is as embedded imperatives, in that the interrogative construction precedes the explicit agent, action and object as a formal addition. The embedded imperative form is, however, less characteristic of attention interrogatives. These frequently are variations of naming or finding games in which the explicit attention verbs such as 'look' or 'see' do not appear, e.g. 'What's this here?' or 'Where's teddy?'

Declaratives provide the mother with another form of 'indirect' command. Taken literally, they usually convey information and thus may seem the least forceful of the various grammatical forms. An action is sometimes specified, again in the manner of an embedded imperative: 'You have to push it right down', but it may be even less explicit, as in 'I think the top comes off'. Attention declaratives are generally used to identify the location of an object: 'There's the wheelbarrow', 'It's over there'. With such statements the mother may be providing the child with information, just as with interrogatives she appears to be asking for information; in each case, however, the intended outcome may be to bring about a change in the child's behaviour regarding the object referred to.

Moodless controls incorporate those clipped utterances that are inserted into a child's ongoing activity in order to modify its progress: 'Careful', 'Over there', 'Round the other way'. The child must relate them to what he is currently doing and perhaps also to a preceding more complete verbal control: 'Push it down . . . gently now'.

Non-verbal controls.　Some of the same classificatory distinctions that we have used for verbal controls can also be made with regard to non-verbal controls (see Figure 2.2). This does not apply, of course, to the formal linguistic categories (imperatives, interrogatives, declaratives and moodless) we have previously discussed; instead, a distinction between *gestures* and *manipulatives* can be usefully made. These two categories differ with respect to whether something, object or child, is directly acted upon or not: gestures, being symbolic in nature, do not generally involve such contact; manipulatives, on the other hand, do entail an action bringing the individual into direct contact with the object.

Gestures are frequently used to supplement verbal controls. As Murphy and Messer (1977) have shown, mothers' use of pointing in order to focus the infants' attention on some feature of the environment tends to be synchronized (in a most precise manner) with verbal references to that feature. Pointing persists as one of the most common

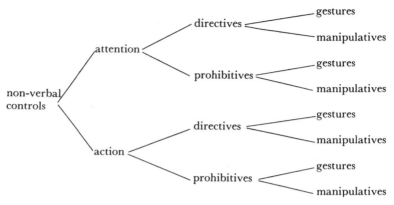

Fig. 2.2   Classification of non-verbal control techniques

discourse gestures, particularly in situations such as that described here where interaction takes place primarily via a number of objects scattered around at a distance. Among other classes of gestures that can be identified are receiving gestures, either of an object (by holding out the hands) or of the child (by beckoning); pantomimes of an action the child is expected to perform upon a toy; and approval or disapproval gestures (e.g. head nodding or finger shaking). All can be said to serve control purposes.

Manipulatives make some form of physical contact with either the child or an object. They may be divided into three classes. *Location* manipulatives result in a changed position for some object relative to the child: the mother may, for example, discretely put a toy within reach of the child or, rather more assertively, pick up a child and carry him away from a door he was attempting to open. This strategy is very typical of interactions with younger infants whose own mobility is limited and whose lack of language comprehension makes verbal controls relatively ineffective. *Demonstrating* manipulatives have an obviously instructive character. The function, structure or properties of some object is illustrated, usually by acting upon the object in question, e.g. the mother guides her child's hands as he attempts a difficult task like spinning a top. *Attracting* manipulatives are used to direct the child's attention towards some object by touching it or moving it about its location. The consequence is to generate a more interesting visual or auditory stimulus; a common example is the shaking of a toy in front of the child.

The other classificatory distinctions made for non-verbal controls are the same as those for verbal controls. Thus the former too may serve either to direct attention to objects or to specify some action. Pointing, for example, is used to attract attention to an object; other gestures, such as pantomimes, indicate actions for the child to perform. Similarly, location manipulatives can direct attention to a toy, while demonstrating manipulatives specify the action that can be performed on that toy. The distinction between directives and prohibitives is also applicable; thus attention to some object may be effectively initiated or terminated by altering its location with respect to the child.

Maternal strategies and child behaviour
A detailed examination of mothers' behaviour makes it very apparent that the techniques used to influence children's activities assume a great many different forms. The mode of the technique (verbal or non-verbal), its positive or negative character (directive or prohibitive), the aspect of the child's behaviour to which it is addressed (attention or action), the construction of the utterance (imperative, interrogative, declarative or moodless) and the nature of the non-verbal technique (gesture or manipulative), all indicate something of the rich stock from which the mother is, potentially at least, able to draw whatever is relevant for any given set of circumstances in order to convey her purpose to the child and affect his behaviour accordingly. And, in particular, it becomes clear that the directness with which she attempts to achieve her purpose is also highly varied: the paradeground-like command that perhaps most people initially associate with the notion of control is in fact observed far less frequently than a great range of highly subtle and indirect tactics that are much less forceful but that, nevertheless, may serve just as effectively as controls.

Such variety raises two main questions. First, how are individual controls organized together into coherent strategies, involving the simultaneous integration of verbal and non-verbal elements and the successive integration of sequences of controls? Second, what determines the occurrence of different controls – in particular, how are they related to ongoing child behaviour? These are both highly complex problems, and we can but briefly touch upon them here.

As to interrelationships among control techniques, it is apparent that individual controls are associated in a far from haphazard manner. Thus gestures rarely occur without some simultaneous, appropriate verbal utterance: a mother pointing to an object will almost invariably accompany her gesture with some reference to the object or at the very least with a request to look at it – even when the child addressed is a pre-verbal infant. The additional information conveyed by non-verbal elements may be particularly useful in cases of ambiguity in speech, such as that resulting from the use of pronouns and of deictic terms. Thus the younger the child the greater the incidence of simultaneous verbal and non-verbal cues that one can expect. And similarly, the sequential arrangement of controls is frequently of an orderly nature; for example, attention controls tend to precede action controls, in that a mother must first ensure that her child's attention is on the appropriate object before she requests him to act upon it. Also, strings of verbal directives all referring to the same object and act (repeated because the child did not comply at once) are rarely identical; invariably the mother will modify her original remark, sometimes by elaborating upon it but often by simplifying it through a process of abbreviation or ellipsis.

In the particular situation observed by us the mother's role was one of initiating and maintaining play around half a dozen or so toys. Under such circumstances a great many of a mother's control utterances are organized in sequences (or 'episodes'), in which all the constituent controls refer to the same object (e.g. 'Go and fetch the ball . . . go on, pick it up . . . bring it over here . . . now throw it to me . . .'). While within each episode the mother's focus remains upon one particular toy, the question arises as to how episodes are first initiated: does the mother decide arbitrarily, bolt-out-of-the-blue fashion when the child is to play with a new toy, or does she take note of what he is currently doing and time her directive accordingly?

We can answer this question by taking the beginning of each episode, i.e. the first utterance that mentions a toy not referred to in the previous episode, and consider what the child is doing at the time. When this analysis is performed it emerges that a considerable proportion of the mothers' verbal controls concerning a new toy follow *an initiative taken by the child*. Thus, for the younger and older children respectively, 59·7 per cent and 74 per cent of these maternal directives occur after the child himself has already made contact with the toy or at least focused upon it. The age difference is particularly notable, for it appears to reflect the generally much more active and exploratory character of the older children's play: with increasing age the child is much more likely to initiate toy shifts himself, the mother merely coming in with requests for new actions.

What happens in the remaining cases, however, when the mother takes the initiative for a toy shift? In most of these instances (87·2 per cent and 78·8 per cent respectively for the two age groups) the shift is attempted with an attention directive; action controls tend to be reserved until attention is captured and focused. In other words, to a child busily engaged with building bricks, the mother will not suddenly shout: 'Kick the ball!'. Rather, having decided it is time he turned to something else, she will first use various attention-attracting devices (verbal and non-verbal) in order gently to introduce the ball, wean him away from the bricks, and only when she has succeeded in doing so will she issue an action directive such as to kick the ball. Such a strategy has, however, to be employed far more frequently with younger children: in our fifteen-months-old group we found mothers using twice as many attention directives as in the twenty-four-months group, despite the fact that action directives occurred with approximately the same frequency. The greater tendency of the younger children to get 'stuck' on a particular toy meant that their mothers had to work harder in tempting them to other toys; in most of such instances, however, they first made sure that the child was oriented to the new toy before indicating some action to be performed upon it.

These observations highlight once again the skill with which mothers phase their own actions and requirements into what the child is doing at the time. Their aim may be to control the child by directing his behaviour into particular channels; more often than not, however, this is accomplished in a most sensitive, not a dictatorial manner.

Conclusions

Mothering is a most varied, multi-faceted activity and its analysis correspondingly complex. It is, therefore, not surprising that different investigators have resorted to different approaches in order to understand its nature and its relationship to child behaviour. These approaches have been described in detail elsewhere (Schaffer, 1977b); they may be roughly grouped into the following four categories:

Mothering as physical care activity, where attention is given primarily to such practices as feeding, weaning and toileting, in that (following Freudian theory) variations in these practices are thought to account for particular personality constellations in later life.

Mothering as a set of attitudes, the crucial variables here being rather broader aspects of the relationship, i.e. dimensions (such as warmth–

coldness and permissiveness–restrictiveness) which are assumed to underlie a wide range of parental behaviour.

Mothering as stimulation, an approach which pays particular attention to the way in which the mother mediates and suitably selects the environmental stimulation the child requires for fostering development.

Mothering as interlocution. It is this approach with which we have been particularly concerned here, for it is based on the notion that mothering is part of an interactional pattern in which both partners must adapt to one another. Just as in a conversation the two interlocutors continually synchronize their responses according to a shared set of rules for regulating the relationship, so mother–child interaction also involves a highly sophisticated integration of the two sets of responses into one consistent flow. As we have seen, much of the responsibility for establishing such interpersonal synchrony during infancy lies with the mother: it is her skill in knowing not only *how* but also *when* to respond that is crucial in maintaining a dialogue.

According to this view, mutuality is the keynote in the relationship between mother and even the very youngest infant. What one does is affected by what the other is doing; neither is acting upon an inert organism. Thus the mother's task, in acting as a socializing agent, is not to create something out of nothing – it is rather to slot her responses into the ongoing stream of the child's behaviour, with due respect to its temporal and content characteristics, in order thus to bring about a 'smooth' interaction and a predictable outcome. The fact that from the beginning an infant is active, not passive, that he is capable of spontaneous, organized behaviour, means that in social interactions he is often an initiator, not merely a responder, and that the mother is thus frequently cast into the role of follower, not leader.

This conclusion is reached by various studies of mother–infant interaction, some of which were described in the earlier part of this chapter. However, while many of these were specifically set up to highlight the infant's determining role, it is noteworthy that even in a situation where the mother is asked to adopt a more assertive, task-oriented part the evidence for mutuality is still to be found. In part this is provided by the way in which the mother times her controls, in that even this type of behaviour is sensitively linked to the child's activity at the time; and in part by the way in which maternal behaviour changes according to the child's age, showing how mother can adjust the nature of her demands to the capabilities of the child. Both points underline the fact that mothers do not act as though they see the child as a mere lump of clay to be shaped at will, but rather that they appear at all times acutely aware of what is appropriate to a given child at a given moment and that they are prepared then to adjust their requirements and actions accordingly.

Socialization thus emerges as a process based on mutuality. It is not an arbitrary imposition by a powerful being on another, utterly passive being. If a mother wishes to bring about some change in her child she needs to start within the context of his own behaviour. Socialization is based on a two-way relationship, and any theoretical model that neglects this basic feature will fail to account for its very essence.

References

Ainsworth, M. D. S. (1974) The development of infant–mother attachment. In B. M. Caldwell and H. N. Ricciuti (eds) *Review of Child Development Research, Vol. 3.* Chicago: University of Chicago Press.

Bernstein, B. (1971) Language and socialization. In N. Minnis (ed.) *Linguistics at Large.* London: Gollancz.

Blurton Jones, N. (ed.) (1972) *Ethological Studies of Child Behaviour.* London: Cambridge University Press.

Bowlby, J. (1969) *Attachment and Loss, Vol. 1.* London: Hogarth.

Bronfenbrenner, U. (1971) *Two Worlds of Childhood: U.S. and U.S.S.R.* London: Allen and Unwin.

Caldwell, B. M. (1964) The effects of infant care. In M. L. Hoffman and L. W. Hoffman (eds) *Review of Child Development Research, Vol. 1.* New York: Russell Sage Foundation.

Clarke, A. M. and Clarke, A. D. B. (1976) *Early Experience: Myth and Evidence.* London: Open Books.

Collis, G. M. and Schaffer, H. R. (1975) Synchronization of visual attention in mother–infant pairs. *Journal of Child Psychology and Psychiatry 16*: 315–20.

Duncan, S. (1973) Toward a grammar for dyadic conversation. *Semiotica 9*: 29–46.

Ervin-Tripp, S. (1976) Is Sybil there? the structure of some American English directives. *Language and Society 5*: 25–66.

Fergusson, C. A. (1964) Baby talk in six languages. *American Anthropologist 66*: 103–14.

Hartup, W. W. (1970) Peer interaction and social organization. In P. H. Mussen (ed.) *Manual of Child Psychology, Vol. 2.* New York: Wiley.

Hoffman, M. L. (1970) Moral development. In P. H. Mussen (ed.) *Manual of Child Psychology, Vol. 2.* New York: Wiley.

Kaye, K. (1977) Toward the origin of dialogue. In H. R. Schaffer (ed.) *Studies in Mother–Infant Interaction.* London: Academic Press.

Kessen, W., Haith, M. and Salapatek, P. H. (1970) Human infancy: a bibliography and guide. In P. H. Mussen (ed.) *Manual of Child Psychology, Vol. 1.* New York: Wiley.

78   Issues in childhood social development

Lamb, M. E. (1976) *The Role of the Father in Child Development.* New York: Wiley.

Le Vine, R. (1969) Culture, personality, and socialization: an evolutionary view. In D. A. Goslin (ed.) *Handbook of Socialization Theory and Research.* Chicago: Rand-McNally.

Mead, M. (1935) *Sex and Temperament in Three Primitive Societies.* New York: Morrow.

Murphy, C. M. and Messer, D. J. (1977) Mothers, infants and pointing: a study of a gesture. In H. R. Schaffer (ed.) *Studies in Mother–Infant Interaction.* London: Academic Press.

Orlansky, H. (1949) Infant care and personality. *Psychological Bulletin 46*: 1–48.

Phillips, J. R. (1973) Syntax and vocabulary of mothers' speech to young children: age and sex comparisons. *Child Development 44*: 182–5.

Schaffer, H. R. (1971) *The Growth of Sociability.* Harmondsworth: Penguin Books.

Schaffer, H. R. (1977a) Early interactive development. In H. R. Schaffer (ed.) *Studies in Mother–Infant Interaction.* London: Academic Press.

Schaffer, H. R. (1977b) *Mothering.* London: Open Books; Cambridge, Mass: Harvard University Press.

Schaffer, H. R. (1978) Acquiring the concept of the dialogue. In M. Bornstein and W. Kessen (eds) *Psychological Development from Infancy.* Hillsdale, NJ: Erlbaum.

Schaffer, H. R., Collis, G. M. and Parsons, G. (1977) Vocal interchange and visual regard in verbal and pre-verbal children. In H. R. Schaffer (ed.) *Studies in Mother–Infant Interaction.* London: Academic Press.

Sears, R. R., Maccoby, E. E. and Levin, H. (1957) *Patterns of Child Rearing.* Evanston, Ill.: Row, Peterson.

Shatz, M. (1978) Children's comprehension of their mothers' question-directives. *Journal of Child Language 5*: 39–46.

Sinclair, J. McH. and Coulthard, R. M. (1975) *Towards an Analysis of Discourse.* London: Oxford University Press.

Snow, C. E. (1972) Mothers' speech to children learning language. *Child Development 43*: 549–65.

Stayton, D. J., Hogan, R. and Ainsworth, M. D. S. (1971) Infant obedience and maternal behavior: the origins of socialization reconsidered. *Child Development 42*: 1057–69.

Stern, D. N., Beebe, B., Jaffe, J. and Bennett, S. J. (1977) The infant's stimulus world during social interaction. In H. R. Schaffer (ed.) *Studies in Mother–Infant Interaction.* London: Academic Press.

Wolff, P. H. (1967) The role of biological rhythms in early psychological development. *Bulletin of Meninger Clinic 31*: 197–218.

Yarrow, M. R., Campbell, J. D. and Burton, R. V. (1968) *Child Rearing: An Inquiry into Research and Methods.* San Francisco: Jossey-Bass.

Zigler, E. F. and Child, I. L. (eds) (1973) *Socialization and Personality Development.* Reading, Mass.: Addison-Wesley.

3 Early social knowledge: the development of knowledge about others

Jeanne Brooks-Gunn
and Michael Lewis

Knowledge of others has been studied under the rubric of social cognition, social perception and person perception. Traditionally studied by those interested in adults, social perception has been defined as 'the process by which man comes to know and to think about the other persons, their characteristics, qualities and inner states' (Tagiuri, 1969, p. 395). Attention has classically been given to the recognition of various emotions exhibited by others and to the ability of persons to judge others' emotional states (Bruner and Tagiuri, 1954; Darwin, 1965; Tagiuri, 1969). In addition, attribution theorists such as Kelley (1973) and Heider (1958) have concentrated on discovering how the individual interprets his own behaviour and that of other people.

The development of such knowledge has been studied in terms of role taking, empathy and person perception, but only recently has it appeared as a separate field of study. This field has been labelled social cognition, and several excellent reviews of the literature on children's understanding of others' thoughts, feelings and intentions have appeared (Chandler, 1977; Shantz, 1975; Youniss, 1975). A current definition of the field is given by Shantz: 'a child's intuitive or logical representation of others, that is, how he characterizes others and makes references about their covert, inner psychological experiences' (1975, p. 258). This definition excludes other important aspects of social cognition. Youniss's definition includes five aspects: a sense of self, of others, of a 'relative social standing', of the knowledge of self vis-à-vis society, and of values and principles (Youniss, 1975). We would agree with Youniss that social cognition (or what we are calling social knowledge) includes more than just knowledge of others. Specifically, the knowledge of self seems to be a crucial aspect of social knowledge (Lewis and Brooks, 1975). Indeed, we would argue that knowledge of others cannot occur without some knowledge of self, for as Mead (1934) and Merleau-Ponty (1964) have stated, knowledge of others is developed through one's interactions with others. Without interaction with the social world there would be little knowledge about it or ourselves.

Besides knowledge of self and others, the child's knowledge of its relationship with others and with the world is a large component of social knowledge. We wish to define relationship rather broadly to include knowledge of relationships with others, with societal institutions and with universal principles. Through interactions with others, the child learns that he has different relationships with different persons and that these relationships differ in terms of the nature of the social object, as well as the nature of function, situation and status. As with knowledge of others, knowledge of relationship involves knowledge of self. Thus, social knowledge contains at least three components – knowledge of self, of others, and of relationships. These three are not independent, but overlap and interact in varying degrees.

As developmental psychologists, we are interested in how each of the three components of social knowledge develops and how the development of each affects the others. The latter point is crucial since different theories of development might predict different developmental sequences. For example, the three components may develop quite separately, they may gradually become differentiated, or they may develop in a parallel fashion, being dependent upon the same underlying cognitive process.

In the following discussion we will examine the development of one aspect of social knowledge – knowledge of others – specifically examining how this knowledge is acquired in the first two years of life. Another question to be examined in this chapter is the identity of the possible cognitive processes underlying the development of knowledge of others. The development of self and of relationship have been reviewed elsewhere (Lewis and Brooks, 1975; Lewis and Brooks-Gunn, in press; Lewis and Feiring, in press).

The development of knowledge of other

Several different topics need to be addressed in the study of infant's knowledge of other. First, the importance of the social world in development needs to be addressed. We will suggest that many tasks are embedded in a social context and that development cannot be understood without reference to the infant's social world. Second, perceived differences between social and non-social objects must be examined, with the suggestion being made that social and non-social objects are perceived differently from an early age. Third, the development of knowledge about others will be examined in terms of the different dimensions that persons possess, dimensions that the infant must learn in order to differentiate among persons. Finally, the importance of situation and function in acquiring knowledge about others will be considered.

Knowledge as embedded in a social context

We believe that most development tasks are embedded in a social context. Indeed, the infant seems to be primed from the very beginning to respond and attend to social situations and persons. The relationship of early structures and preferences to social knowledge has been shown in a variety of diverse studies. For example, hemispheric differentiation for processing speech and non-speech sounds (Molfese, 1972), early interaction patterns (Sander, 1977; Lewis and Freedle, 1973; Stern, 1974), and shape, colour and movement preferences (Bornstein, 1977; Fantz, 1963, 1966) all move the newborn toward examination of and interaction with other humans rather than other objects.

The past two decades of infancy research have demonstrated greater perceptual and cognitive abilities than previously imagined. At the turn of the twentieth century, William James described the infant's world as a 'blooming, buzzing mass of confusion'. The infant was described as an insensate organism without any organized experience or properly functioning sensory apparatus. In contrast, research has shown the young infant to be an intact organism, one who has sensory abilities and who can process information and who can learn. In the sensory modalities, the infant can see a static object placed approximately seventeen cm from its eyes fairly well, although there are limits on tracing focusing speed (Fantz, 1958; Fantz and Nevis, 1967; Salapatek and Kessen, 1966). From the moment of birth the infant is capable of processing complex visual information and it shows preferences for complexity over simple stimuli (Kagan and Lewis, 1965; Kessen et al., 1970). Moreover, the same sophistication of other sensory systems has been shown for the auditory, olfactory and tactile modalities (c.f. Graham et al., 1968; Engen and Lipsitt, 1965; Bell, 1965). In terms of learning capacities, infants are thought to be capable of classical conditioning although this learning is influenced by a variety of factors (Fitzgerald and Brackbill, 1976). The instrumental conditioning literature indicates that very young infants have the ability to alter their behaviour as a function of environmental demands – a basic biological definition of intelligence. For example, Siqueland (1968) and Bruner (1968) both report research where the sucking response was used to alter the visual field by increasing the illumination of a picture on a screen in one case and focusing a picture in the other. In these studies, intentional, organized and complex cognitive activity was demonstrated.

Many of these early sensory and learning capacities are directed at attending to and interacting with the social world. The sensory abilities and preferences of the young infant direct him toward other persons. The human voice, the shape of the human face, the movement of the eyes and mouth, the contrast of the eye area, and the visual acuity range all make interaction with others, especially caretakers, likely. In addition, intersensory integration occurs at an early age (Aronson and Rosenbloom, 1971; McGurk and Lewis, 1974). Finally, a number of investigators (Brazelton et al., 1974; Stern, 1974; Lewis and Freedle, 1973) have demonstrated that complex interactional patterns between caregiver and infant are established very early. Sensory dysfunction first leads to impairment in the social realm, as has been demonstrated in Fraiberg's (1974) work with blind infants.

Evidence of knowledge of others in terms of differentiation has been demonstrated in numerous studies. Brooks and Lewis (1976) have demonstrated that infants in the first year of life already have an understanding of the face–body relationship; the presentation of a child-sized adult (a distortion of normal face–body relationships) elicits surprise and attention. Bronson (1975) has found that infants were capable of recognizing strangers as early as three months of age. And year-old infants have knowledge of and a preference for other social objects besides their mothers; for example, unfamiliar peers are responded to quite differently from and are preferred to adults (Lewis et al., 1975).

Within the opening months of life, the infant both has the capacity – in terms of sensory ability and cognitive skills – and the motivation to acquire vast amounts of information about its social world. Moreover, the infant is no passive recipient of information from its world; rather, he actively seeks stimulation and utilizes it as a function of his individual plans, personality and cognitive organization.

Social and non-social knowledge

Even though most knowledge is presented to the infant in a social context, one still needs to ask whether or not the infant perceives a difference between social and non-social objects. We believe that social and non-social knowledge are different, since the former implies a similarity between the perceived and the perceiver – both are human (c.f. Tagiuri, 1969; Hamlyn, 1974). The notion of similarity implies that the infant must know that he is human before the two types of knowledge would be perceived as different. Therefore, social knowledge will not be perceived as different from object knowledge until the infant has some primitive notion of self and has some notion that he and others are similar.

In addition, differentiation between social and non-social events will change as the infant acquires new social knowledge and increases his cognitive capacity. For example, animals may be perceived as persons by young children, since animals respond in similar ways to persons (i.e. they provide contingent feedback and can both respond and initiate an interaction) and because children see others treating animals as human (e.g. family pets are treated as members of the family and certain television shows portray animals as humanlike). Only as more information about what is human is acquired would animals be classified as non-human.

The above discussion leads to the question of what characteristics are unique to humans. Very few non-social objects in the environment provide consistent and responsive feedback and even objects that *do* provide contingent feedback usually require the organism to either initiate the interaction or to respond in an appropriate manner. Only self and others are able to emit a multitude of responses contingent on situational cues that are not highly stylized.

Given that children do learn to differentiate between social and non-social stimuli, at what age does this first occur? Evidence regarding the preference for social stimuli in the first month of life is conflicting. Fantz (1963), Fitzgerald (1968), and Stechler and Latz (1966) report that infants younger than one month prefer social to non-social stimuli, while Fantz (1966), Hershenson (1965), Salzen (1963), Thomas (1965), Wilcox (1969) and Spitz and Wolf (1946) do not. By two months of age, it seems clear that infants can differentiate between social and non-social objects (Carpenter, 1973; Fantz, 1966; Gibson, 1969). An immobile, unsmiling and silent real face will elicit a smile by six weeks (Ambrose, 1961).

Koopman and Ames (1968) outline three general theories that may be evoked to account for the discrimination of social objects. First, the organism may be innately predisposed to respond to human features (Bowlby, 1969; Spitz and Wolf, 1946). The human face would act as an innate releasing mechanism for increased attention or positive affect. Second, social preference may result from progressively learned differentiations of the physical characteristics of the face (Gibson, 1969). A third theory, which incorporates both ethology and learned differentiations, states that preferences for social stimuli are determined by the physical properties of the face. In fact, movement and contrast seem to be the characteristics that first hold the neonate's attention (Bond, 1972; Fantz, 1966; Haith, 1966; Kagan, 1970; Salapatek and Kessen, 1966) and, of course, the human face amply provides this type of stimulation.

Having established that infants at very early ages can differentiate between social and non-social objects, investigators have asked about the parts of the face that generate the most interest. When a live face is presented, smiles are most easily elicited by a nodding motion and a voice (Polak et al., 1964; Salzen, 1963; Wolff, 1963). It is interesting that a high-pitched voice is more effective than a low-pitched one, a characteristic that often differentiates between males and females. The facial characteristic that is most preferred and most easily elicits smiling is the eyes. Eye-to-eye contact elicits smiles by five weeks of age (Wolff, 1963). Bergman et al. (1971) have studied scanning patterns of infants viewing a live face. Infants younger than seven weeks examine high contrast borders while attention is shifted to the eye section of the face in older infants. The eye scan increases if a human voice is presented with the face. The same preference for the eye is reported by Donnee (1973) for photographic faces. Ahrens (1954) reports that infants smile more at the eye than at the mouth–nose section, while Wilcox (1969) found no fixation differences for the same comparison.

However, Fantz (1963) and Ahrens (1954) found that a dot pattern approximating the eye configuration elicits greater attention than other patterns. Caron et al. (1973) have attempted to delineate further the salience of various structural features of the face. Using a habituation paradigm, four- and five-month-olds were presented with one of sixteen distortions of schematic faces. At four months of age the eyes are more salient than the mouth area and facial contour is more salient than inner facial elements. By five months these differences are no longer apparent.

That the face becomes integrated in the form of a schema is demonstrated by the research comparing infants' responses to regular and scrambled faces. In general, infants under six months of age prefer to look at regular facial representations (Fantz, 1965, 1966; Haaf and Bell, 1967; Kagan et al., 1966; Lewis, 1969) while this preference seems to diminish in the second six months of life (Kagan, 1970; Lewis, 1969). Kagan and Lewis have explained the shifts in attentional preference in terms of a discrepancy hypothesis. As the infant becomes older, with a highly developed schema of face, it becomes interested in moderately discrepant events such as facial distortions.

As stated earlier, intersensory integration of features also appears in the first six months of life, as infants respond to the mismatch of mothers' face and voice (McGurk and Lewis, 1974; Waite and Lewis, 1977) and of a midget's height and facial cues at least by six months of age (Brooks and Lewis, 1976).

Dimensions of social objects

Not only must the infant learn to differentiate among social and non-social objects, but he must differentiate among different social objects. The infant comes into contact with a vast array of social objects – parents, friends, relatives, peers and strangers. How does the child go about differentiating among these social objects?

One way to explore social object differentiation is to study social dimensions. The study of social dimensions may be more complex than the study of stimulus properties of non-social objects. Properties such as colour, shape, size, configuration and number of elements have all been studied as they may be systematically varied in order to study differentiation and salience. Social dimensions on the other hand are more complex, as they contain a number of stimulus properties; for example, colour, shape and size may all be included in one social dimension.

Three dimensions that most would agree are social in nature are learned in every culture and are acquired quite early; they are familiarity, age and gender. *Familiarity* has been studied the most extensively, involving recognition of the primary caregiver and differentiation between the caregiver and strange social objects. Both indices of familiarity have been studied under the rubric of attachment (Bowlby, 1969; Ainsworth, 1972) and dependency (Gewirtz, 1972). Usually differentiation is thought to occur after the infant has an internal representation of the mother that serves as a comparison point. Many studies have shown differentiation of mother and stranger by at least three months of life (c.f. Bronson, 1972; Banks and Wolfson, 1967). Infants also differentiate between familiar and strange peers (Lewis et al., 1975). Within the familiarity dimension, they respond differently to their mothers and fathers in live situations (Lamb, 1976a), in photographs (Lewis and Brooks, in press) and in verbal labelling situations (Brooks and Lewis, 1975). Some researchers have suggested studying familiarity as a continuum rather than as a dichotomous function (c.f. Rosenthal, 1973). For example, a grandparent may be more familiar than a neighbour or mailman who are in turn more familiar than the doctor, and so on. Such a framework could be used to study the familiarity dimension with greater precision.

Gender is the second dimension that is hypothesized to provide cues for the infant. Since infants may be socialized differentially as a function of their sex (Lewis, 1972a, 1972b; Moss, 1967; Robson et al., 1969), gender may be especially salient in differentiating among other social objects. A variety of properties may be gender-relevant, including reproductive differences, dress, hair, voice and height cues. Biological reproductive differences between men and women do not seem to be noticed by children until the third or fourth year of life, suggesting that infants use culture-related cues and facial voice and height cues to differentiate between the genders.

Gender differentiation has been studied using photographic and live representations of men and women, boys and girls. In general, adults are differentiated on the basis of gender earlier than are children. Infants have been shown to respond differentially to men and women in studies investigating reactions to the approach of strangers, with the men eliciting more negative responses (Benjamin, 1961; Lewis and Brooks, 1974; Morgan and Ricciuti, 1969; Shaffran and Décarie, 1973). These differences appear to be accounted for by height and voice cues (Brooks and Lewis, 1976). Boy and girl children have not been found to elicit different responses (Greenberg et al., 1973; Lewis and Brooks, 1974). Representations of male and female faces yield similar findings. In a series of studies, Fagan (1972) presented four-, five-, and six-month-old infants, representations of adult females, adult males and infants. In general, the younger infants did not discriminate among conditions while the older ones exhibited gender differentiation. Six-month-olds also differentiated between male and female photographs vis-à-vis vocalizations in a study by Kagan and Lewis (1965). In a recent study of nine- to twenty-four-month-olds' responses to facial representations, we found that attention and affect were not directed to male and female strangers differentially but that verbal labels were. By eighteen months of age, when most of the infants had some utterances in their verbal repertoire, infants labelled adults correctly on the basis of gender 90 per cent of the time, using 'mommy' or 'lady' for the female adult and 'daddy' or 'man' for the male adult. Of the infants who had the labels for boy and girl, approximately 80 per cent applied them correctly to the pictures of children (Lewis and Brooks, 1974; Brooks and Lewis, 1975).

The gender dimension also seems to be relevant to the infant himself. Money et al. (1957) report that gender reassignment is possible in the beginning of life without psychological consequences, but that children over eighteen months of age often have difficulty with such reassignments. In addition, older infants who have boy and girl labels in their verbal repertoire are able to label themselves correctly in the second half of the second year (Lewis and Brooks, 1974; Lewis and Brooks, in press). With increasing age and cognitive capacity, the concept of gender becomes stable and invariant (c.f. Kohlberg, 1966) for both the self and for others.

Social objects also differ with respect to *age*, a dimension that, like gender, has many properties. Height, facial characteristics, vocalizations and dress may all provide cues for distinguishing between persons of different ages. The infancy literature suggests that age is used to categorize the social world quite early. Fagan (1972) found that six-month-old infants could distinguish between an adult and a baby in two- and three-dimensional representations, while we found that nine- to twelve-month-olds could differentiate between photographs of baby and adult faces (Lewis and Brooks, 1974). In addition, our infants preferred to look at and to smile at the baby than the adult. In terms of labelling behaviour, verbal eighteen- to twenty-four-month-olds always labelled pictures of adults and babies correctly (Brooks and Lewis,

1975). In terms of situations involving real babies and adults, twelve-month-old infants clearly prefer to interact with strange babies than with strange adults (Lewis et al., 1975; Brooks-Gunn and Lewis, in press; Lenssen, 1973).

Even though infants can easily differentiate between babies and adults, they do have some difficulty differentiating between older children and adults. In our studies child–adult differentiation does not consistently occur until the second half of the second year using photographic representations. Even our verbal infants sometimes mislabel the pictures of children, using 'mommy' or 'daddy' rather than 'boy' or 'girl' (Brooks and Lewis, 1975). In live approaches, the younger infant (nine to twelve months of age) is easily able to respond differently to children and adults (Greenberg et al., 1973; Brooks and Lewis, 1976; Lewis and Brooks, 1974). These findings suggest that height, movement and voice cues (cues not present in photographic representations of faces) may be very important in the first year, while facial, hair and style cues (cues that are present in pictures) become more salient in the second year. However, extreme differences in facial, hair and style cues (i.e. between baby and adult) are responded to in the first year.

We would suggest that these three dimensions – age, familiarity and gender – could be conceptualized as a three-dimensional space in which most of the social objects in the child's world could be placed. As the child's social world becomes more complex and as these dimensions become more differentiated, more and more social objects may be added or their placement in the space more differentiated. As young–old becomes more continuous, children, adolescents and grandparents are probably differentiated from the original baby–adult classification. Although the gender dimension is dichotomous, the young child may perceive it to be more continuous, e.g., a mother may be more 'female' than a five-year-old girl. Therefore, one might expect gender to become more dichotomous with increasing age, an expectation that is borne out in the literature on gender constancy (c.f. Kohlberg, 1966). Figure 3.1 presents a possible placement of several objects within the proposed three-dimensional model.

Social functions

Social functions also provide information about others. Although the importance of situations has been recognized (Lewis, in press), resulting in the study of the infant in a variety of situations (i.e., the mother and

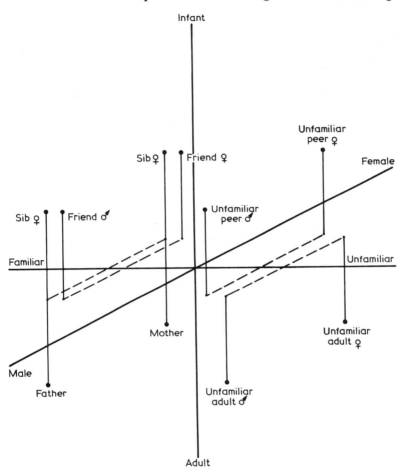

Fig. 3.1   Possible placement of social objects in a 3-dimensional space (from Lewis and Feiring, in press)

child have been observed in free-play situations, in separation and reunion sequences, and in the presence or absence of a stranger), a similar analysis using functions has not been carried out. This limitation has had important consequences for the theoretical models that have been considered, leading to a restricted view of infants' social knowledge. The restricted view of function also has affected the number of social objects in the infant's world that have been examined. For example, nurturance and protection, functions of the mother, have been alluded to in the vast attachment literature. But what about play and exploration, functions that may be provided by other social objects? The realization that play is important, for example, has led to a renewal of interest in knowledge of peers, the origins of friendship, and the importance of siblings (c.f. Lewis and Rosenblum, 1975).

Thus, in any analysis of social knowledge, the range of social functions and situations, as well as social objects, must be considered (Lewis and Feiring, in press). Although different social objects may be characterized by particular social functions, it is often the case that social objects, functions and situations are only partially related (Lewis and Weinraub, 1976). Consequently, the identity of the social object does not necessarily define the type or range of its social functions. For example, 'mothering' (a function) and mother (an object) have been considered to be highly related. Some recent work with other social objects indicates that fathers (Parke and O'Leary, 1975) are very competent in 'mothering'. At the same time, some social objects may be more closely tied to a specific function. For example, prior to technological advances, the feeding function required the mother (however, the existence of wet-nurses may make the relationship between object and function less than perfect even in this relatively straightforward example).

As noted above, social functions have not yet been systematically studied. We would define social functions as those activities that take place within the network which involve other social objects.[1] Functions that do not rely on the direct or indirect involvement of other social objects are not social functions. While social functions involve other social objects, the presence of another social object may not be necessary; for example, social imitation may occur in the absence of the other social object, but would still be considered a social function.

Besides involving social objects, social functions have been thought of as having some specific use for the organism's social survival. Communication and play are usually thought of as facilitating some aspect of development or growth. For example, it is commonly believed that we ask questions only to obtain information. Recently, Garvey (1977), Lewis and Cherry (1977) and Lewis (1977) have suggested that communication also has a function in the act of maintaining social contact. That is, a significant function of question asking may be in its social facilitation as well as in its information-producing capacity. Play behaviour can also be argued to have as a goal the establishment and maintenance of social relations (Mueller and Vandell, in press) rather than only the acquisition of skills. Thus, a function may have both social and non-social aspects, our primary interest being in the former. Social functions take place with social objects and may be important because they facilitate and maintain the relationship between these objects.

While we do not feel that a list of functions can be adequately realized, the following is an attempt to delineate some of the more important ones in the infants' world.

Protection. This function would include protection from potential sources of danger, including animate and inanimate sources.

Caregiving. This function refers to a set of activities which centre around biological needs relating to bodily activities.

Nurturance. This is the function of love, or attachment, as specified by Bowlby (1969) and Ainsworth (1969).

Play. This function refers to activities that have no immediately obvious goal and are engaged in for their own sake.

Exploration/learning. This function involves the activity of finding out about the environment through either watching others, asking for information or engaging in information acquisition with others.

While functions as they relate to different objects have not been extensively studied, mothers' behaviour toward their children in different situational contexts, in which social function has been captured in part, has been examined (Lewis and Freedle, 1973, 1977). In one study the conversational relationship between dyads, twelve-week-old infants and their mothers, was examined when the infant was on its mother's lap (presumably when she wished to interact, e.g. play function), and when the infant was in an infant seat (presumably when the mother wishes to do housework and keep an eye on her child, e.g. protective function). In the former context, maternal initiation of contact with and responsivity toward the infant were many times greater than under the latter function, even though the amount of vocalization the mother produced was not different. Such differences could affect the infant's knowledge about mother. Another example involves differentiation of function within a social dimension. Mothers and fathers are both familiar persons, but they tend to differ vis-à-vis the functions they perform; for example recent research suggests that fathers' modal interaction can be characterized as play, mothers' as nurturing or caregiving (Lamb, 1976b).

The problem of function and object relationship has been specifically addressed in a recent study by Edwards and Lewis (in press). Thirty-two children between 3 and 4 years of age were asked to choose which stranger – a peer (3 years old), an older child (7 years old) and an adult (20 years old), all the same sex as the subject – they would approach in order to (1) obtain help, (2) engage in play, or (3) obtain information on how an object worked. The strangers were represented pictorially. Both girls and boys chose to obtain help more from the adult than either child, chose to play with a peer more than an adult or older child, and chose to obtain information more from an older child than an adult. It is especially interesting that children may choose other children over adults for information-seeking as well as play. Thus, different social objects were seen as having clearly different functions by 3 to 4 years of age.

If we are to understand the child's social behaviour and social knowledge some analysis of the array of social objects and functions needs to be undertaken. Mothers, fathers and peers have been studied, but not in terms of function, while siblings, grandparents, uncles, aunts and cousins have all but been ignored. Much work is necessary, especially since children at very young ages understand and utilize social dimensions (see Figure 3.1) and that young children have significant emotional ties with many social objects.

Cognitive processes

In order to understand the development of knowledge of other, the cognitive processes[2] that may be necessary for this knowledge must be explored. We believe that the infant actively constructs social knowledge and is not a passive recipient of incoming information (see Lewis and Brooks, 1975, for a complete discussion of this issue).

Although we hold to a learning position, ethological theories may also explain some early social object differentiation. Ethological theories are usually evoked to explain affective responses to others, specifically fear of the strange and attachment to a caregiver. Fear of the unfamiliar is thought to be adaptive since it strengthens the attachment bond and protects the infant from harmful situations. However, differentiation of familiar and unfamiliar can and usually does occur without the expression of fear (c.f. Rheingold and Eckerman, 1973; Lewis and

Rosenblum, 1974), age and gender within the unfamiliarity dimension are responded to differentially and not all are responded to negatively; i.e. some strange social objects elicit negative affect which others do not (c.f. Lewis and Brooks, 1974; Morgan and Ricciuti, 1969; Shaffran and Décarie, 1973). Thus, differentiation within the familiarity–unfamiliarity dimension does not seem to be entirely accounted for by ethological theory.

Consider also infant responsiveness during the first year of life to the social dimension of age. Infants respond more positively to children than to adults, but do not do so to a child-sized adult (Brooks and Lewis, 1976). The facial configuration of the young may elicit positive affect. Hess (1970) and Lorenz (1943) have suggested that the quality of 'babyishness' may release protective or maternal responses in adults. The infant data suggest that young facial features may elicit positive affect, although we doubt that this releaser is protective in nature. However, the ethological position does not entirely explain the infants' responses to the child-sized adult, who was clearly responded to differently to a normal-sized child or adult. This latter finding suggests that infants in the first year have integrated at least two characteristics into their schema of person–facial configuration and height.

The cognitive capabilities available to the infant are actively utilized and are further enhanced by interaction with the social world. It is our belief that cognitive principles are more likely to account for social differentiation than ethological principles. Four cognitive processes are hypothesized to underlie the development of knowledge of others: permanence, schema development, generalized expectancies and contingencies, and self comparison. Each process will be discussed.

Permanence

Permanence involves the recognition that objects and people exist even when perceptually absent. In other words, one attribute of all social and non-social objects is existence, existence that is separate from oneself and that has continuity through time and space (Piaget, 1952). The development of this concept has been studied in infancy, usually by transforming an object and/or by testing its conservation. Following Piaget, an object is hidden using visible or invisible displacements, and the infant's search strategies are examined. If the infant searches, then knowledge of the object's existence is inferred. Person permanence may develop at the same time or earlier than object permanence, as Piaget

(1947) has hypothesized. Person permanence, although methodologically more difficult to examine than object permanence, also has been examined recently. Bell (1970) and Décarie (1965) have demonstrated that person and object permanence exhibit similar developmental patterns. In addition, their data suggest that person permanence often develops earlier than object permanence, probably due to the salience, the frequency of interaction, the contingency offered by people and the affectual relationships developed between infant and specific persons. This last factor seems to be especially important as is demonstrated by Bell's (1970) finding that person permanence only developed earlier than object permanence in infants who were securely attached to their mothers. Thus, both object and person permanence have been demonstrated empirically and theoretically.

Little is known about the development of the concept of permanence of self, though such a concept may be a prerequisite to understanding the permanent existence of others. Unfortunately, an empirical test of self permanence is difficult to construct. However, if object and person permanence are developing concurrently, it is not unreasonable to hypothesize a parallel development of self permanence. Self permanence may be inferred through some of our work on visual self recognition, which shows the beginnings of such recognition around eight to nine months, the same age at which object and person permanence are first demonstrated (Lewis and Brooks, in press).

Schema development

Development involves the notion that internal representations, or schemata, are developed from interaction with the world. These schemata are used to make sense of incoming information, with the information being compared to the internal representation. In terms of knowledge of other, differentiation of familiar and unfamiliar persons has been thought to depend on such a process.

A more specific variant of this position is the incongruity or discrepancy hypothesis. Negative affect directed toward the unfamiliar has been studied vis-à-vis discrepancy (Hebb, 1946, 1949). The hypothesized sequence of events is as follows: through repeated encounters, an internal representation of a familiar person is developed and becomes the standard against which incoming information is compared. This provides the basis whereby strange and familiar persons are differentiated. The familiar comparison figure is usually thought to be the mother, but schemata for other familiar persons could certainly exist. Until an appropriate schema is formed, differentiation of social objects cannot develop.

The hypothesis holds that the relationship between affect and discrepancy is thought to be curvilinear. Neither the thoroughly familiar nor the entirely novel arouse negative affect. However, a moderately discrepant event, one which is sufficiently like a familiar person to engage the related schema but sufficiently different also to engage incompatible processes, is experienced as anxiety provoking and fearful (Hebb, 1946). However, beyond this general statement, the relationship between discrepancy and affect has never been quantified.

The incongruity hypothesis has also been used to explain attentional, as well as affective responses. Experience with the environment leads to the formation of internal representations which are defined in terms of the distinctive elements of the event. The schemata are not constant, changing as more information is processed. Organisms attend to events that are moderately discrepant from the existing schema and ignore familiar events that do not elicit interest and highly discrepant events that cannot be processed. Kagan (1970) presents evidence for this version of the discrepancy hypothesis from observing infants' fixation times to pictures of regular and scrambled faces. The one-week-old infant looks at the faces and meaningless stimuli equal amounts of time, the four-month-old looks longest at the regular human face, and the older infant looks longest at the scrambled face. When the face schema is emerging, the regular face is preferred; when the face schema is established, moderate discrepancies are preferred.

There are various problems with the incongruity hypothesis, which have been discussed in an earlier paper (Lewis and Brooks, 1975). In terms of a more general theory of schema development, one of the major difficulties involves the possible number of internal representations. Although early social schemata are usually discussed primarily in terms of the mother, other schemata may exist. For example, an infant might have a schema for father, grandparent, sister, brother, to name a few. If infants have many different internal representations, how are we to predict which will be used in any given situation?

Alternatively, schema development and comparison may involve social dimensions as well as schemata for specific persons. If dimensions are used in conjunction with specific schemata, then the infant may not compare all strangers to a schema of mother, but may first make a general familiarity–unfamiliarity judgement. Thereafter, if the stranger is a female adult, the schema of mother may be important, but if the stranger is a child, a male, or an elderly adult, then another schema may be deployed. In addition, different comparisons, involving the same social objects, may involve different social dimensions. If the infant is encountering his mother, his uncle and a strange adult female, the mother and uncle would be judged as similar if familiarity–unfamiliarity were the dimension, the mother and the strange adult female if gender were the dimension being used. Thus, the infant's cognitive strategy and the situation need to be taken into account in order to specify which schema or social dimension is being utilized in any comparison.

Self as a comparison figure

An infant may also compare social objects with internal representations of self. Self as a schema or internal representation is considered as separate from the preceding discussion of schema development since the self representation is somewhat different. We have suggested (Lewis and Brooks, 1975; Lewis and Brooks-Gunn, in press) that self knowledge has at least two aspects – the existential self, or the self as separate from other, and the categorical self, or the categories by which one defines himself. Both are thought to develop in the first year of life, with the existential self development involving the initial differentiation of self from others and categorical self development involving the first categories that the infant uses to define himself. Both are necessary for knowledge of other.

Without differentiation of self and other, neither can be known. Thus, knowledge of self and other are highly dependent on one another. Mead (1934), Hamlyn (1974) and Merleau-Ponty (1964) have all discussed the complex interrelationship of self and other. The development of permanence, discussed earlier, may underlie the early differentiation of these two objects.

Categories of self are believed to be related to knowledge of others. We believe that the social dimensions used to categorize the world are also used to categorize oneself. Thus, as the infant is learning about gender and age as social dimensions, dimensions that he can use to categorize other, he is also learning that he too can be categorized in like fashion. For example, he learns that he is young and that he is a male. The findings cited earlier on the use of social labels illustrate this point: infants label pictures of themselves (as well as others) correctly in terms of age and gender.

The fact that infants categorize themselves is thought to be of particular importance in that this knowledge may result in preferences for certain social objects. Preferences for social objects have been repeatedly demonstrated in infancy and early childhood. Specifically, infants prefer interacting with and looking at unfamiliar infants and children rather than unfamiliar adults (c.f. Lewis and Brooks, 1975; Brooks and Lewis, 1976; Greenberg et al., 1973; Lewis and Brooks, 1974; Fantz, 1958), while toddlers and young children prefer interacting with same-sex to opposite-sex playmates (Abel and Sahinkaya, 1962; Langlois et al., 1973). Thus, those who are *like oneself* are preferred, at least for certain functions. As the child develops a notion of self, he also comes to value himself. By inference, those who are like self are also valued. Thus, preferences arise out of the valuation of self and the knowledge that self and a specific other both possess similar properties, i.e. gender, age, or perhaps even a specific affective relationship (i.e. parent and infant, brother and sister, etc.). Thus, with increasing knowledge about oneself, differentiation of and preferences for social objects will begin to develop.

Generalized contingencies

Another method by which the infant comes to know the social world is through the establishment of contingent relationships between his own behaviour and that of other persons. Contingency is not only important because of its reinforcing properties but because it is instrumental in establishing a generalized expectancy (Lewis and Goldberg, 1969) about the actions of social objects and establishes specific contingency patterns with different social objects.

Contingency is developed through interaction with the social world. Not only does the infant act on social objects but social objects, unlike most non-social ones, act on the infant. Indeed, ontogenetically the infant is first acted on and introduced into an interactive mode, being both responder to and initiator of action in its social world (Stern, 1974; Lewis and Freedle, 1973). Only following this is he capable of producing these contingencies through his own behaviour with inanimate objects. Thus, intentional instrumental behaviour proceeds from the social contingencies that the infant is initially presented with rather than from the accidental discoveries of contingency (Lewis, 1976).

The contingency provided by social objects provides an opportunity to learn about the nature of social objects. There is evidence that the contingency provided by the mother is responded to very early, suggesting its importance in the first year of life. For example, Moss (1967) suggests that if the mother responds to the infant's signals in a contingent fashion she gradually acquires secondary reinforcement value. It might be argued that the mother's acquisition of reinforcement value is an indication that the infant has learned to expect contingent outcomes. The degree or *speed* with which she becomes a secondary reinforcer may be the measure of the effects of contingency and the learning of action–outcome. Since there is ample evidence that the mother acquires secondary reinforcing value very quickly – within the opening weeks or days of life – it might be inferred that contingency begins quite early.

Several studies suggest that contingent responding has an effect on the infant in the first months of life. Bell and Ainsworth (1972) demonstrated that reinforcement or responsivity to an infant cry in the first quarter of the first year of life did not lead to more crying in the last quarter but rather to more communicative skill. Instead of increased crying, an outcome predicted from reinforcement principles, these infants learned that their behaviour had outcomes and from this developed new skills. Lewis and Goldberg (1969) report that contingent responding is significantly related to the infant's ability to distribute its attention in an efficient and adaptive fashion. Three-month-old infants who received more contingent responses from their mothers were those infants who were more interested in the world around them, were more attentive, and exhibited greater habituation to redundant information. In a recent study of the relationship between mother–infant relationship and infant's cognitive performance at three months, maternal responsivity to an infant behaviour was found to be significantly more predictive of the infant's cognitive performance than the mother's frequency of behaviour (Lewis and Coates, 1976; Lee-Painter and Lewis, 1974; Lewis, 1976).

These data suggest that by three months of age the contingent nature of the maternal response is significantly related to the infant's developing skills in other areas not reinforced by the mother's behaviour. These correlations cannot be considered causal, since it may be the case that attentive or skilled infants elicit more response behaviour rather than the reverse. However, the data are suggestive in pointing out the early age by which contingency awareness may be established. We would suggest that the infant learns about the social nature of the world through such contingent interactions and further that individual differences in several different factors of contingency (i.e. consistency and latency of response) teach the child about differences between social objects. For example, strangers are not as responsive to an infant's signals as is the mother. The importance of contingency and social object is demonstrated by the fact that an infant becomes very distressed when his mother acts in a non-contingent manner but does not become distressed if a stranger does so. In fact, the infant will probably try to engage the stranger a few times, then just turn away.

Summary

We have argued that social knowledge, or what others have called social cognition, includes the infant's knowledge of others, self and the relationship between self and others. Only through interaction with the social world does the infant come to know himself, others and relationships. These three areas of social knowledge are, then, interrelated by process and definition.

In our discussion of knowledge of others, it is clear that the very young infant has the sensory capacity and the cognitive ability to form complex notions about others, that these capabilities turn him toward the social world, and that social dimensions such as age, gender and familiarity are utilized very early. Moreover, as we have tried to indicate, social objects interact with one another over functions and situations, each of which define the nature of social objects. Thus, the matrix of social objects, functions and stimulus dimensions, as well as his perceptual cognitive capacities, all direct the infant to his primary task, of adaption to his social environment.

Notes

1 A more complete discussion may be found in Lewis and Feiring (in press).
2 Although we are labelling these processes cognitive, they may be social in nature. In fact, the term 'social cognitive processes' may be more accurate. However, since others have used this term to mean 'knowledge of others', it is not used here in order to reduce terminology confusion.

* This paper was supported in part by a grant from the Foundation for Child Development to Michael Lewis.

100   Issues in childhood social development

References

Abel, H. and Sahinkaya, R. (1962) Emergence of sex and race friendship preferences. *Child Development 33* : 939–43.

Ahrens, R. (1954) Beitrage zur entwickiung des physiognomie und mimikericennes. *Zeitschrift für experimentelle und angewandte psychologie 2* : 412–54.

Ainsworth, M. D. S. (1969) Object relations, dependency, and attachment: a theoretical review of the infant–mother relationship. *Child Development 40* : 969–1025.

Ainsworth, M. D. S. (1972) Attachment and dependency: a comparison. In J. L. Gewirtz (ed.) *Attachment and Dependency*. Washington: Winston. 97–138.

Ambrose, J. A. (1961) The development of the smiling response in early infancy. In B. M. Foss (ed.) *Determinants of Infant Behavior*. New York: Wiley. 179–96.

Aronson, E. and Rosenbloom, S. (1971) Space perception in early infancy: perception within a common auditory-visual space. *Science 172* : 1161–3.

Banks, J. H. and Wolfson, J. H. (1967) Differential cardiac response of infants to mother and stranger. Paper presented at the Eastern Psychological Association meetings, Boston, April.

Bell, R. Q. (1965) The prone head reaction in the human newborn: relationship with sex and tactile sensitivity. *Child Development 36* : 943–6.

Bell, S. M. (1970) The development of the concept of object as related to infant–mother attachment. *Child Development 41* : 291–311.

Bell, M. and Ainsworth, D. (1972) Infant crying and maternal responsiveness. *Child Development 43* : 1171–90.

Benjamin, J. D. (1961) Some developmental observations relating to the theory of anxiety. *Journal of the American Psychoanalytic Association 9* : 652–68.

Bergman, T., Haith, M. M. and Mann, L. (1971) Development of eye contact and facial scanning in infants. Paper presented at the Biennial meeting of the Society for Research in Child Development, Minneapolis, April.

Bond, E. K. (1972) Perception of form by the human infant. *Psychological Bulletin 77* (4): 225–45.

Bornstein, M. H. (1977) Chromatic vision in infancy. In H. W. Reese and L. P. Lipsitt (eds) *Advances in Child Development and Behavior, Vol. 12*. New York: Academic Press.

Bowlby, J. (1969) *Attachment and Loss. Attachment, Vol. 1*. New York: Basic Books.

Brazelton, T. B., Koslowski, B. and Main, M. (1974) The origins of reciprocity: the early mother–infant interaction. In M. Lewis and L. Rosenblum, *The Effect of the Infant on its Caregiver, Vol. 1*. New York: Wiley.

Bronson, G. W. (1972) Infants' reactions to unfamiliar persons and novel objects. *Monographs of the Society for Research in Child Development 47* (148).

Bronson, W. C. (1975) Developments in behavior with age mates during the second year of life. In M. Lewis and L. Rosenblum (eds) *Friendship and Peer Relations: The Origins of Behavior, Vol. IV*. New York: Wiley.

Brooks, J. and Lewis, M. (1974) Attachment behavior in thirteen-month-old, opposite-sex twins. *Child Development 45* : 243–7.

Brooks, J. and Lewis, M. (1975) Person perception and verbal labeling: the development of social labels. Versions of this paper were presented at both the Society for Research in Child Development meetings, Denver, Colo., April 1975 and the Eastern Psychological Association meetings, New York, NY, April 1975.

Brooks, J. and Lewis, M. (1976) Infants' responses to strangers: midget, adult and child. *Child Development* 47: 323–32.

Brooks-Gunn, J. and Lewis, M. (in press) The effects of age and sex on infants' playroom behavior. *Journal of Genetic Psychology.*

Bruner, J. (1968) *Processes of Cognitive Growth: Infancy.* (Vol. III, Heinz Weiner Lecture Series.) Clark University Press with Bane Publishers.

Bruner, J. S. and Tagiuri, R. (1954) The perception of people. In G. Lindzey (ed.) *Handbook of Social Psychology, Vol. 2.* Cambridge, Massachusetts: Addison-Wesley. 601–33.

Caron, A. J., Caron, R. F., Caldwell, R. C. and Weiss, S. J. (1973) Infant perception of the structural properties of the face. *Developmental Psychology 9*: 385–400.

Carpenter, G. C. (1973) Mother–stranger discrimination in the early weeks of life. Paper presented at the Biennial meeting of the Society for Research in Child Development, Philadelphia, March.

Chandler, M. J. (1977) Social cognition: a selective review of current research. In W. F. Overton and J. M. Gallagher (eds) *Knowledge and Development, Vol. 1, Advances in Research and Theory.* New York: Plenum.

Darwin, C. (1965, originally 1895) *The Expression of the Emotions in Man and Animals.* Chicago: University of Chicago Press.

Décarie, T. G. (1965) *Intelligence and Affectivity in Early Childhood: An Experimental Study of Jean Piaget's Object Concept and Object Relations.* New York: International Universities Press.

Donnee, L. H. (1973) Infants' developmental scanning patterns to face and nonface stimuli under various auditory conditions. Paper presented at the Biennial meeting of the Society for Research in Child Development, Philadelphia, March–April.

Edwards, C. P. and Lewis, M. (in press) The social world of the young child: concepts of age groups and age functions. Paper presented at a Conference, The Origins of Behavior: The Social Network of the Developing Infant, Educational Testing Service, Princeton, NJ, December 1977. In M Lewis and L. Rosenblum (eds) *The Social Network of the Developing Infant.* New York: Plenum.

Engen, T. and Lipsitt, L. P. (1965) Decrement and recovery of responses to olfactory stimuli in the human neonate. *Journal of Comparative and Physiological Psychology 59*: 3–13.

Fagan, J. F. (1972) Infants' recognition memory for faces. *Journal of Experimental Child Psychology 14*: 453–76.

Fantz, R. L. (1958) Pattern vision in young infants. *Psychological Review 8*: 43–7.

Fantz, R. L. (1963) Pattern vision in new born infants. *Science 140*: 296–7.

Fantz, R. L. (1965) Visual perception from birth as shown by pattern selectivity. *Annals of the New York Academy of Sciences 118*: 793–814.

102 Issues in childhood social development

Fantz, R. L. (1966) Pattern discrimination and selective attention as determinants of perceptual development from birth. In A. M. Kidd and J. L. Rivoire (eds) *Perceptual Development in Children.* New York: International University Press.

Fantz, R. L. and Nevis, S. (1967) Pattern preferences and perceptual–cognitive development in early infancy. *Merrill-Palmer Quarterly 13* : 77–108.

Fitzgerald, H. E. (1968) Autonomic pupillary reflex activity during early infancy and its relation to social and nonsocial visual stimuli. *Journal of Experimental Child Psychology 6* : 470–82.

Fitzgerald, H. E. and Brackbill, Y. (1976) Classical conditioning in infancy: development and constraints. *Psychological Bulletin 83* (3) : 353–76.

Fraiberg, S. (1974) Blind infants and their mothers. In M. Lewis and L. Rosenblum (eds) *The Effect of the Infant on its Caregiver : The Origins of Behavior, Vol. I.* New York: Wiley. 215–32.

Garvey, C. (1977) The contingent query: a dependent act in conversation. In M. Lewis and L. Rosenblum (eds) *Interaction, Conversation and the Development of Language : The Origins of Behavior, Vol. V.* New York: Wiley.

Gewirtz, J. L. (1972) Attachment, dependence and a distinction in terms of stimulus control. On the selection and use of attachment and dependence indices. In J. Gewirtz (ed.) *Attachment and Dependency.* Washington: Winston. 139–215.

Gibson, E. J. (1969) *Principles of Perceptual Learning and Development.* New York: Appleton-Century-Crofts.

Graham, F. K., Clifton, R. K. and Hatton, H. M. (1968) Habituation of heart rate response to repeated auditory stimulation during the first five days of life. *Child Development 39* : 35–51.

Greenberg, D. J., Hillman, D. and Grice, D. (1973) Infant and stranger variables related to stranger anxiety in the first year of life. *Developmental Psychology 9* : 207–12.

Haaf, R. A. and Bell, R. O. (1967) The facial dimension in visual discrimination by human infants. *Child Development 38* : 893–9.

Haith, M. M. (1966) The response of the human newborn to visual movement. *Journal of Experimental Child Psychology 3* : 235–43.

Hamlyn, D. W. (1974) Person-perception and our understanding of others. In T. Mischel (ed.) *Understanding Other Persons.* Totowa, New Jersey: Rowman and Littlefield. 1–36.

Hebb, D. O. (1946) On the nature of fear. *Psychological Review 53* : 259–76.

Hebb, D. O. (1949) *The Organization of Behavior.* New York: Wiley.

Heider, F. (1958) *The Psychology of Interpersonal Relations.* New York: Wiley.

Hershenson, M. (1965) Form perception in the human newborn. Paper presented at the Second Annual Symposium, Center for Visual Science, University of Rochester, June.

Hess, E. H. (1970) Ethology and developmental psychology. In P. Mussen (ed.) *Carmichael's Manual of Child Psychology, Vol. I.* New York: Wiley. 1–38.

Kagan, J. (1970) The determinants of attention in the infant. *American Scientist 58:* 298–306.

Kagan, J., and Lewis, M. (1965) Studies of attention in the human infant. *Merrill-Palmer Quarterly 11* : 95–127.

Kagan, J., Henker, B., Hen-Tov, A., Levine, J. and Lewis, M. (1966) Infants' differential reactions to familiar and distorted faces. *Child Development 37*: 519–32.

Kelley, H. H. (1973) The processes of causal attribution. *American Psychologist 28*: 107–28.

Kessen, W., Haith, M. A. and Salapatek, P. H. (1970) Human infancy: a bibliography and guide. In P. H. Mussen (ed.) *Manual of Child Psychology, Vol. 2*. New York: Wiley. 287–446.

Kohlberg, L. (1966) A cognitive–developmental analysis of children's sex-role concepts and attitudes. In E. E. Maccoby (ed.) *The Development of Sex Differences*. Stanford: Stanford University Press. 82–173.

Koopman, P. R. and Ames, E. W. (1968) Infants' preferences for facial arrangements: a failure to replicate. *Child Development 39*: 481–95.

Lamb, M. (1976a) Effects of stress and cohort on mother– and father–infant interaction. *Developmental Psychology 12*: 435–43.

Lamb, M. (ed.) (1976b) *The Role of the Father in Child Development*. New York: Wiley.

Langlois, J., Gottfried, N. and Sear, B. (1973) The influence of sex of peer on the social behavior of preschool children. *Developmental Psychology 8*: 93–8.

Lee-Painter, S. and Lewis, M. (1974) Mother–infant interaction and cognitive development. Paper presented at the Eastern Psychological Association meetings, Philadelphia, April.

Lenssen, B. G. (1973) Infant's reactions to peer strangers. Unpublished manuscript.

Levi-Strauss, C. (1962) *The Savage Mind*. Chicago, Ill.: University of Chicago Press.

Lewis, M. (1969) Infants' responses to facial stimuli during the first year of life. *Developmental Psychology 1*: 75–86.

Lewis, M. (1972a) Parents and children: sex-role development. *School Review 80* (2): 229–40.

Lewis, M. (1972b) State as an infant–environment interaction: an analysis of mother–infant interaction as a function of sex. *Merrill-Palmer Quarterly 18*: 95–121.

Lewis, M. (1976) The origins of self competence. Paper presented at the NIMH Conference on Mood Development, Washington, D.C., November.

Lewis, M. (1977) Early socioemotional development and its relevance for curriculum. *Merrill-Palmer Quarterly 23*, 4: 279–86.

Lewis, M. (in press) Situational development and the study of behavioral development. In L. Pervin and M. Lewis (eds) *Perspectives in Interactional Psychology*. New York: Plenum.

Lewis, M. and Brooks, J. (1974) Self, other, and fear: infants' reactions to people. In M. Lewis and L. Rosenblum (eds) *The Origins of Fear: The Origins of Behavior, Vol. II*. New York: Wiley. 195–227.

Lewis, M. and Brooks, J. (1975) Infants' social perception: A constructivist view. In L. Cohen and P. Salapatek (eds) *Infant Perception: From Sensation to Cognition, Vol. II*. New York: Academic Press. 101–43.

Lewis, M. and Brooks-Gunn, J. (in press) *Social Cognition and the Development of Self*. New York: Plenum.

Lewis, M. and Cherry, L. (1977) Social behavior and language acquisition. In M. Lewis and L. Rosenblum (eds) *Interaction, Conversation, and the Development of Language: The Origins of Behavior, Vol. V.* New York: Wiley.

Lewis, M. and Coates, D. (1976) Mother–infant interaction and infant cognitive performance. Paper presented at the Sixth Annual meeting of the International Primatological Society, Cambridge, England, August.

Lewis, M. and Feiring, C. (in press) The child's social world. Chapter to appear in R. M. Lerner and G. D. Spanier (eds) *Contributions of the Child to Marital Quality and Family Interaction through the Life-span.* New York: Academic Press.

Lewis, M. and Freedle, R. (1973) Mother–infant dyad: the cradle of meaning. In P. Pliner, L. Krames and T. Alloway (eds) *Communication and Affect: Language and Thought.* New York: Academic Press. 127–55.

Lewis, M. and Freedle, R. (1977) The mother and infant communication system: the effects of poverty. In H. McGurk (ed.) *Ecological Factors in Human Development.* Amsterdam: North-Holland. 205–15.

Lewis, M. and Goldberg, S. (1969) Perceptual–cognitive development in infancy: a generalized expectancy model as a function of the mother–child interaction. *Merrill-Palmer Quarterly 15* (1): 81–100.

Lewis, M. and Rosenblum, L. (1974) *The Origins of Fear: The Origins of Behavior, Vol. II.* New York: Wiley.

Lewis, M. and Rosenblum, L. (eds) (1975) *Friendship and Peer Relations: The Origins of Behavior, Vol. IV.* New York: Wiley.

Lewis, M. and Weinraub, M. (1976) The father's role in the infant's social network. In M. Lamb (ed.) *The Role of the Father in Child Development.* New York: Wiley. 157–84.

Lewis, M., Young, G., Brooks, J. and Michalson, L. (1975) The beginning of friendship. In M. Lewis and L. Rosenblum (eds) *Friendship and Peer Relations: The Origins of Behavior, Vol. IV.* New York: Wiley. 27–66.

Lorenz, K. Z. (1943) Die angeborenen formen möglicher erfahrung. *Zeitschrift für Tierpsychologie 5*: 235–409.

McGurk, H. and Lewis, M. (1974) Space perception in early infancy: perception within a common auditory–visual space? *Science 186* (4164): 649–50.

Mead, G. H. (1934) *Mind, Self, and Society.* Chicago: University of Chicago Press.

Merleau-Ponty, M. (1964) *Primacy of Perception.* J. Eddie (ed.) and W. Cobb (trans.). Evanston: Northwestern Universities Press.

Molfese, D. L. (1972) Cerebral Asymmetry in Infants, Children, and Adults: auditory evoked responses to speech and noise stimuli. Unpublished doctoral dissertation, Pennsylvania State University.

Money, J., Hampson, J. G. and Hampson, J. L. (1957) Imprinting and the establishment of gender roles. *A. N. A. Archives of Neurology and Psychology 77*: 333–6.

Morgan, G. A. and Ricciuti, H. N. (1969) Infants' responses to strangers during the first year. In B. M. Foss (ed.) *Determinants of Infant Behavior, Vol. 4.* London: Methuen.

Moss, H. A. (1967) Sex, age, and state as determinants of mother–infant interaction. *Merrill-Palmer Quarterly 13*: 19–36.

Mueller, E. and Vandell, D. (in press) Infant–infant interaction. In J. Osofsky (ed.) *Handbook of Infant Development.* New York: Wiley.

Parke, R. D. and O'Leary, S. (1975) Father–mother–infant interaction in the newborn period: some findings, some observations, and some unresolved issues. In K. Kreigel and J. Meacham (eds) *The Developing Individual in a Changing World, Vol. II.* Social and environmental issues. The Hague: Mouton.

Piaget, J. (1947) *The Psychology of Intelligence.* New York: Harcourt, Brace.

Piaget, J. (1952) *The Origins of Intelligence in Children.* New York: International University Press.

Polak, P. R., Emde, R. N. and Spitz, R. A. (1964) The smiling response to the human face, II. Visual discrimination and the onset of depth perception. *Journal of Nervous and Mental Disorders 139:* 407–15.

Rheingold, H. L. and Eckerman, C. O. (1973) Fear of the stranger: a critical examination. In H. W. Reese (ed.) *Advances in Child Development and Behavior, Vol. 8.* New York: Academic Press.

Robson, K. S., Pederson, F. A. and Moss, H. A. (1969) Developmental observations of diadic gazing in relation to the fear of strangers and social approach behavior. *Child Development 40:* 619–27.

Rosenthal, M. K. (1973) Attachment and mother–infant interaction: some research impasse and a suggested change in orientation. *Journal of Child Psychology and Psychiatry 14:* 201–7.

Salapatek, P. and Kessen, W. (1966) Visual scanning of triangles by the newborn. *Journal of Experimental Child Psychology 3:* 113–22.

Salzen, E. A. (1963) Visual stimuli eliciting the smiling response in the human infant. *Journal of Genetic Psychology 102:* 51–4.

Sander, L. W. (1977) The regulation of exchange in the infant–caretaker system and some aspects of the context–content relationship. In M. Lewis and L. Rosenblum (eds) *Interaction, Conversation, and the Development of Language: The Origins of Behavior, Vol. V.* New York: Wiley.

Schaffer, H. R. (1966) The onset of fear of strangers and the incongruity hypothesis. *Journal of Child Psychology and Psychiatry 7:* 95–106.

Shaffran, R. and Décarie, T. (1973) Short-term stability of infants' responses to strangers. Paper presented at the Society for Research in Child Development meetings, Philadelphia, March–April.

Shantz, C. U. (1975) The development of social cognition. In E. M. Hetherington (ed.) *Review of Child Development Research, Vol. 5.* Chicago: University of Chicago Press. 257–323.

Siqueland, E. R. (1968) Conditioned sucking and visual reinforcers with human infants. Paper presented at Eastern Regional meeting, Society for Research in Child Development, Worcester, Massachusetts, April.

Spitz, R. and Wolf, K. (1946) The smiling response: a contribution to the ontogenesis of social relations. *Genetic Psychology Monographs 34:* 57–125.

Stechler, G. and Latz, E. (1966) Some observations on attention and arousal in the human infant. *Journal of the American Academy of Child Psychiatry 5* (3): 517–25.

Stern, D. (1974) Mother and infant at play: the dyadic interaction involving facial, vocal, and gaze behaviors. In M. Lewis and L. Rosenblum (eds) *The*

Effect of the Infant on its Caregiver: The Origins of Behavior, Vol. I. New York: Wiley. 187–214.

Tagiuri, R. (1969) Person perception. In G. Lindzey and E. Aronson (eds) *The Handbook of Social Psychology.* Reading, Mass.: Addison-Wesley. 395–449.

Thomas, H. (1965) Visual-fixation responses of infants to stimuli of varying complexity. *Child Development 36*: 629–38.

Waite, L. H. and Lewis, M. (1977) Intermodal person schema in infancy: perception within a common auditory-visual space. Paper presented at the Eastern Psychological Association meetings, Boston, Massachusetts, April.

Wilcox, B. M. (1969) Visual preferences of human infants for representations of the human face. *Journal of Experimental Child Psychology 7*: 10–20.

Wolff, P. H. (1963) Observations on the early development of smiling. In B. M. Foss (ed.) *Determinants of Infant Behavior, Vol. II.* New York: Wiley.

Youniss, J. (1975) Another perspective on social cognition. In A. D. Pick (ed.) *Minnesota Symposium on Child Psychology, Vol. 9.* Minneapolis: University of Minnesota Press.

4 The child's perception of other people

Colin Rogers

The socially experienced and cognitively matured adult perceives other people on at least two levels. People are perceived first in terms of their physical characteristics and in terms of what they typically do, and second as psychological entities. The actions of other people are not merely observed, they are also interpreted. These interpretations involve the making of inferences of thoughts, feelings and, most importantly, intentions. We, as adults, analyse the actions of others in causal terms and utilize the information thus obtained to produce impressions of others that include dispositional characteristics, these being typically expressed in the form of personality traits.

Heider (1958), whose work has inspired the currently burgeoning research area collectively labelled Attribution Theory, referred to these dispositional characteristics as '. . . the invariances that make possible a more or less stable, predictable and controllable world'. As Mischel (1968) has argued, these invariances may well have more to do with the characteristics of the perceiver than the perceived. The behaviour of other people may well lack the consistency (both temporally and trans-situationally) that the attribution of stable traits to them would imply. However, if we, as individuals, need to attempt to predict and possibly control the behaviour of those other people, then a conceptualization of others that is essentially invariant is the most economical way of achieving this. Mischel's objections to the use of trait terms to account for personality characteristics are directed at the professional psychologist, not at the man-in-the-street, or the 'naive psychologist'. The naive psychologist has a more limited range of concern than his professional counterpart, wishing usually only to predict the behaviour of those people with whom he is personally involved and only in those situations that are relevant to his own needs. While a conceptualization of human action in terms of dispositions may be inadequate for the professional, it has served the naive psychologist well.

The notion of perceived invariance in the behaviour of other people has recently been taken up by Livesley and Bromley (1973) in their study of the development of person perception. Their work will be discussed in more detail below, but essentially they show that while a fifteen-year-old's description of another person is integrated and coordinated around one or two central themes, the child of nine or ten years will produce a list of relatively poorly organized personality characteristics and the seven-year-old hardly refers to such characteristics at all, his descriptions consisting predominantly of references to physical characteristics and routine actions. This developmental sequence is interpreted by Livesley and Bromley as following from the older child's recognition of the essentially invariant nature of human action. The child's focus of attention shifts from the discrete and directly observable action itself to the underlying intentions.

Given the analysis of person perception presented by Heider, the young child's relatively low use of dispositional characteristics in his descriptions of others will place him at some disadvantage relative to the older child and adult. The young child will be less able to predict the behaviour of others across a range of situations and will consequently be less able to control his own behaviour with respect to the reactions to it of others.

A developmental study of the process of person perception is therefore of immediate importance. The child, in common with the adult, will react not to other people directly, but to his own impressions of those other people. If we wish to understand the social behaviour of children we must also attempt to understand *their* understanding of other people's behaviour. A developmental study of person perception will also provide useful tests of the adequacy of our understanding of similar processes in adults. We must begin our investigations into the development of person perception with an examination of the end products of the process – children's descriptions of other people.

Of the studies investigating the way in which children describe others, Livesley and Bromley (1973) have reported the most extensive and most recent example. They put forward the view that it is essential to allow the child freedom to describe others in his own terms. The ideal research design is, in their view, a simple one. Tell the child what people you want him to describe and then examine in detail what he has to say. As a first step it would appear that such an approach is indeed likely to be maximally useful; it will be argued below, however, that it is by no means sufficient if we are to be able to interpret the significance of any age-related changes that such a methodology might detect.

Given the fact that there have been very few studies of this type to date, the consensus amongst them is impressive. Watts (1944), in an inadequately reported study, shows that up to six or seven years of age the child describes others almost exclusively in terms of their physical characteristics, personality characteristics being used to an increasing extent from eight years and above. The child also comes to differentiate people more clearly from each other and, principally from the age of eleven years onward, to accept that both desirable and undesirable traits can co-exist in the same person.

Scarlett et al. (1971) analysed descriptions given by boys aged six, nine and ten to eleven years. The six-year-olds predominantly described others in egocentric terms, e.g. 'He hits me!' Nine-year-olds also used these statements to a predominant extent but also used an increasing number of non-egocentric but concrete statements e.g. 'He plays ball'. The oldest children predominantly used abstract constructs e.g. 'He is intelligent'.

Peevers and Secord (1973) obtained descriptions from five age groups ranging from kindergarteners to college students. Again, older children used more dispositional items and made fewer egocentric statements. Dispositional characteristics were rarely explicitly mentioned by the younger children but they would frequently imply them. For instance, they will state that 'He is always fighting' rather than 'He is aggressive'.

Brierley (1967) used a form of the repertory grid test, rather than freely written descriptions. Subjects, both boys and girls, were aged seven, ten and thirteen years. The seven-year-olds mainly produced constructs concerned with social roles (29 per cent of the total number produced) and appearance (32 per cent). The nine-year-olds mainly produced behaviour constructs (40 per cent) and social role constructs (27 per cent). The thirteen-year-olds mainly produced behaviour constructs (41 per cent) and personality constructs (40 per cent). Only

9 per cent of the seven-year-olds' constructs and 19 per cent of the ten-year-olds' constructs could be classified as personality constructs.

As indicated above, the most extensive study to date using the free descriptions approach is Livesley and Bromley (1973). Subjects were classified into yearly age intervals ranging from seven to fifteen years as well as into sex and higher/lower IQ categories. Each subject described eight people personally known to the child, who would fit each of the possible categories obtained from people who the child liked/disliked, who were the child's peer or an adult and who were of the same/opposite sex. The analysis of the ensuing data is too complex to be done justice here. Most importantly they show a significant age-related increase in the use of 'central' statements (i.e. statements concerned with personality traits, attitudes, motives and values). Only 22 per cent of the statements made by seven-year-olds could be classified as central compared to 43 per cent for the eight-year-olds and 46 per cent for the fifteen-year-olds. Girls used a greater number of central statements but not a higher proportion. A greater number of central statements were addressed to males but a higher proportion to females and both a higher number and proportion of central statements were made in descriptions of peers as compared to adults. While Peevers and Secord (1973) found more dispositional statements being used in descriptions of disliked others, Livesley and Bromley found no such effect.

The general developmental trend identified by these studies is clear in spite of the differences in detail that exist between them. The descriptions given by the young child are essentially concrete. Thus a person is described *predominantly* in terms of his or her size, colouring, name, age, clothes, home, possessions and so on. There is an apparent inability to differentiate the person clearly from his surroundings. As the child gets older so more abstract notions are included in his descriptions of others. Initially such abstract descriptions are simple. Most importantly they appear to be univalent. Other people are described as being essentially either all good or all bad, as liked or disliked. The personality characteristics that they are assumed to have apply in an all-or-none fashion. The child does not attempt to qualify his statements, neither does he attempt to draw attention to seemingly conflicting elements in another person's make-up.

In many respects the appearance of divalent descriptions, where both good and bad, desirable and undesirable aspects of another person's character are recognized and some attempt to integrate them is made, is the achievement of the young adolescent. It is an achievement that requires the ability to form high level, abstract concepts about others that conceptualize behaviour as an essentially invariant reflection of underlying dispositions. These changes are to be seen as changes in emphasis on the part of the child. The seven-year-old's description of others are not usually totally lacking in personality descriptors and a substantial proportion of the descriptions given by adults consists of descriptions of physical characteristics. However, the relative balance between the two types of statement is as indicated above.

While there is general agreement concerning the nature of this age-related change it is, as yet, unclear as to whether the change is gradual or abrupt. Livesley and Bromley (1973), using free description data, obtain an abrupt change between seven and eight years. Brierley (1967), using the repertory grid technique, reports a more gradual change in the extent to which personality terms are used between the ages of seven and thirteen years. These differences may well be attributable to the different methodologies and content analysis systems employed. Salmon (1976) has suggested that the repertory grid test may be particularly difficult for young children and could therefore be expected to underestimate their performance. However, the nature of the developmental change, whether gradual or abrupt, is clearly a matter for future empirical resolution.

Irrespective of the rate of development, substantial changes in the nature of children's descriptions of other people do take place. What is to be made of them? The type of descriptive terms with which one is concerned here is accorded a central role in the person perception literature. These abstract, dispositional terms are of importance due to the expectancies associated with them (Warr and Knapper, 1968). To say that a person is 'diligent' tells us that we can expect him to behave in certain ways under certain conditions. Armed with such information it is possible to predict how the person to whom it is applied will behave. Such predictions enable us in turn to regulate our own behaviour towards the other person. It was for exactly this reason that the early person perception research was concerned with attempts to identify the good judge of other people. Such a good judge would be able to predict accurately the behaviour of others in a variety of settings.

As stated above, doubts exist as to the validity of trait-type descriptions of personality for the professional psychologist. However, the naive psychologist has different concerns and, as argued by Jones and Nisbett (1971), the presence of one's self in a series of interactions with the same individual(s) lends to them a certain degree of consistency that may well validate a trait-based account of human behaviour, and allow reasonably accurate predictions of the behaviour of others.

It is within this conceptual framework, one that is also supported by the work following from Kelly (1955), that the relative absence of dispositional terms from the descriptions of others given by young children becomes crucial. The young child who does not use such terms in his descriptions will be relatively unable to understand, predict and influence the behaviour of others across a range of different situations. His knowledge of others will be situation specific.

Up to this point one has assumed that the way in which a child represents others in his descriptions of them can be considered to be equivalent to his actual perceptions of them. In other words that his descriptions of others will represent the way in which he actually understands their ongoing behaviour. This is a long-standing problem within the psychology of person perception and one which becomes crucial when a developmental perspective is adopted; at the same time it is potentially solvable. It is a problem that becomes crucial in as much as the communicative powers of the young child are clearly limited in comparison to those of an adult (e.g. Flavell, 1968). It becomes potentially solvable when one moves from an analysis of the complete descriptions that young children might give of others to an analysis of the ways in which those descriptions have been built up, in other words as one moves from a study of impressions to a study of impression formation. Initially one will still be dependent upon the child's communicative abilities, but as a clearer understanding of the processes of impression formation is established this dependence will be reduced.

Where to begin? The traditional adult-orientated study of person perception has identified a number of sources of information that may be available to the individual seeking to attribute dispositions to another. Many of these sources, however, would appear to be of only minor significance from a developmental point of view. What eludes the young child is the very concept of a disposition, or more accurately the recognition of the usefulness of such a concept. This is the conclusion frequently drawn by those who have identified an increase in the use of dispositional terms with age. Livesley and Bromley, for example, state that the young child will find the behaviour of other people particularly puzzling and inconsistent due to an inability to detect the underlying similarities in a series of apparently different behaviours.

It is unlikely then that much progress will be made by examining, for example, the extent to which a young child will infer dispositional characteristics from a person's appearance. For the adult this would appear to be a particularly important source of information regarding the dispositional characteristics of others. Yet in this case the adult would have already formulated the concept of a dispositional characteristic. The appearance of a person is simply used as a convenient, shorthand method for making assumptions about the person's dispositions. When more reliable information becomes available, through processes of social interaction, the impressions based on appearance may well be superceded (e.g. Argyle and McHenry, 1971). It is the process by which dispositions are abstracted from ongoing behaviour that is of importance from a developmental perspective. Attribution theory (see Jones et al., 1971; Harvey et al., 1976) suggests at least one possible line of investigation. As mentioned above Heider, the founder of attribution theory, was concerned with the way in which the ordinary person, the naive psychologist, seeks out invariance in the behaviour of other people. The attribution of dispositional characteristics to others represents the most important way in which this perception of invariance is achieved. The theory is concerned with the way in which these attributions are made.

The naive psychologist, in observing the behaviour of other people, is confronted with a potentially bewildering variety of actions in an equally broad range of situations. Stability and consistency can be achieved by attempting a causal analysis of this behaviour. Basic, dispositional causal factors will be seen to exercise their influence upon behaviour in a consistent, if complex, manner across a variety of situations.

Much of the complexity involved in the relationship between the invariant dispositions and varying behaviour is due to the existence of other causal factors. Heider (1958) draws a broad distinction between personal (internal) and impersonal (external) causal factors. The problem confronting the naive psychologist observing an instance of behaviour is, first, to determine the relative importance of both internal and external factors and, second, to determine which examples of each are present. More recent theoretical formulations have been primarily concerned with the former of these two problems and have attempted to demonstrate the 'lawfulness' of such causal attributions.

Kelley (1971) argues that the decision to attribute an act to either an internal or external cause can be seen to be controlled by three general principles of covariation, discounting and augmentation. The covariation principle states that acts will be attributed to the causal factors with which they are seen to covary, even though this does not logically present 'proof' of a causal relationship. The discounting principle states that confidence in an attribution is reduced if other plausible causal factors are present. The augmentation principle states that confidence in an attribution will be increased if other causal factors are present that would normally inhibit the observed behaviour.

An earlier analysis by Jones and Davis (1965) is concerned with factors determining the extent to which an attributed internal cause might be seen to represent an underlying intention or disposition.

This brief account cannot do justice to the complexity of attribution theory. However, it serves to highlight the way in which an understanding of the nature of one individual's interpretation of the actions of others relates to the dispositions that he might later attribute to those others. If dispositional characteristics are to be attributed to another person then the actions of that other person need to be interpreted in terms of internal causal factors, particularly intentions. Given this analysis, together with the finding that young children make comparatively few dispositional attributions, one can go on to ask to what extent the latter finding might be due to an inability on the part of the young child to conceptualize the behaviour of others in terms of thoughts, feelings and, most importantly, intentions.

Faced with a paucity of research dealing directly with the child's person perceptions, writers such as Livesley and Bromley have turned to the extensive moral judgement literature for clues regarding the child's ability to utilize information concerning the intentions of others.

Piaget's (1932) assertion that the child of seven years and below would be less likely to take the intentions of a possible transgressor into account in the making of moral judgements has received considerable support (Gutkin, 1972; Hebble, 1971; Hoffman, 1970). Piaget's original study involved the presentation of two simple stories to a child. In one the 'hero' had acted with good intentions but had brought about markedly negative consequences. In the second the 'hero' acted with less than honourable intentions but caused less negative consequences. On being asked to state which of the two was the naughtier, children below the age of eight typically select the character associated with the worst consequences, irrespective of his intentions, while children above the age of eight select the character with the worst intentions.

There are several problems associated with this research. Constanzo et al. (1973) have pointed out that Piaget's initial study, and many of the ensuing replications, are designed so as to confound the two factors of intentionality and seriousness of the consequence. Armsby (1971) has shown that the original research fails to distinguish adequately between 'good' and 'bad' intentions and presents evidence to show that if this is done six-year-old children are more likely to make their moral judgements on the basis of the actor's intentions, as long as the damage caused is relatively slight. Chandler et al. (1973) show that if the information is presented to the children via videotape rather than in the form of written stories, the incidence of mature, intention-based judgements will again increase for the younger children. Berg-Cross (1975) has shown that six-year-olds will respond to the intention information if they are asked to rate stories singly rather than make comparisons between pairs. Berndt and Berndt (1975) point out that much of the moral judgement research has confused the concepts of 'intention' and 'motive'. The former refers to the intentional–accidental distinction and the latter to the various reasons an individual might have for acting in a particular manner.

More importantly, Farnhill (1974) and Imamoglu (1974) have shown that the relatively low use which the younger child makes of information concerning the intentions of the actor is related more to the nature of the moral judgement situation rather than to the cognitive inadequacies of the child. Farnhill shows that the extent to which the child will use the intention information depends on the type of judgement that he is asked to make. He had his subjects observe an actor carrying out a task which, in one condition, was deliberately performed badly. The bad performance also involved damaging various objects. The subjects were then asked either to make a moral evaluation of the actor, or to judge how useful that actor might be in helping the subject perform a task similar to the one in which the actor had been engaged. The results indicate that use of the intention information is greater when the child is making judgements about the usefulness of the actor than when he is making a moral evaluation of him.

Imamoglu (1974) presents evidence that shows why this might be. Investigating the moral judgements of children aged five to eleven years she found that all children would take longer to respond to accidental rather than intentional acts, indicating at least some awareness of differences between the two. While five-year-olds failed to take the actor's intentions into account when judging the *act*, they did so when they evaluated the *actor* (on a like–dislike scale). In addition to making moral judgements on their own behalf, the children were also asked to state how various adult characters (e.g. mother, schoolteacher, policeman) would rate the actors. Children were found to expect the adults to make less use of the intentional information than they did themselves. The results obtained by Farnhill and Imamoglu show that children as young as five or six years of age can, and sometimes will, differentiate intentions from consequences, but that they appear to learn from their social environment that intentions are frequently less important.

Weiner and Peter (1973) present similar evidence in a study concerning achievement judgements. In assessing the extent to which somebody else deserves credit for being successful young children initially pay little attention to the amount of effort exerted; it is the outcome that determines the child observer's reactions. By ten or twelve years of age, however, the child has become increasingly influenced by the amount of effort exerted by the actor and less so by the success or failure achieved. Up to this point the parallel with the typical findings concerning intentions and outcomes in the moral judgement sphere seems clear. However, after the age of twelve, Weiner and Peter report that the child comes to pay relatively less attention to effort expenditure and reverts to the earlier, more immature, style of judgement, where outcomes primarily determine the reaction. Weiner and Peter suggest that the child learns through experience in school that it is outcome that counts!

The conclusions to be drawn from these studies is that the young child is in fact aware of the nature and significance of intentions. They are not completely beyond his comprehension. Whether he makes reference to other people's intentions or not, however, will be situationally determined. Accordingly, if we wish to know to what extent a young child will infer intentions in situations relevant to person perception we must look directly at those situations, and not to attempt to extrapolate from other areas.

More direct evidence on this point comes from a study by Flapan (1968). Male subjects aged six, nine or twelve years were shown two extracts from a film showing everyday, domestic scenes involving parents and their children. Following the showing of each film episode the children were asked to describe what they had seen and were then questioned concerning the feelings, thoughts and intentions of the actors in the film. The children's free descriptions were then content analysed. Three main categories were used for this content analysis, *Reporting and Describing* statements, *Explaining* statements and *Inferring and Interpreting* statements.

Most of the results discussed by Flapan are in the form of descriptive trends rather than statistically significant differences. Initially, the six-year-old child is primarily concerned with the overt, factual elements of the interactions portrayed in the film episodes. He is concerned with what happened and with directly observable consequences rather than with why it happened and more subtle consequences. The nine- and twelve-year-olds show an increased concern with the covert psychological aspects of the interactions. The thoughts, feelings and intentions of the film actors are mentioned spontaneously by an increasing number of children.

Interestingly, the differences observed by Flapan are primarily between the six-year-olds and the two older age groups. This corresponds closely to the findings of Livesley and Bromley (1973) who also found a sudden increase in the use of central statements in the descriptions of others at around eight years. However, only a few of the differences alluded to by Flapan actually obtain significance in the statistical sense. The two older groups significantly more often explained events in situational terms and more of the older children inferred the feelings, thoughts and expectations of the actors in the film. A similar pattern of results was obtained when the children's answers to specific questions were analysed. The six-year-old children showed themselves to be largely unable to answer questions concerning the feelings of other people or to give explanations for their behaviour. The nine-year-olds mentioned 'obvious' feelings and explained other people's actions primarily in terms of situational factors. The twelve-year-olds talked of 'non-obvious' feelings that they had presumably inferred and also referred to more complex feelings. This latter trend again corresponds to findings from research looking at children's impressions of others, divalent descriptions being mentioned more frequently by older children. In accounting for other people's behaviour the twelve-year-olds primarily responded in 'psychological' terms. Apart from giving interjudge reliability figures, Flapan does not subject the data to any statistical analysis.

One further point of interest arises from Flapan's study that is worth mentioning. The responses of the children, at all age levels, were more sophisticated when they were replying to questions than when they were giving their own, unprompted accounts. This finding has important implications for further research. It will be necessary to decide whether it is the maximum performance of which children are capable that is of interest or the lower level performance that is observed when the children are given few prompts. It is difficult to resolve this issue at present. The difficulty, in part, reflects our lack of understanding of the precise nature of the phenomenon under investigation. If the main concern of person perception research is to determine how one person typically describes another, and how such descriptions may vary from one set of circumstances to another, we require to know what people typically do. However, the process of obtaining one person's descriptions of another is merely a means to an end. The ultimate concern is with the use that an individual typically makes of the available information about the other person. In this sense, it would seem that availability of the relevant information does not necessarily correspond to its being in a form whereby it can be readily passed on to a third party in the form of a description.

In other words, in asking one individual to describe another, we may be asking him to perform tasks which are importantly different from the normal requirements of the person perception process: his descriptions of another may not therefore accurately reflect the amount and type of information that he would usually utilize. Such issues are of considerable importance when one is dealing with young children since they are less skilled at presenting what they know in a form useful to a third party (e.g. Flavell, 1968).

If person perception research is concerned, at least in part, with the use to which people put available information about others then, ideally, the researcher would know of all the information available. The research problem to be addressed would then become one of determining the circumstances under which certain parts of the available information package were used and precisely how they were used. Obviously we are obliged to work with approximations to such an ideal. In the case of developmental research where children are used as subjects, it would seem that a closer approximation to this ideal will be achieved by determining the child's level of *competence*, by prompting if necessary, rather than by only determining his typical level of *performance* by the use of free descriptions. In this respect, the procedure adopted by Flapan of specifically questioning the child on aspects of his understanding of other people appears fruitful.

While generally of interest, Flapan's study is marred by a limited statistical analysis of the data. For example, no indication is given of the relevant frequency with which the various categories are used, instead we are only told how many children from each age group use each category at least once. More fundamentally, her classifications must be questioned. The distinction between 'obvious' and 'non-obvious' intentions is particularly problematic. In this study, feelings and intentions were so classified from an adult perspective. It is by no means clear that what is obvious to an adult will also be obvious to a young child. Flapan's results are, therefore, somewhat equivocal and difficult to interpret. The attribution theory analysis of person perception discussed above highlights the importance of inferences of individual intentions in the process of forming dispositional impressions of others. In as much as studies of children's descriptions of others agree in showing a marked increase with age in the use of dispositional statements, so we would expect Flapan's research to show a similar age-related increase in the ability to infer intentions as a means of accounting for individual actions. Her data only partially fulfil this expectation. There are trends in the expected direction but these are not sufficiently pronounced. Recent research by the present author has addressed these issues and will be discussed below.

Information processing in the development of person perception

The analysis presented so far does not make reference to the information processing capabilities of the child. Rather it has been concerned with the nature of the information that the child has to process. Person perception research has frequently been concerned with the way in which given information about others is processed (e.g. Anderson, 1974; Warr and Knapper, 1968; Wyer, 1970). In their model of person perception Warr and Knapper stress the importance of the 'processing centre'. An important function of this centre is the integration of incoming information about other people. The information is combined and elaborated. Studies of the 'processing centre' (e.g. Anderson, 1974; Warr, 1974) have shown that incoming information tends to be combined in a 'lawful' and predictable manner. For example, if it is known how an individual will rate various single trait terms with respect to how likeable these are, it is possible to predict how he would rate them, in the same respect, in various combinations. However, in this area, age-related differences in performance have so far only received scant attention, and the studies that have been carried out have produced results that are less than uniform.

One of the most thoroughly investigated models of information integration is the 'weighted averaging' model proposed by Anderson (see, for example, Anderson, 1974). Items of information are individually evaluated and weighted, and these weighted evaluations are then averaged to obtain evaluations of combinations of items. This model has closely matched judgements made by adults across a variety of situations. Butzin and Anderson (1973) have shown the model to apply to children as young as five years. However, in this study the children were making judgements about the attractiveness of toys. While the results may demonstrate that children are capable of making this sort of judgement about objects it is not clear that they will actually do so when making judgements about people. However, further evidence comes from Hendrick et al. (1975) who obtained ratings from children aged five to eleven of people described by trait words presented singly or in pairs. The judgements made by all age groups closely approximated the predictions derived from an averaging model. Furthermore, a test–retest procedure showed that the ratings obtained were reasonably stable.

On the basis of this limited data it would seem that children are capable of combining information from a number of sources from at least five years of age in much the same way as adults. We might assume, then, that they will be able to elaborate on information obtained on separate occasions and build up a more generalized impression of a person's character, an impression that would, due to its generality and wider data base, have more predictive validity.

However, the two studies cited above are both somewhat artificial and one of them is only tangentially related to person perception. Gollin (1958) presents more directly relevant information. He had boy and girl subjects aged ten, thirteen and sixteen years, observe four films showing a boy behaving well on two occasions and badly on the other two. The children's accounts of what they had seen were analysed to determine the extent to which they attempted to integrate and account for the apparently discrepant behaviour. Of the ten-year-olds only 2 per cent of the boys and 2 per cent of the girls introduced conceptual terms to account for the observed discrepancies. By age thirteen these figures had increased to 9 per cent and 21 per cent for boys and girls respectively and to 39 per cent and 64 per cent for sixteen-year-olds.

Children had to write their accounts of what they had seen and this may have suppressed their performance. However, it seems clear that when asked to *account* for observed differences in behaviour, even children in early adolescence perform at a low level. Whether the ability to verbalize a reason for discrepant behaviour or the ability to make combined judgements is more central in the development of person perception remains undemonstrated but if competence rather than performance is to be our main concern then perhaps Hendrick et al. are closer to the mark than Gollin.

The development of impression formation

For adults impression formation can be seen to involve the ability to interpret the behaviour of others in causal, psychological terms, in terms of thoughts, feelings and intentions. The child's ability to make such inferences has been primarily investigated in relation to the making of moral judgements; the prime lesson from this area of research being that contextual factors greatly determine the extent to which a child will utilize information concerning intentions. The child's failure to do so is not therefore necessarily due to cognitive incapacity. A more plausible explanation is that the child fails to take intentions into account, not because he is unable to comprehend them, but because he does not perceive them as salient.

It is reasonable then to assume that the child's use of inferences of thoughts, feelings and intentions in his perceptions of other people will similarly be subject to strong contextual and situational inferences. In a series of studies to be discussed below, Rogers (1977) undertook, among other things, to investigate the extent of the validity of this assumption.

In the first of these studies three groups of children aged five, eight and ten years of age were told four short, simple stories accompanied by cartoon strips illustrating the central events in each story. The stories as presented to the children made reference only to the explicit, directly observable behaviour of the characters involved. The child's task was to infer the implicit, psychological substructure. Each story had two variants, half of the subjects in each age group being exposed to one, half to the other. In one variant the central character was an adult; in the other, a child. With this exception both variants were identical. Pilot work had shown that adults would interpret the two variants at the level of thoughts, feelings and intentions quite differently, the interpretation being determined by the age of the central character. Following the narration of each story the children were asked to retell it and were also questioned about specific points. In both cases the children were encouraged to infer thoughts, feelings and intentions.

Content analysis of responses revealed relatively minor changes in the extent to which children made inferences of thoughts, feelings and intentions. There were no age-related differences in the proportionate use of these three inference types. However, when the actual inferences made were examined more closely (by utilizing the children's responses to specific questions) clear age-related differences did emerge. Essentially the five-year-old children failed to differentiate between the two variants and attributed childlike intentions and reactions to the adults. The eight and ten-year-old children's responses increasingly approximated to those provided by an adult control group.

While the five-year-olds were no less capable than the older children of extracting information from the stories in order to make any inferences, they were less sensitive to the contextual requirements, principally the age of the actor. More than anything else this probably reflects their relative lack of social experience. Through the processes of exposure and reciprocal interaction the young child achieved an understanding of the motives of his peers that still eludes him with respect to adults. In this respect, the most important aspect of age development is not in the extent to which intentions and other psychological states are inferred, but in the extent to which those inferences made can be considered to be appropriate.

A second study adopted a similar strategy to the first. Again two variants of simple, factual, illustrated stories were narrated to five, eight and ten-year-old children. The two variants were identical except that one was preceded by a dispositional statement pertaining to one of the major characters (e.g. 'John is a shy boy'). Having been narrated the story children were asked to select one of two alternative endings. Pilot work with adults had shown that the choice of ending was crucially determined by the presence or absence of the dispositional statement. Children were also asked to elaborate on the thoughts, feelings and intentions of the characters in the stories.

While the ten-year-olds made significantly more, and a significantly greater proportion of all three inference types, there were no differences in the ability of children to select an appropriate ending for the story. So while five-year-old children may only very rarely spontaneously produce dispositional statements, they can (at least with the statements employed in this study) utilize them in an appropriate manner.

However, in order to be able to function effectively in ongoing social situations the child needs to do more than infer discrete intentions to account for discrete events. He needs to be able to perceive the behaviour of others as being essentially invariant by detecting the common underlying intention that links, or may be inferred to link, two or more action sequences. A third study investigated aspects of this process.

Different children from the same age groups as before were presented with three one-sentence stories. Each story involved a mother and her daughter. In each case the mother did something to the daughter and the children were told both *what* she did and *why* she did it. The triad of stories was so constructed that three pairs could be formed; one pair illustrated the same intention but different action, another pair the same action but different intentions and the final pair had neither intention nor action in common. Children were told that two of these stories involved the same mother and were asked to indicate which pair they thought this would be. It can be seen that the children could either match stories on the basis of intentions, action or neither (the random match).

Children from all age groups made the random match significantly less frequently than the other two, but while the eight and ten-year-olds matched on the basis of common intention the five-year-olds matched on the basis of common action. Thus the five-year-old, who has been shown to be capable of both inferring intentions and utilizing dispositional statements, perceives trans-situational consistency in terms of action rather than intention. They appear to experience difficulty in linking disparate actions by common, underlying intentions. This interpretation is further supported by the finding that children at all ages who had initially made an action match had difficulty in seeing any similarity in the intention pair while those who had made an intention match could more readily perceive the similarity of the action pair.

A fourth study further illustrates the young child's limitations with respect to integrating information concerning the dispositions and actions of another person. Subjects aged five to sixteen were narrated one of two pictorially illustrated stories. One portrayed a mother acting in a kindly manner towards a child and the other showed her acting in an unkind manner (helping the girl up from the floor and knocking her down respectively). The children were asked to make several judgements about the event, particularly to rate the kindness of the action and their expectations concerning the mother's general degree of kindness.

Evidence from this and other studies (e.g. Kagan, 1956; Kagan and Lemkin, 1960; Mott, 1954) shows that even the five-year-old child has a relatively clearly formed impression of a mother as a kind and nurturant person. However, the five-year-olds in particular were largely incapable of integrating this preconception with the evidence from the unkind story. Thus, although the five-year-olds gave the most extreme negative rating to the unkind *act* they alone judged this mother to be generally kind. Unlike the older children, the five-year-olds seemed to make very little attempt to temper their judgements concerning the nature of the act with information pertaining to the general characteristics of the actor. In response to questioning, however, the five-year-olds were able to switch from one source of information to another (the act or the characteristics of the actor) in a manner perfectly suited to the nature of the particular question asked.

Towards an overview of the development of person perception

The six- or seven-year-old's perception of other people can be distinguished from those of other children and adults in three aspects. First, the *content* of his impressions will frequently be different. When he uses trait terms to describe another person he will use simple, unqualified, univalent ones. When he infers psychological states to others he will often infer states that are different from those inferred by older children; for example he will infer childish motives to adults. These differences may sometimes, but need not always, be deficiencies. There will be occasions, for example, when the inferences that a young child does make about another will lack predictive value because they are inappropriate.

Possibly however, this lack of predictive value is perceived as a greater problem by us than it is by the young child. The second way in which the five-year-old differs from older children is with respect to *orientation*. The younger child is more concerned with the immediate and the concrete; the older child, and increasingly the adult, with the longer term and the abstract. Thus for the young child what happens is often more important than *why* it happens. People are more readily described in terms of their physical rather than their personality characteristics.

These differences are not entirely due to cognitive incapacities on the part of the young child. Five- and six-year-olds can, and do, infer and utilize information regarding intentions. They can, and do, utilize information regarding dispositions. It is for this reason that the term 'orientation' is used to describe this set of age-related differences.

Thirdly, the young child differs from those older than him with respect to his *information processing skills*. Of the three, this is the most difficult to summarize. On the one hand a recent study by Shultz and Mendelson (1975) has shown that children as young as three years can make quite complex causal judgements about physical events; we have also seen how Butzin and Anderson (1973) have shown young children to integrate information in a manner that matches a statistical model which in turn matches the integrations of adults. On the other hand, Berndt and Berndt (1975) have shown that while preschool children can understand the concepts of intention and motive they cannot work with complex motives, there being simply too many items of information for the child to cope with. Further, the studies of Gollin (1958) and Rogers (1977) discussed above have revealed information processing inadequacies on the part of the young child. While the young child can often select the most appropriate item of information available with which to operate, he will also be frequently unable to process adequately all the information available.

Clearly the young child is limited by his cognitive resources. Equally clearly we will not come to understand these limitations fully by considering the child's information processing skills in isolation. The three elements of content, orientation and information processing highlighted above form part of a closely interdependent system. In certain respects the content of the child's perception of others will limit the development of his orientation towards the perception of others. If the intentions he infers to others are inappropriate then they will lack predictive value which in turn will inhibit the establishment of an orientation that is concerned with the long term; it is also clear, however, that until the child is orientated towards the long term he is unlikely to establish any content that is relevant to that orientation.

Similar interdependencies can be seen to exist with respect to the child's information processing skills; if the child is not orientated towards the long term he will not attempt to synthesize discrete intentions into generally applicable dispositions, but without carrying out the necessary information processing how does he come to acquire a new orientation?

Recognition of these problems brings us back to a consideration of the functions of person perception. We, as adults, perceive people as we do in order to be able to predict the behaviour of others, control our own behaviour with respect to others, and influence the behaviour of others. We can only assume that this is equally applicable to young children.

As Smith (1974) has pointed out, we know very little about the natural social behaviour of children. Yet causal observation tells us that the social world of children is not chaotic. Therefore, if their social behaviour is mediated by their perceptions of others then these perceptions must be suited to that function of mediating social behaviour. Clearly, the social world of the child undergoes many dramatic changes between the ages of five and ten. The child moves out from the comparatively sheltered and limited environment of the family home to the more complex and varied world of the school. Adolescence brings further and equally dramatic changes.

It is suggested that changes in the child's social life act as the impetus for change on his perceptions of other people. The task ahead for those investigating the development of these perceptual processes should involve a mapping out of the relationships between perception and behaviour and the changes that occur in both.

We have seen on a number of occasions that the way in which a child perceives a particular situation is partly determined by the nature of that situation. This is perhaps most clearly demonstrated by Farnhill's (1974) study. What is now required is a systematic extension of this type of work. How will the child's own informational needs vary as a function of various situational characterstics? Will the child regard the intentions of others as being more salient when engaged with them in long rather than short tasks? Will the intentions of peers always be more salient than those of adults? It should be possible to devise research designs that would enable the investigator to manipulate the possible informational requirements of his subjects so as to determine how different subjects attempt to fulfil those requirements.

Eventually we wish to understand how the child's changing perceptions of other people enable him to function in such complex social situations as a school or a friendship group. To do this we must seek to understand the relationships that exist between content, orientation and information processing and the ways in which all of

these are influenced by the functional requirements of the diversity of
social contexts in which children find themselves.

References

Anderson, N. H. (1974) Algebraic models in perception. In E. C. Carterett and
M. P. Friedman (eds) *Handbook of Perception, Vol. 2.* New York: Academic
Press.

Argyle, M. and McHenry, R. (1971) Do spectacles really affect judgements of
intelligence? *British Journal of Social and Clinical Psychology 10*: 27–9.

Armsby, R. E. (1971) A re-examination of the development of moral
judgements in children. *Child Development 42*: 1241–8.

Berg-Cross, L. (1975) Intentionality, degree of damage and moral judgements.
Child Development 46: 970–4.

Berndt, T. J. and Berndt, E. G. (1975) Children's use of motives and
intentionality in person perception and moral judgements. *Child Development
46*: 904–12.

Brierley, D. W. (1967) The Use of Personality Constructs of Children of Three
Different Ages. Unpublished Ph.D. thesis, University of London.

Butzin, C. A. and Anderson, N. H. (1973) Functional measurement of children's
judgements. *Child Development 44*: 529–37.

Chandler, M. J., Greenspan, S. and Barenboim, C. (1973) Judgements of
intentionality in response to videotaped and verbally presented moral
dilemmas: The medium is the message. *Child Development 44*: 315–20.

Constanzo, P. R., Cole, J. D., Grumet, J. F. and Farnhill, D. (1973) A re-
examination of the effect of intent and consequences on children's moral
judgement. *Child Development 44*: 154–61.

Farnhill, D. (1974) The effects of social-judgement set on children's use of
intent information. *Journal of Personality 42*: 276–89.

Flapan, D. (1968) *Children's Understanding of Social Interaction.* New York:
Teachers' College Press.

Flavell, J. H. (1968) *The Development of Role-Taking and Communication Skills in
Children.* New York: Wiley.

Gollin, E. S. (1958) Organizational characterstics of social judgement: a
developmental investigation. *Journal of Personality 26*: 139–54.

Gutkin, D. C. (1972) The effect of systematic story changes on intentionality
in children's moral judgements. *Child Development 43*: 187–95.

Harvey, J. H., Ickes, W. J. and Kidd, R. F. (1976) *New Directions in Attribution
Research, Vol. 1.* Hillsdale, New Jersey: Lawrence Ellbaum.

Hebble, P. (1971) The development of elementary school children's judgement
of intent. *Child Development 42*: 1203–15.

Heider, F. (1958) *The Psychology of Interpersonal Relations.* New York: Wiley.

Hendrick, C., Franz, C. and Hoving, K. (1975) How do children form
impressions of persons? They average. *Memory and Cognition 3*: 325–8.

Hoffman, M. (1970) Moral development. In P. H. Mussen (ed.) *Carmichael's
Manual of Child Psychology, Vol. 2.* New York: Wiley.

Imamoglu, E. (1974) Children's Understanding of Intentionality. Unpublished Ph.D. Thesis, University of Strathclyde.

Jones, E. E. and Davis, K. E. (1965) From acts to dispositions: the attribution process in person perception. *Advances in Experimental Social Psychology 2*: 219–66.

Jones, E. E., Kanouse, D. E., Kelley, H. H., Nisbett, R. E., Valins, S. and Weiner, B. (eds) (1971) *Attribution: Perceiving the Causes of Behaviour.* Morristown: General Learning Press.

Jones, E. E. and Nisbett, R. E. (1971) The actor and the observer: divergent perceptions of the causes of behaviour. In E. E. Jones, D. E. Kanouse, H. H. Kelley, R. E. Nisbett, S. Valins and B. Weiner (eds) *Attribution: Perceiving the Causes of Behaviour.* Morristown: General Learning Press.

Kagan, J. (1956) The child's perceptions of the parent. *Journal of Abnormal and Social Psychology 53*: 257–8.

Kagan, J. and Lemkin, J. (1960) The child's differential perception of parental attributes. *Journal of Abnormal and Social Psychology 61*: 440–7.

Kelley, H. H. (1971) Attribution in social interaction. In E. E. Jones, D. E. Kanouse, H. H. Kelley, R. E. Nisbett, S. Valins and B. Weiner (eds) *Attribution: Perceiving the Causes of Behaviour.* Morristown: General Learning Press.

Kelly, G. A. (1955) *The Psychology of Personal Constructs.* New York: Norton.

Lerner, E. (1937) The problem of perspective in moral reasoning. *American Journal of Sociology 43*: 248–69.

Livesley, W. J. and Bromley, D. B. (1973) *Person Perception in Childhood and Adolescence.* London: Wiley.

Mischel, W. (1968) *Personality and Assessment.* New York: Wiley.

Mott, S. N. (1954) Concept of mother – a study of four and five year old children. *Child Development 25*: 99–106.

Peevers, H. and Secord, P. F. (1973) Developmental change in attribution of descriptive concepts to persons. *Journal of Personality and Social Psychology 26*: 120–8.

Piaget, J (1932) *The Moral Judgement of the Child.* London: Routledge and Kegan Paul.

Rogers, C. (1977) The Development of the Child's Understanding of Other People. Unpublished Ph.D. Thesis, University of Leicester.

Salmon, P. (1976) Grid measures with child subjects. In P. Slater (ed.) *Explorations of Intrapersonal Space, Vol. 1.* London: Wiley.

Scarlett, H. H., Press, A. N. and Crockett, W. H. (1971) Children's descriptions of peers: a Wernerian developmental analysis. *Child Development 42*: 439–53.

Shultz, T. R. and Mendelson, R. (1975) The use of covariation as a principle of causal analysis. *Child Development 46*: 394–9.

Smith, P. (1974) Ethological methods. In B. Foss (ed.) *New Perspectives in Child Development.* Harmondsworth: Penguin.

Warr, P. B. (1974) Inference magnitude, range and evaluative direction as factors affecting the relative importance of cues in impression formation. *Journal of Personality and Social Psychology 30*: 191–7.

Warr, P. B. and Knapper, C. (1968) *The Perception of People and Events.* New York: Wiley.

Watts, A. F. (1944) *The Language and Mental Development of Children.* London: Harrap.

Weiner, B. and Peter, N. (1973) A cognitive developmental analysis of achievement and moral judgements. *Developmental Psychology 9*: 290–309.

Wyer, R. S. (1970) Information redundancy, inconsistency and novelty and their role in impression formation. *Journal of Experimental Social Psychology 6*: 111–27.

5 Children and their friends[1]

Willard W. Hartup

Peer relations contribute substantially to the development of social competencies in children. Capacities to create and maintain mutually regulated relations with others, to achieve effective modes of emotional expression, and to engage in accurate social reality-testing derive from interactions with other children as well as from interaction with adults.

Considerable concern has been evidenced in both the scientific literature and the popular media about 'cross pressures' between adult–child relations and peer relations. In point of fact, the outcomes of peer interaction are concordant with adult–child interaction more often than discordant. Certain norms emerge in one context or the other – e.g., friends may be chosen in accordance with peer norms while educational objectives are established on the basis of adult values (Brittain, 1963). Friendship choices, however, are approved by children's parents more often than not. Similarly, educational aspirations are more likely to be consistent with the values of the peer culture than inconsistent with them.

Misunderstandings concerning the concordances in child–child and adult–child relations are among the most common misunderstandings about child development. These mistakes have generated several attitudes which have negative implications for social policy: (a) ignore children's peer interactions in the belief that, in the long run, such experiences will have little impact on the child, and/or (b) suppress such influences because they are a bothersome nuisance, and may even be unhealthy. Educators systematically fail to train children in the most basic social skills (Combs and Slaby, 1977). At the same time, Byzantine mechanisms are erected for constraining peer socialization in schools, recreation centres and social clubs. Long lists of rules govern children's behaviour at meal times, on the school bus, on the playground and in the lavatory. No modern school can exist without rules but prevailing attitudes foster the suppression of peer relations in child development rather than their constructive exploitation. Such attitudes are strange in light of the evidence. Successful social experiences are more than superficial luxuries to be enjoyed by some children and not by others.

In this essay, the functions of peer relations in child development will be examined. The correlates and consequences of socialization with other children will be considered along with the nature of child–child interaction in relation to developmental status. Modelling, tutorial and cognitive mechanisms in peer interaction will be elucidated and conditions making for effective peer relations in childhood will be summarized. Major findings concerning the origins and nature of children's friendships will be reviewed. The entire essay underscores the thesis that, in all cultures, peer relations affect the course of socialization as profoundly as any social events in which children participate.

What is a peer?

Children's institutions are age-graded in most Western cultures. Child care centres, schools, sports teams, clubs and camps are composed of enclaves in which chronological age ranges across only a few months or years. Since child–child relations have been studied most intensively in schools and child care centres, our research literature is a same-age literature. It would seem that agemates have greater significance in children's socialization than non-agemates and that peer relations consist mainly of interactions among children of the same chronological age.

Actually, children of the same chronological age differ greatly in size, intellectual capacities, physical skills and social abilities. One child may be considerably brighter than average; another may exhibit unusually low levels of social skill; and another may be noticeably less attractive than the other children enrolled in his/her class. These individual differences generate large differences in the social interaction that ensues within same-age classrooms. Peer-like behaviour, then, should be considered only as social activity in which the actions of one child represent a status that is similar to the actions of another child. Considering also that children may be peer-like in one situation (e.g. the classroom) but not in another (e.g. the playground), it is probably best to designate children as peers who interact at comparable levels of behavioural complexity (Lewis and Rosenblum, 1975). 'Peers' may be children of the same age, or they may not.

While most children's institutions are age-graded, street societies are more diverse. Barker and Wright (1955) found that approximately 65 per cent of children's interactions with other children involved individuals who differed in age by *more* than twelve months. Similar surveys have not been conducted in other cultures (this survey was conducted in a small town in the midwestern United States) but it is safe to say that most children's societies are heterogeneous rather than homogeneous with respect to chronological age.

Contemporary observations of the !Kung San (Bushmen) in the Kalahari Desert show that multiage play groups are ubiquitous in that culture, consisting mostly of siblings and cousins ranging in age from late infancy to adolescence (Konner, 1975). Smaller subgroups with restricted age ranges sometimes can be observed, but most social contacts in this ancient culture are mixed-age. In other 'Third World' cultures, where women are assigned major responsibilities in agricultural activity, infant and toddler care is assigned to 5- and 8-year-old children (Wenger and Whiting, 1977). These 'child nurses' are responsible for entertaining, carrying, feeding and bedding down the infants and young children in their care. Children's socialization thus seems to have evolved under conditions favouring the multiage group, partly because the populations in hunter-gatherer societies (from which modern man evolved) are not sufficiently concentrated to supply huge numbers of agemates.

Mixed-age societies are well suited to the young child's needs. Social adaptation requires skills in both seeking help (dependency) and giving it (nurturance); being passive and being sociable; being able to attack others (aggression) and being able to contain one's hostility; being intimate and being self-reliant. Since there is a greater likelihood that some of these behaviours will occur in interaction with younger children than with older children (e.g. nurturance), some in interaction with agemates rather than non-agemates (e.g. aggression), and some in interaction with older children rather than younger children (e.g.

dependency), mixed-age social contacts would seem to serve children in ways that same-age contacts cannot. Overall, the evidence suggests that social development is facilitated both by interaction with agemates and with non-agemates.

Mixed-age social interaction differs qualitatively and quantitatively from same-age interaction. In one study (Lougee et al., 1977), observations were conducted of pairs of nursery school children who were not well acquainted with each other. In some dyads, the individuals differed by 16 months of age; in others, the children differed by 2 months or less. Social interaction was least frequent in 3-year-old same-age dyads, intermediate in dyads containing a 3-year-old and a 5-year-old, and most frequent in dyads of 5-year-old children. Certain children showed accommodation in the mixed-age situation to the social needs of their partners; others did not. Other investigators (Langlois et al., 1978) have shown that, when children are well acquainted with each other, the amount of social interaction in same-age dyads is more frequent than in mixed-age dyads – among 3-year-olds as well as among 5-year-olds. In addition, verbal communication is adjusted qualitatively according to the age difference existing between partners (Shatz and Gelman, 1973; Lougee et al., 1977).

Same- and mixed-age interaction also differs among elementary school children. Both second- and fifth-graders were found to work harder at simple tasks when social rewards were supplied by a non-agemate than by an agemate (Ferguson, 1965). And, in a social problem-solving task (Graziano et al., 1976), the individual contributions of third-graders were shown to vary according to the composition of the group: singleton status (i.e. being the only third-grader in a triad) was associated with greater speed, success and task persistence than was majority status (i.e. being a majority member in a triad).

Long-term consequences of same- and mixed-age interaction are different. Suomi and Harlow (1972) demonstrated that the untoward effects of prolonged isolation on the social development of Rhesus monkeys can be reversed by a carefully managed programme of cross-age peer contact involving the isolated animal and a *younger* monkey. Such programmes ameliorated the effects of social isolation more effectively than other rehabilitation efforts, including exposure to same-age or older animals. Although 'non-programmed' contact with normal agemates can increase the sociability of very unsocial preschool children (Koch, 1935), exposure to a younger child may produce greater changes in sociability, just as with the non-human primates.

One research team (Furman et al., 1978) located twenty-four socially withdrawn children in seven child care centres by means of observations conducted over five-week periods. (These children may be considered social isolates but were not autistic or emotionally disturbed.) For 8 children, an intervention was devised consisting of ten daily play sessions involving a second child who was 15 months younger than the subject. Another 8 children participated in daily play sessions with a child who was within 3 months of the subject's own age. The remaining children received no treatment. Significant improvement in sociability occurred in both experimental groups as contrasted to the no-treatment group (which did not change), but greater increases in sociability occurred among the children exposed to younger 'therapists' than among those exposed to same-age 'therapists'. Non-programmed interaction with younger children, indeed, promotes social competence in some situations more effectively than experience with agemates.

In other instances, social learning occurs more effectively in interaction with older children: for example, reciprocal imitation is more characteristic of children's interactions with older children than with younger children (Thelen and Kirkland, 1976). Older children are more effective models than younger children (Peifer, 1971), although this difference in effectiveness is greater in situations calling for difficult perceptual judgements or complicated skills than in situations calling for declarations of personal preferences or tastes (Lougee, 1978). In tutoring situations, children prefer to be taught by children older than themselves (Allen and Feldman, 1976).

All in all, the existing data show that social behaviour in same- and mixed-age conditions is not identical, and that social adaptation is facilitated by both same-age and mixed-age interaction. What is a peer? Certainly not each child with whom a child interacts. Rather, the term *peer relations* delimits those social relations in which equivalence in development and social status characterizes the participants.

The importance of peer relations

What are the derivatives of peer interaction? Is the isolated child 'at risk' for psychopathology? For deviant behaviour? For inadequate social adjustment? Following is a letter[2] from a farmer in the midwestern United States that summarizes the evidence bearing on these questions:

DEAR DR

I read the report in the Oct. 30 issue of _____ about your study of only children. I am an only child, now 57 years old and I want to tell you some things about my life. Not only was I an only child but I grew up in the country where there were no nearby children to play with. My mother did not want children around. She used to say 'I don't want my kid to bother anybody and I don't want nobody's kids bothering me.'

. . . From the first year of school I was teased and made fun of. For example, in about third or fourth grade I dreaded to get on the school bus to go to school because the other children on the bus called me 'Mommy's baby.' In about the second grade I heard the boys use a vulgar word. I asked what it meant and they made fun of me. So I learned a lesson – don't ask questions. This can lead to a lot of confusion to hear talk one doesn't understand and not be able to learn what it means . . .

I never went out with a girl while I was in school – in fact I hardly talked to them. In our school the boys and girls did not play together. Boys were sent to one part of the playground and girls to another. So, I didn't learn anything about girls. When we got into high school and the boys and girls started dating I could only listen to their stories about their experiences.

I could tell you a lot more but the important thing is I have never married or had any children. I have not been very successful in an occupation or vocation. I believe my troubles are not all due to being an only child, but I do believe you are right in recommending playmates for preschool children and I will add playmates for the school agers and not have them strictly supervised by adults. I believe I confirm the experiments with monkeys in being overly timid sometimes and overly aggressive sometimes. Parents of only children should make special efforts to provide playmates for [their children].

Sincerely yours,

Experimental evidence in support of the letter-writer's conclusions is scarce. In studies with monkeys, to which the writer alludes, Harlow (1969) deprived young animals of peer contact for varying lengths of time. Wariness and hyperaggressiveness characterized those animals not having contact with agemates through the first four to eight months of life – both in their initial contacts with other animals and for some time thereafter. Deprivation studies have not been conducted with children, but various experiments confirm that children are effective socialization agents vis-à-vis each other: (a) peer reinforcement can be ✳ used to shape a wide variety of social behaviours (Wahler, 1967); (b) peer models are effective instruments of behaviour modification (Hartup and Lougee, 1975); and (c) peer tutors can be used to bring about an extensive range of motivational and cognitive changes in both younger and older children (Allen, 1976). The bulk of the evidence concerning the significance of peer interaction in social development is correlative rather than experimental; causal inferences are thus difficult to make. The literature nevertheless indicates that peer relations are embedded centrally in the socialization of the child.

Long-term longitudinal investigations demonstrate that peer relations in childhood are prognostic indicators of social conduct in adolescence and adulthood. Roff (1961) studied a sample of servicemen who were former patients in a child-guidance clinic. Men receiving 'bad conduct' discharges were more likely to have been rated by their childhood counsellors as having poor peer adjustment than men with successful service records. In other work, this investigator and his colleagues (Roff et al., 1972) obtained significant correlations between childhood peer acceptance and delinquency in adolescence. Among upper lower-class and middle-class boys, delinquency rates were higher among children who were not accepted by their peers than among those who were. Among lower-class subjects, *both* highly accepted and highly rejected individuals had higher delinquency rates than those who were moderately accepted by the peer culture. Individual case records suggested that social deviance was more widely generalized among the rejected lower-class boys since the records indicated that the ultimate adjustment of the peer-accepted individuals would be better than the rejected ones, even though delinquency rates in early adolescence were similar.

Ratings of peer acceptance in childhood are predictive of later mental health status. Again, using adult males who were seen as children in child-guidance clinics, Roff (1963) found that poor peer relations were predictive of adult neurotic and psychotic disturbances of a variety of types, as well as disturbances in sexual behaviour and adjustment. Kohn and Clausen (1955) reported that a much higher proportion of adults diagnosed as psychotic were social isolates as children than was the case for a normal control sample. And, in an extensive prospective study (Cowen et al., 1973), poor peer adjustment in the third grade was revealed as an excellent predictor of emotional difficulties in early adulthood. A variety of measures were accumulated on the children, including IQ scores, school grades, achievement test results, school attendance records, teacher ratings and peer ratings (i.e. nominations by other children for positive and negative roles in a class play). Eleven years later, community mental health registers were examined to locate those individuals then consulting a mental health professional. Of all the measures secured in the third grade, the best predictor of adult mental health status was the peer rating. Subjects listed in the mental health registers were over two-and-one-half times as likely to have been nominated for the 'bad' roles in the third-grade class play than subjects not appearing in these registers.

Once again, it should be emphasized that the evidence linking peer relations to emotional vulnerability is correlational in nature. Emotional vulnerability (or its precursors) could lead to poor peer relations as well as the reverse. Simple unidirectional interpretations of the research results are probably not as sensible as interpretations positing reciprocal causation. Coupled with the animal experiments, however, the correlational studies suggest a causal link between the social and affective domains in human development. It is worth noting that no evidence exists to contradict the hypothesis that peer relations play a central role in personality development (Roff et al., 1972).

Specific social competencies seem to derive from peer interaction as well as more general social orientations. 'Sociability', in contrast to social withdrawal, is positively related to social acceptance and negatively related to anxiety and instability. In Bronson's (1966) study of 'central orientations' among children between the ages of 5 and 16, the dimension *reserved-sombre-shy/expressive-gay-socially easy* was associated with an inward-looking social orientation, high anxiety, and low activity. In later childhood, reservedness was associated with vulnerability, lack of dominance, cautiousness and instability. Peer acceptance has also been found to be positively correlated with the amount of neutral social interaction in which the child engages (Furman, 1977) and the extent to which the child provides positive social rewards for other children (Hartup et al., 1967). Thus, the child's willingness to engage in social activity is related to generalized social effectance.

Children learn to master aggressive impulses within the context of peer relations. Field studies show that rough-and-tumble play occurs among juveniles in all primate species but seldom occurs between parents and their offspring. Such activity promotes the acquisition of a repertoire of effective aggressive behaviours and also establishes necessary regulatory mechanisms for modulating aggressive affect

(Harlow, 1969). Aggression occurs more frequently in child–child interaction than in adult–child interaction in many different cultures (Whiting and Whiting, 1975), and observational studies in the United States have shown clearly that feedback from other children escalates and de-escalates rates of aggression among nursery school children (Patterson et al., 1967).

The rough-and-tumble activity necessary for effective aggressive socialization is not compatible with the constraints built into adult–child relations. Family relations, for example, exist to protect the child from danger, ensure an adequate food supply, and provide the child with an opportunity to learn certain skills (e.g. language). Attachments accommodate these ends. These attachments, however, cannot be maintained concurrently with uninhibited aggression. Parents cannot execute parental functions when children are completely aggressive, and children cannot thrive in the care of abusing parents. Aggression, then, is antithetical to the maintenance of attachments. Children need some other social context in which to learn aggressive behaviours and to manage aggressive affect. Because peer interaction provides an opportunity to experiment aggressively with co-equals (i.e. individuals whose cognitive abilities and social skills are comparable to one's own), this social context seems well adapted to such socialization requirements.

Peer interaction contributes to the individual's sexual socialization. Although gender-typing first occurs in interactions between the child and its parents (Money and Ehrhardt, 1972), the peer culture extends and elaborates this process. Social rewards are exchanged within the peer culture according to the gender-appropriateness of the child's behaviour (Fagot and Patterson, 1969) and peer models also contribute to the formation of appropriate sexual attitudes (Kobasigawa, 1968). Sexual experimentation is pervasive in child–child interactions and must be seen as contributing positively rather than negatively to socialization (Kinsey et al., 1948).

Peer relations contribute to the emergence of so-called 'social intelligence'. Children who are able to 'take the role of the other' are more socially active than less able role-takers and are more competent in social exchanges with other children (Gottman et al., 1975). In addition, peer interaction is associated with moral reasoning. Keasey (1971) studied fifth- and sixth-graders, finding that those who belonged to many social organizations had higher moral judgement scores than those who belonged to fewer clubs. Children with higher moral judgement scores were also rated as more popular than those with lower levels of moral judgement. Whether advances in moral judgement are derivatives of peer interaction as Piaget (1932) suggested, though, is still an open question. Club membership may lead to changes in the nature of the child's moral thinking but advances in moral reasoning may also facilitate entrance into the peer culture. In any event, the evidence indicates that peer interaction and moral development are linked, consistent with the hypothesis that opportunities for social exchange among co-equals contribute constructively to changes in the structure of moral thought.

The association between peer relations and other dimensions in intellectual development is not clear. Competencies in social relations do not bear a consistent relation to IQ nor to academic achievement. Similarly, the evidence does not show that peer interaction is a major vehicle for the 'decentration' in cognitive abilities that occurs in middle childhood (see Hartup, 1976). Since general intelligence is consistently related to sociometric status, however, it may not be argued that intellectual abilities and social competencies have no bearing on one another.

The evidence suggests that whenever give-and-take is an essential element in a social skill, peer relations contribute to social competence. Reciprocal elements in peer interaction would seem to underlie both aggressive and sexual socialization, as well as the socialization of moral values. In other instances (e.g. altruistic behaviour), the peer culture seems to contribute to socialization through the complementary quality of mixed-age interaction. In all cases, however, peer interaction is laced with different sanctions and prohibitions from those marking the child's interactions with adults. Child–child relations contain residuals of reciprocity even when social hierarchies are extremely rigid. Egalitarianism is the cornerstone of socialization in the peer culture.

Developmental course

Differentiation in the social relations of children begins in babyhood. By at least the third quarter of the first year, the mother has usually been selected as an object of specific attachment and, when given the opportunity to interact with her or another baby, the year-old infant will remain in proximity and attend mostly to her (Eckerman et al., 1975; Lewis et al., 1975). Nevertheless, babies are responsive to one another: by two or three months of age, babies orient to the movements of other infants and, at about five months, to the cries of other babies

(Bridges, 1933; Vincze, 1971). No one has yet demonstrated that babies under six months of age interact synchronously, but it is clear that the vigour and the 'meshing' of infant–infant interactions increases rapidly during the second six months of life.

Infancy studies

Maudry and Nekula (1939) observed babies between 6 and 25 months using a 'baby party' technique. Babies between the ages of 6 and 8 months ignored about half of one another's overtures, and the social interactions that occurred resembled contacts made with play materials (i.e. exploratory looking and manipulation). Fighting increased (mostly over toys) between 9 and 13 months, decreasing afterward. Much positive attention was given to peers in addition to the negative interaction but the role of toys in the social intercourse of children under the age of one year is not well understood. Most of the evidence suggests that babies are interested in each other *per se*, engaging in mimicry and taking turns, but many of these social behaviours are object-centered (Mueller and Lucas, 1975; Eckerman, 1977).

Repeated exposure changes the quality of peer interaction among babies. Becker (1977) arranged for sixteen pairs of 9-month-old infants to meet for 10 play sessions, followed by a meeting with a new partner. Control pairs met twice, at intervals matching the beginning and ending sessions of the experimental pairs. Peer-oriented behaviour increased in quantity, complexity and degree of social engagement among the experimental subjects but not among the controls. Social exposure effects were observed with the new infant in addition to the familiar infant; thus, the results suggest a general social learning phenomenon rather than the associative learning of specific behaviours directed toward a specific infant.

Peer experience results in individual differences in social interaction among babies. Lee (1973) studied five babies ranging between 8 and 10 months at the beginning of the study and who attended a day care centre. Social activity had the same qualities noted earlier (Maudry and Nekula, 1939), but differentiation based on both attraction and rejection occurred during six months' attendance at the centre. One baby was more consistently approached than the other members of the group, and one was more consistently avoided. The most preferred infant was a responsive social partner who interacted non-assertively with the other babies and whose social involvements were reciprocal. The least preferred infant was nearly asocial: both the intensity and extensiveness of his involvements depended on whether or not he himself had initiated the interaction. One cannot assert definitely that these individual differences precipitated the budding friendships that were observed. But 'personal styles' clearly distinguished two babies from the other members of this group.

Mueller and Lucas (1975) assert that one of the most dramatic changes occurring in peer interaction during the second year is the emergence of complex contingencies in socially directed behaviours which are tangentially related to toys (and other non-social objects). Imitation becomes more common and better coordinated; responsibilities for the maintenance of social interchanges are more commonly shared; and social interchanges increase in both dimensionality and organizational complexity. Reciprocity and complementarity in play interactions emerge late in the second year as revealed in organized role relations such as 'chaser' and 'chased' or 'giver' and 'receiver'. Seemingly, children coordinate their social actions to their social complements in a manner which resembles the coordination of mental schemes based on non-social objects.

These progressions were studied with six male toddlers who were members of a play-group when between 16 and 22 months of age (Vandell, 1977). Video-taped records were made at 16, 19 and 22 months in various dyadic combinations and analyzed in terms of the incidence of both simple and coordinated actions by individual children as well as contingencies (i.e. co-occurrence within three seconds) occurring in the activities of the two children. Frequencies of both simple and coordinated behaviours increased over the five-month period as well as the number of interaction initiations and terminations. Concurrently, interaction sequences became longer and involved an increased number of actor exchanges. The frequency of object-related acts also increased, indicating that non-social objects retain an important role in peer relations during the second year. But the data show that the complexity and coordination of social activity changes markedly during this time (see also Bronson, 1975). Social interaction in larger groups is dyadic and qualitative changes in the interaction are more visible in these dyadic exhanges than in social behaviour in group situations (Vandell and Mueller, 1977).

Qualitatively, peer interaction during the second year is both similar and dissimilar to the child's interactions with adults. Eckerman et al. (1975) studied 14 pairs of same-age toddlers: 10 to 12, 16 to 18, and 22 to 24 months of age. The children, who were not previously acquainted, met together for twenty minutes in the presence of their mothers. Peer-related behaviours occurred in over 60 per cent of the observations at each age, indicating that young children have considerable salience for one another. More important, however, the observations revealed that behaviours observed in the child's interactions with the mother (e.g. smiling, vocalizing and touching) also occurred with peers, but not as frequently as with the mother. Interaction with play materials occurred more often in peer interaction than in mother–child interaction. These observations confirm the hypothesis that the early stages of peer interaction are object–centered, and it is clear that different controlling mechanisms mark the mother–child system and the child–child social system.

These investigators also found that peer interaction differed from the children's interaction with strange adults. During exchanges between children there was little crying and fussing, much synchronous use of the play materials, give-and-take with materials, and struggles. Among the older children, coordinated activity with the toys was observed and the children's imitative use of the materials showed the interaction to be socially regulated. Most common in peer interaction, in contrast to stranger–child interaction, was use of play materials. Here, again, is confirmation of the hypothesis that peer interaction becomes increasingly 'coordinated' during the second year, as well as evidence showing that the young child's commerce with other children is structured differently from commerce with adults.

Studies of preschool and nursery school children

Evidence with three- and four-year-old children also suggests that peer-directed behaviour does not duplicate adult-directed behaviour. Rarely do three-year-olds express affection verbally, hug one another, or cling to each other (Heathers, 1955). Affection-seeking, in general, declines during the preschool years, and kisses, hugs, clinging, and 'I love yous' never enter the repertoire of child–child relations to the extent that they remain in adult–child relations. In extreme circumstances, intensive clinging and proximity-maintenance may occur in peer interaction. Freud and Dann (1951), who studied six young children reared together in a concentration camp during World War II, found them to be avoidant and aggressive in their attitudes towards adults, but strongly attached to one another. Positive feelings were centered in their own group and the children seemed to care only for each other and not at all for anybody or anything else. But such circumstances are seldom encountered. While this 'experiment of nature' shows that children have the capacity to serve as their own socializing agents, the literature indicates that adults and children usually contribute different competencies in the course of socialization.

Both the incidence of social encounters and their nature continue to change during the years from three through six. In nursery schools (where most studies have been conducted) the frequency of both positive and negative social interactions changes. Smith and Connolly (1972) studied social interaction in forty children ranging in age from 2 years 9 months to 4 years 9 months in three day nurseries. Staring, crying, sucking, pointing and submissive-flight behaviours occurred less frequently among the older children while talking to other children and social play were increasingly common. Similar results were obtained in another investigation based on twelve 2-year-olds and thirteen 4-year-olds (Blurton Jones, 1972). Older children engaged more frequently in talking, playing with other children (including rough-and-tumble play), and other social behaviours such as smiling and laughing. Less frequent among the older children were crying, watching other children, having toys taken, and orienting to the teacher (see also Heathers, 1955; Parten, 1932).

Four types of positive exchanges were studied in an investigation of seventy 3- and 4-year-old children (Charlesworth and Hartup, 1967): *giving positive attention and approval, affection and personal acceptance, submission,* and *giving tangible objects.* Such behaviours occurred at significantly higher rates among the 4-year-olds than among 3-year-olds, even though exchange rates varied from classroom to classroom and from activity to activity. Rates of initiating positive overtures were also strongly correlated with rates of receiving such initiations ($r = 0.75$). Total frequencies of aggression – particularly object-related aggression – also increase between the ages of 2 and 4 years but then decline (Dawe, 1934; Walters et al., 1957; Blurton Jones, 1972; Hartup, 1974). Age changes in aggression, however, are not the same in girls and in boys and incidence of aggression at no time exceeds positive or neutral interactions (Walters et al., 1957; McGrew, 1972).

With increasing age, children participate more readily in associative and cooperative activities and less readily in idleness, solitary play, parallel play and on-looker behaviour (Parten, 1932). Assuming that cooperative and associative play require more advanced cognitive skills than the other play categories, these data have been regarded widely as social reflections of cognitive changes occurring during the preschool years. Recent observations (Barnes, 1971; Smith and Connolly, 1972; Blurton Jones, 1972) show similar developmental progressions, although one or two investigators have suggested that there may be higher cognitive and task-oriented demands contained in solitary play than believed earlier. Role-taking skills, however, are negatively related to parallel play and positively related to associative play, confirming the hypothesis that associative activity represents relatively more mature peer interaction than parallel activity (Rubin et al., 1976).

Normative action is visible in nursery school groups to a greater extent than can be observed in toddler interaction. Merei (1949) reported that preschool children formed normative traditions including seating orders, possession of objects, ceremonies connected with toys, belongingness, and rituals in games. More recently, Lakin et al. (1977) studied normative behaviour in same-age groups in various Israeli *kibbutzim*: $1\frac{1}{2}$–2 years; 2–$2\frac{1}{2}$; $2\frac{1}{2}$–3; and 3–$3\frac{1}{2}$. Observations revealed significantly more frequent assignment and execution of clear-cut roles, rule-enforcement and rehearsal, and helping behaviour in the older groups than in the younger ones. Monitoring activities (similar to onlooker behaviour) occurred less frequently in the older groups.

Perhaps the most extensive norms to manifest themselves during this time are related to sex. Boys play more frequently with boys than with girls; girls play more often with other girls. Sex differences become stronger as children enter middle childhood, but they are also visible in most groups of toddlers and preschool children. The nature of social activity also varies according to sex (Shure, 1963; Edelman and Omark, 1973). To a considerable extent, these early divisions are based on shared interests among children of the same sex rather than avoidance of the opposite sex. But, whatever the basis, sex-role norms manifest themselves in the peer interactions of very young children.

Later childhood

Qualitative changes in social interaction continue beyond the nursery school years. Observations conducted in child care centres showed that instrumental aggression (i.e. agonistic behaviour aimed at the retrieval of an object, territory or privilege) was instigated more consistently by goal-blocking among 4-year-olds than among 7-year-olds, and that aggressive acts among the older children were more likely to be hostile (i.e. person-directed) than among the younger children (Hartup, 1974). The aggression of the preschool-aged children had a direct, instrumental quality in contrast to the aggression of the older children which was a mixture of both object-oriented and person-oriented harm-doing. Apparently, elementary school children and adolescents are better able to engage in the role-taking and attributions leading to hostile aggression than younger children are.

Cognitive capacities also constrain children's evaluations of each other's aggression. Rule and Duker (1973) studied reactions to stories in which the consequences of aggression were described as either serious or less serious. Certain stories ended with the aggressor's victim falling and scratching his leg (for example) while others ended with the victim's suffering a broken leg. Eight-year-olds regarded the aggression resulting in serious outcomes as 'more naughty' than aggression leading to less serious outcomes. Outcome made no difference in the evaluation of aggression by the 12-year-old children. Either children become more callous to serious injury as they grow older (not unlikely) or their capacity to subjugate outcome to intention increases in making moral judgements, as suggested by Piaget (1932).

Normative activity in child–child relations becomes more salient and more complicated in middle childhood. While nursery school children share interests and conform to common rules, these activities are not extensive and the hierarchization in social organization is relatively weak. Both explicit and implicit values are shared more commonly by individual members in societies of older children and adolescents. For normative activity to develop, however, children must share common goals. In one experiment (Sherif et al., 1961), twenty-two boys were recruited for an experimental summer camp, divided into two aggregates, removed to separate campsites, and observed over several weeks. Opportunities to engage in common activities within each aggregate transformed the group structures in a very short time – status hierarchies became evident, norms emerged, and in-group feelings were manifest. Normative activity increased (e.g. group names were adopted) when the groups accidently discovered one another. Athletic competitions, rigged so that neither group won nor lost consistently, led to hostility between the groups. Inter-group fights were common; name calling and vandalism were frequent. To reduce the inter-group conflict, the experimenters tried non-programmed interaction between groups; the conflict merely accelerated. Only cooperative interaction, in which members of the two groups were required to work together toward a superordinate goal (e.g. restoring the camp water supply), reduced the conflict. The achievement of harmonious inter-group relations, then, required an opportunity to work toward common ends. Whether children's ages constrain such group dynamics is unknown since this experiment was conducted with 11-year-old boys only. These results have long been assumed to apply to the societies of both children and adolescents, as well as to the social behaviour of adults.

Some aspects of group interaction undergo change during adolescence. Twenty groups, each including four individuals, were constituted from nursery schools, elementary schools and university classes and asked to create stories based on pictures (Smith, 1960). Across these groups, chronological age was positively correlated with both amount of social activity ($r=0.81$) and amount of task-related behaviour ($r=0.64$). The groups of 5-year-olds were much less coordinated in the manner in which new ideas were introduced than were groups of older children and adolescents, as well as less cooperative and more autonomous in terms of individual activity. The younger children behaved like aggregates of independent persons whereas the older children manifested reciprocal social relations. In another study (Smith, 1973), five-person same-age groups ranging in age from 5 to 20 years were studied while they made interpretations for a Rorschach card. Once again, interaction and task-related behaviour increased with age, at least through early adolescence. But the social interaction became more 'mature' in several other ways: (a) within-groups variance in the interaction was lower in the older groups; and (b) behaviours such as unifying actions, use of acknowledgements, signalling that one understands, asking for opinions, and exchanges of questions were more common in the adolescents' groups than in the children's groups. Both studies suggest that group problem-solving becomes more coordinated with increases in age.

Social hierarchies can be observed in children's societies, even when the individual members are 2-, 3- and 4-year-old children. Sociometric scores (i.e. indices of social status or popularity) are somewhat less stable in groups of nursery school children than in groups of older children although considerable stability exists even in the choices of very young children. Marshall and McCandless (1957a) found stability coefficients ranging from 0.22 to 0.74 in various nursery school classes tested at twenty-day intervals. Also, Hartup et al. (1967) reported a test-retest correlation of 0.68 for one group of preschoolers retested after a five-month interval. Hierarchies based on rejection choices are not as stable as hierarchies based on positive choices.

Dominance hierarchies have been studied in both preschool children and elementary school children. Strayer and Strayer (1976) and Strayer (1977) studied three classes of dominance interactions – attacks, threats and object/position struggles. The observations in these studies centred on instances of 'somebody wins, somebody loses' rather than instances of individual aggression. Linear dominance structures were identified in a number of day nurseries enrolling 3- and 4-year-old children, but the existence of these hierarchies was not established with every measure. In two instances, for example, a linear status structure emerged from observations of attack and threat interactions, but a different structure emerged from observations of object struggles (Strayer and Strayer, 1976). Among elementary school children, the three conflict measures converged to yield one single linear dominance structure. Such structures emerge early in young children's groups, solidifying relatively rapidly in the early stages of group interaction (Harris, 1977).

Developmental changes in group structures are also revealed in studies of *perceived* dominance (Edelman and Omark, 1973). Paired comparisons, in which each child in a classroom was asked to compare himself with every other child in terms of 'Who is toughest', revealed a clear developmental progression in the number of children who independently agreed that one child was tougher than the other. Percentages of dyads agreeing in this manner were 40 per cent among nursery school children; 62 per cent among kindergarten children; 66 per cent, 72 per cent, 72 per cent and 73 per cent among first-, second-, third- and fourth-graders, respectively. Comparing the results from the observational studies with the results based on perceived dominance, it appears that behavioural interaction may produce dominance structures earlier than the children's application of dominance constructs to themselves and their classmates. Scattered work suggests that structures in children's groups may also be based on affiliation and altruism, but these conclusions remain unconfirmed, and their developmental implications unexplored (Strayer, 1977; Wareing, 1977).

To summarize: the current literature suggests that the development of peer relations proceeds from simple organizations to complex hierarchies, from loosely differentiated interchanges to differentiated interaction, and from primitive awareness of the needs of others to reciprocal relations based on complex attributions. Adolescent peer relations resemble the peer relations of young children in many ways but both dyadic interaction and group structures change enormously as children mature.

Family relations as antecedents of peer interaction

Adult–child and child–child relations are neither wholly independent nor wholly interdependent in child development. Experiences within each social system affect the other. Lieberman (1976) examined the relation between the nature of the 3-year-old child's attachment to the mother and social competence in the nursery school. Observations of mother–child interaction were conducted in the home and observations of behaviour with an agemate were conducted at school. Children whose attachments to the mother were rated as 'secure' were more responsive to other children and engaged in more protracted social interactions than did children who were not securely attached. Also, those children whose mothers arranged contacts with other children in the home were more mature in their responsiveness to other children in the school. Here, then, is evidence that the security of the child's attachment to the mother provides an effective basis for interaction with other children. At the same time, providing direct practice in child–child interaction also contributes its share.

Research with older children is consistent with the results based on younger children. Using interview and sociometric methods to study a sample of elementary school boys and their parents, Winder and Rau (1962) found that both the mothers and fathers of 'likable' children expressed low demands for aggression and tended not to use aggressive punishment. The mothers infrequently deprived their sons of privileges, had high self-esteem, and were well adjusted themselves. The fathers of the high status children also gave favourable evaluations of their sons' competence and provided high levels of supportive reinforcement. The distinctive qualities in the socialization of these high status boys thus included discouragement of antisocial behaviour, small amounts of frustration and punishment, and supportive reinforcement. Similar results were obtained by Baumrind (1967, 1971) in her studies of instrumental competence. Children rated as self-reliant, self-controlled and explorative had *authoritative* parents (i.e. mothers and fathers who exerted control over the child and demanded independence, but who were also warm, rational and receptive to the child's feelings and points of view. Such a child-rearing orientation contrasted sharply with the orientations expressed by the parents of less competent children.

Impulsive-aggressive children, for example, lived with *permissive* parents, while conflicted-irritable children were raised by *authoritarian* parents.

Satisfactory home lives, continuing from early childhood through later childhood, are thus predictive of good peer relations. Prospective studies are needed, however, to establish more clearly whether effectiveness in peer relations derives directly from parent–child relations or whether these social systems are linked reciprocally. The available evidence suggests a synergism between the adult–child and child–child social systems which extends from the earliest years of childhood.

What are friends?

Friendship is only a little less interesting than love to laymen and literary artists. While the analytic tools of social science have been applied to love with some regularity (cf. Rubin, 1973), these tools have seldom been used to study friendships. And yet it is difficult to underestimate parents' worries about their children's friends. Having friends is considered to be a significant social achievement, an indicator of social competence, and a mark of positive mental health. Not having friends brings children to consulting psychologists. And, yet, little is known about friendship formation in children, the age-related vicissitudes of friendship, and the characteristics of children who have many mutual friends as compared to those who do not. Sociometric analysis has been used extensively to study social acceptance and popularity in children, but having friends is not the same as being popular. Friendliness may be a major correlate of social acceptance (Moore, 1967) but one does not have to be popular to be a friend.

What are friendships? First, friendships are dyadic. One may have affectionate and trusting relations with a triad (or a larger group), but friendships are specific attachments not unlike the attachments existing between child and mother or between husband and wife. Like other attachments, friendships involve maintaining contact with the other person as well as sharing affects, concerns, interests and information (Hess, 1972). We expect to enjoy our friends, to trust them and for them to provide a variety of gratifications to us. Even children stress attributes like 'brave', 'kind', 'loyal', and 'true' in describing their friends, along with 'friendliness' and 'similarities' in various attributes (Austin and Thompson, 1948).

Friendships are constrained in ways which are different, though, from other attachments. First, friendships are volitional; they may be $\divideontimes$ terminated by a single defection. The friendship dyad is extremely vulnerable and, unlike the parent–child dyad or the marriage dyad, it has no legal safeguards against dissolution. Second, friends cannot rely $\divideontimes$ on sanctions against abuse or neglect and can claim no special rights, obligations or privileges. Friendships require continuous reaffirmation, a process in which both parties must participate (Hess, 1972). Friendships are fragile, even though the shared affects, gratifications and intellectual stimulation within them may be as intense as the stimulation inherent in familial attachments.

Friendships are governed by different rules from other social relations. Children understand these rules as well as adults. In one study (Cabral et al., 1977), sixty-four subjects between the ages of 7 and 17 were given three stories in which a child shares confidential information with a parent, a friend and an acquaintance. Later, the child discovers that the confidence has been breached. The subjects were asked to describe which participant would act first, what the action would be, what effect the broken confidence would have on the relationship, and how the problem would be resolved. Children at all ages differentiated the three relationships in terms of these outcomes. Parents, for example, could use private information publicly; if they broke confidence with the child it was usually thought to be for the child's own good. Friends were not believed to have the same rights; they must abide by reciprocal agreements – clearly indicating that *friendship* relations are *reciprocal* relations. Acquaintances were considered to be free to break confidences but, if they would do so, the action could prevent the acquaintanceship from becoming a friendship. Breaking a confidence was seen as affecting each relationship differently: parent–child relations would eventually return to normal but friendships would be adversely affected; acquaintanceships would be affected adversely or terminated. Resolution of broken confidences also differed: parents were expected to rationalize their actions, while apologies or the passage of time were believed necessary to resolve the crisis between friends; most children could not think of resolution strategies that apply to acquaintanceships. Clearly, the mutual trust existing between friends is not the same as the mutual trust existing between family members, and this trust also differs from the behavioural code that governs more ephemeral social relations.

Children's conceptions of friendship have been explored by studying the manner with which friends are talked or written about. Descriptions of 'best friends' are elicited and contrasted with descriptions of other children – either strangers or acquaintances. Such techniques have been used most extensively with elementary school children and adolescents since obtaining reliable verbal material from younger children is very difficult. Recent studies show that the conceptual system used by children to describe their friends, as well as specific expectations, undergo systematic changes with increasing age.

Bigelow and La Gaipa (1975) asked 480 Canadian school children in Grades 1 through 8 to think about their best friends (same-sex) and to write an essay about what they expect in their friends that is different from their expectations about acquaintances. The essays were coded on twenty-one dimensions of friendship expectation representing various levels of abstraction and various conditions favouring social attraction. 'Onset' consisted of the grade level at which a given expectation occurred with an incidence significantly greater than zero. Significant increases with age (grade) were obtained on sixteen friendship expectations, with onset grades occurring as shown in Table 5.1.

Table 5.1   Onset grades for age-increasing friendship expectations

Dimension	Onset grade
Friend as help-giver*	2
Share common activities*	2
Propinquity*	3
Stimulation value	3
Organized play	3
Demographic similarity	3
Evaluation*	3
Acceptance*	4
Admiration*	4
Increasing prior interaction*	4
Loyalty and commitment*	5
Genuineness*	6
Friend as receiver of help	6
Intimacy potential*	7
Common interests*	7
Similarity in attitudes and values	7

Adapted from Bigelow and La Gaipa (1975). Used with permission.
*Also increased with age in a cross-validation study (Bigelow, 1977).

Many friendship expectations recognized by older individuals were missing in the expectations of younger children. Whether these missing expectations were also missing in the overt social relations of the younger children is not known. But the various attributions applied by adults to their friends clearly 'clock in' at different times during childhood and adolescence. Close examination of these age-related changes suggests a transition from egocentric to sociocentric notions about friendship, and from sociocentric to empathic expectations.

Cross-validation of these results was conducted with a sample of 480 Scottish children (Bigelow, 1977). Eleven of the twenty-one friendship expectations were found to increase with age in this sample, too (see Table 5.1). Onset occurred at similar ages in the two cultures as indicated by a rank-order correlation of 0·78. In only two instances (friend as help-giver and increasing interaction over time) was there a rank-order difference in the two distributions of more than one rank. Consequently, relatively high concordance marked the developmental progression within nine of the friendship expectations. Cluster analyses reveal that friendship expectations evolve in three loose 'stages': (a) a *reward-cost stage* indicated by the appearance of common activities, propinquity and similar expectations – occurring about Grades 2 and 3; (b) a *normative stage* in which shared values, rules and sanctions are evident in friendship expectations – occurring about Grades 4 and 5; and (c) an *empathic stage* in which understanding, self-disclosure and shared interests emerge – somewhere around Grades 6 and 7. Recall, however, that not all friendship expectations changed with age. Among both the Canadian and Scottish children, several basic expectations, including ego reinforcement and reciprocity, were mentioned at all ages. Affective elements thus become associated with friendship very early (and remain so) while cognitive elements change in accordance with the reorganizations that occur in general intellectual development.

Selman and his associates (Selman, 1976; Selman and Jaquette, 1977) also argue that children's conceptions of friendship become increasingly differentiated with increasing age. 'Friendship awareness' was explored within a larger investigation of stages and sequences in 'interpersonal awareness' including: (a) self- and individual awareness, (b) understanding of friendship relations, and (c) awareness of group relations. Assuming that children's conceptualizations within these domains are tied to perspective-taking and its development, these investigators argue that interpersonal awareness emerges in a series of stages differing qualitatively from one another and occurring in invariant, hierarchical sequence. These hierarchies are believed to be based on: (a) awareness of the psychological interdependence between persons, (b) awareness that social action occurs within social systems, and (c) increased sensitivity to the thoughts, generalized expectations and attributions of others. Based on this arm-chair analysis of social behaviour and its development, along with large numbers of preliminary interviews and observations, five stages of friendship awareness have been identified. Note the similarity between the progression outlined in Table 5.2 and the progression obtained by Bigelow (1977).

Table 5.2 Sequentially ordered stages in friendship awareness and perspective-taking

Stage	Friendship awareness	Perspective-taking
0	Momentary physical playmate	Undifferentiated; egocentric
1	One-way assistance	Subjective; differentiated
2	Fairweather cooperation	Reciprocal; self-reflective
3	Intimate; mutual sharing	Mutual; third-person
4	Autonomous interdependence	In-depth; societal

Adapted from Selman and Jaquette (1977). Used with permission.

Selman and Jaquette (1977) then conducted interviews with a normative sample of 225 individuals, ranging in age from $4\frac{1}{2}$ to 32 years, including 48 males who were interviewed twice across a two-year interval. Preliminary analyses have revealed monotonic increases in friendship awareness scores between the ages of 6 and 15. The average increase amounts to nearly two stages – from average scores near Stage 1 to averages near Stage 3. Friendship awareness lagged somewhat behind individual awareness but moved somewhat in advance of awareness of group relations. Correlations of friendship awareness with individual and group awareness approximated 0·80 (controlling for IQ) and 0·70 (controlling for chronological age). There was a considerable range in age among subjects scoring within each stage of awareness, although the longitudinal results showed advances across stages rather than random fluctuations (these analyses were based on summary interpersonal awareness scores rather than on friendship awareness scores). Of the 48 children included in the longitudinal study, 8 remained at the same level, 37 advanced by less than a full stage, and 3 advanced a full stage or more during the two-year interval.

Peevers and Secord (1973) examined written descriptions of liked and disliked peers by kindergarten children, third- and seventh-graders, senior high school students and university students. Four dimensions of these descriptions changed with age: (a) *descriptiveness* – the older children and adolescents described both friends and enemies with more frequent use of differentiated statements and less frequent use of undifferentiated ones; (b) *personal involvement* – older subjects included themselves in the descriptions more frequently than younger subjects did; (c) *consistency* – both positive and negative descriptors were used more consistently by third- and seventh-grade children than by kindergarten children or older adolescents (the former were erratic in their descriptions while the latter were more differentiated than were their childhood counterparts); and (d) *depth* – older subjects described both friends and non-friends in terms of situational and temporal vicissitudes rather than in terms of invariant personality characteristics. Livesley and Bromley (1973) found that the number of constructs used by their subjects (320 children between the ages of 7 and 15) increased with age and, in several other studies (cf. Supnick, 1964), a shift from the use of egocentric and concrete terms to decentered, abstract constructs has been noted.

In addition, children and adolescents describe their friends differently from non-friends. Peevers and Secord (1973) found that fewer trait names were used to describe non-friends than friends, with this difference being greater among adolescents than among younger children. Disliked children were described more egocentrically than were liked children, although these descriptions did not differ from one another in either consistency or depth. Livesley and Bromley (1973) observed that more statements were used to describe liked than disliked persons. This difference characterized descriptions of both children and adults made by boys, but only the descriptions of adults made by girls. Finally, Supnick (1964) compared the descriptions of liked and disliked children by boys who were approximately 7, 9 and 11 years old. She discovered that the two older groups used more constructs to describe both liked boys and liked girls than to describe disliked children, but this difference was obtained among the youngest subjects in their descriptions of girls only. Clearly, the conceptual system applied by children to their friends differs from the system applied to other categories of persons. Most writers have reasoned that children have more extended and varied experiences with their friends than with other individuals, conditions that supply the child with more information to be used in describing friends than non-friends.

Similar reasons would account for the differences that have been found in content analyses of children's descriptions of friends and non-friends. Personality attributes, intellectual abilities, achievements, preferences, aversions, interests, social roles and comparisons with self are all used more commonly to describe liked than disliked persons, while references to appearance, actual incidents, specific behaviour inconsistencies, self-attitudes, relations with others and evaluations are more common in descriptions of disliked than liked persons (Livesley and Bromley, 1973; Austin and Thompson, 1948). These differences characterize elementary school children as well as adolescents, although the terms employed by older individuals are more abstract and less egocentric than the terms used by younger ones.

Considerable agreement exists, then, in the literature on children's descriptions of their friends: with age, increases occur in the number of interpersonal constructs used, the flexibility and precision with which they are used, the complexity and organization of information and ideas about one's friends, the level of analysis used in interpreting the behaviour of other individuals, the recognition of certain attributes as characteristic of friends. Most writers assume that age differences in children's conceptions of their friends are derivatives of more general changes in cognitive and language development. No one knows, as yet, the extent to which these changes are linked to social experience.

Individual differences in friendship expectations remain unexplored, and the implications of such differences for the regulation of friendship relations and social status are unclear. Perspective-taking skills are correlates of social acceptance (Gottman et al., 1975) and children's ideas about helpfulness are also correlated with social status (Ladd and Oden, 1977). But skills in interpersonal observation and description may be indirectly, rather than directly, related to social behaviour.

Children and their friends

Two methods of identifying childhood friendships dominate the literature: (a) sociometric tests (Moreno, 1934); and (b) moving sociometrics – direct observations of children's interactions with each other (Marshall and McCandless, 1957b). These techniques have been used in large numbers of studies dealing with popularity (as well as other dimensions of sociometric status). Interview and observational measures of sociometric choice are moderately correlated with each other among preschool and elementary school children (McCandless and Marshall, 1957).

Although 'best friend' relations among preschool children are relatively stable over several weeks' duration (Marshall and Mc-Candless, 1957a), there is a direct relation between age and amount of fluctuation in these choices. Using large samples of school children in the United States, Horrocks and Thompson (1946) and Thompson and Horrocks (1947) found more frequent fluctuations among 11- to 15-year-olds than among 16- to 18-year-olds. The younger children chose the same individual as a best friend about 50 per cent of the time when sociometric tests were given at two-week intervals. Older children, however, chose the same individual between 60 per cent and 90 per cent of the time. Whether behaviour with one's friends fluctuates in relation to age is not known. Fewer fluctuations occur among girls than among boys, a difference that has been found among both younger and older children (Hartup, 1970).

Related to the sex differences observed in friendship fluctuations, are sex differences in the *intensiveness/extensiveness* of friendship relations. In a factor analytic study of 62 children between the ages of seven and eight, Waldrop and Halverson (1975) found that intensiveness in the child's peer relations (as rated from the mother's mentions of best friends and their importance to the child) loaded highly on a peer-orientation factor only for girls. In contrast, ratings of extensiveness (the degree to which the child participated in group activities and games) appeared on the peer-orientation factor only among boys. 'Intensive' girls also were more socially competent than less intensive girls and 'extensive' boys were more socially at ease than less extensive boys.

Eder and Hallinan (1977) then predicted that sociometric tests with preadolescents should indicate that girls, more frequently than boys, are involved in triads in which a single dyadic friendship exists to the exclusion of the remaining member. Friendship choices were obtained in the standard manner in five classrooms and all possible same-sex triads in each classroom were examined for the existence of mutual sociometric choices. The number of triads encompassing an exclusive dyadic friendship were divided by the total number of same-sex triads existing in the class. The proportion of exclusive dyadic friendships was greater for girls than for boys in four classrooms. Concordantly, participation in non-exclusive friendships within same-sex triads was more common among the boys than among the girls. Even more interesting, the results of seven sociometric tests administered over the school year showed that, when triadic relations were not initially exclusive, there was a high probability that girls would move toward more exclusive social relations with the passage of time. Conversely, boys initially in non-exclusive triads either did not develop exclusive interactions or became more expansive in their choices as the school year progressed. The determinants of these sex differences are obscure, although it has been suggested that play activities encourage boys to develop non-exclusive social relations while, at the same time, such activities encourage girls to form more intensive social relations. According to this argument, once friendships are formed, sex divisions encourage additional sexual differentiation in behaviour and *vice versa*.

Which children have friends?
Dozens of personal characteristics are correlated with sociometric status (i.e. popularity): physical attractiveness, children's names, social class background, intelligence, friendliness, social assertiveness, and endorsement of conventional social values (see Hartup, 1970). Although research indicates that well-endowed children have more friends than children who are less favourably endowed, such data do not indicate whether the nature of friendships varies according to these same characteristics. Certain attributes are mentioned by *both* popular and non-popular children as reasons for choosing their friends – e.g. Austin and Thompson (1948) found that positive personality characteristics such as 'kindness' and 'loyalty' accounted for approximately 50 per cent of the reasons given by sixth-graders for choosing a friend, with 'friendliness' accounting for 15 per cent of these reasons. While sociable children are more likely to be involved in mutual friendships than less sociable children, 'nice guy' qualities seem to be attributed to friends regardless of actual sociability.

Similar results have been obtained with 'kindness'. Mannarino (1976) studied social sensitivity in 92 children, 30 of whom were involved in reciprocal friendships. Altruism was measured with two instruments – a paper-and-pencil inventory and a modification of the prisoner's dilemma game. Both measures showed that children who were chums were more altruistic than were children who were not chums. But, the Austin and Thompson (1948) data confirm that children also attribute 'kindness' to their friends. Kind children, then, are both more likely to have friends than unkind children and to be perceived as 'kind' by their friends. Little more can be concluded about kindness and children's friendships: whether children will sacrifice their own possessions more readily to assist a friend than a non-friend is unknown; whether children will disclose information more readily to a friend than an acquaintance is unknown; whether social interaction between friends is better 'meshed' than the interaction between acquaintances is also unknown.

Similarly, attractive, bright, middle-class children have a wider network of best friends than children who are unattractive, dull and lower-class. Very little is known, however, about the manner in which attributions about attractiveness and intelligence are altered when children 'make friends'. Important issues need research attention in this area.

Do friends resemble one another?

Few data exist concerning friendship relations in mixed-sex situations because most children's friendships are same-sex. Except for chronological age, no characteristic is more extensively shared by friends than gender (see Hartup, 1970).

Most investigators have reported positive correlations between the ages of best friends – both young children and adolescents (Challman, 1932; Furfey, 1927). These correlations are modest in magnitude because the sociometric data were obtained within age-graded classrooms; the restricted age ranges in these classrooms attenuate such correlations greatly as contrasted with situations in which entire schools (for example) were examined for such concordance.

Children and their friends resemble one another in racial characteristics. Both early sociometric studies (e.g. Criswell, 1939) and more recent ones (e.g. Asher, 1973) have shown that, in integrated classrooms, children make fewer cross-race friendship selections than would be expected by chance. Cross-race selections occur, with selection of white children by black children exceeding the number of reverse selections. But cross-race choices, at least in United States schools, are much rarer among secondary school children than among younger children (Asher et al., 1977). Considerable evidence suggests that the social attitudes underlying racial cleavages vary with age: among young children, racial cleavages are based on shared attitudes and affects rather than strong inter-racial hostility. Negative racial attitudes become increasingly salient, however, in the friendship selections of older children.

Behavioural similarity is not as consistent between best friends as similarity in sex, age and race: (a) Positive correlations between best friends' IQs have been reported by some investigators but not others (see Hartup, 1970), and it is doubtful that similarity in intellectual ability is a strong factor in friendship selection when chronological age is held constant. (b) Sociability appears to be more similar among pairs of friends than among pairs of non-friends, but the capacity for organized cooperative activity is particularly salient in boys' friendships while general social participation is significant in girls' (Challman, 1932). (c) Sociometric status has not been established as more similar among friends than non-friends (Thorpe, 1955). (d) Similarity in attitudes and values is related to social attraction. Byrne and Griffitt (1966) showed that sociometric preference is a linear function of perceived similarity in social attitudes among children ranging from the fourth through the twelfth grade, as well as among university students. And, in another study, preferences for camp activities were observed to be similar between children and their sociometric nominees (Davitz, 1955) even though perceived similarity was greater than actual similarity. The interests of mutual friends has not been studied except that Haller and Butterworth (1960) reported positive correla-tions between friends in occupational and educational aspirations. These correlations were higher when the friends' values were supported by parental values than when parental attitudes were discordant. Behavioural similarity, then, may be maximized between friends when children are exposed to concordant norms in other contexts. Shared *absence* of concordant norms in other social situations, however, does not seem to attentuate the similarity between friends in educational values.

Considerable attention has been given to the complementarity–congruence issue in sociometric research, although such studies with children are rare (see Hartup, 1970). Does behavioural similarity foster friendships? Or, does behavioural complementarity stimulate social attraction? Izard's (1960) work with adolescents suggests that the personality profiles of friends are similar rather than complementary. No evidence exists for younger children other than the results cited above. Certainly, broad areas of shared attributes and values must exist between children and their friends since such similarities are defining characteristics of friendship. But 'best friends' are not carbon copies of one another – obviously. The significant issue to be studied, then, is the relative importance of various attributes known to increase or decrease social attraction rather than similarity and/or complementarity *per se*.

Behaviour with friends

Behaviour with acquaintances differs from behaviour with strangers beginning in babyhood. Lewis et al. (1975) studied seven babies who were observed once with 'friends' and once with 'strangers'. The friends were familiar children between 7 and 20 months who had visited the subject at least once each week during the previous two months and twice each week for two weeks prior to the observation. Strangers were matched with the friends according to sex and age. Proximal activities – body contact, proximity and touching – were more frequently directed toward friends than toward strangers, as were gesturing and imitative interactions. Looking at the other child did not differ according to friendship status, and differences in play and affective interaction were minimal. In turn, the friends directed more proximal behaviours toward the target children than did strangers and, in addition, more frequent positive affects. Distal interactions and play behaviours did not differ in the overtures of friends and strangers. Target-to-friend behaviours and friend-to-target behaviours are not independent in these data. Social commerce was nevertheless more visible between children who were acquainted than between children who had never seen one another before.

Familiar peers are 'secure bases' in distress situations. In a study of 108 children enrolled in Soviet nursery schools (Ipsa, 1977), children were matched with either a classmate or another child enrolled in a different nursery class. Observations were conducted in the presence and absence of a responsive adult. Children in the familiar peer condition evidenced very little distress at departure of the adult, while children paired with unfamiliar peers were upset by her departure. Older children were less upset by the adult's absence than were the younger children, but the effects of peer familiarity were observed at all ages.

The literature on familiarity and social attraction among older children is inconsistent – sometimes attraction is positively associated with familiarity (Scholtz and Ellis, 1975) and sometimes negatively (Cantor, 1972). Recent data (Kail, 1977) based on children's preferences for peers of the same- or opposite-sex, demonstrate that the effects of familiarity interact with individual differences in both the target children and their acquaintances. Among children in Grades 1 through 6, those with strong sex-typed preferences showed increased liking for same-sex faces as a function of familiarity but decreased liking for opposite-sex faces. For less strongly sex-typed children, however, familiarity did not affect attraction.

Familiarity and friendship are not the same thing. Does the social behaviour of children with their friends differ from their behaviour with non-friends? The evidence is scattered and thin. Children receive distinctive feedback contingencies from their friends as contrasted to their parents (Cohen, 1962) and will work harder at simple operant tasks to achieve exposure to a photograph of a friend than exposure to a photograph of a neutral peer (Horowitz, 1962). But the effectiveness of social rewards is not always greater in exchanges between friends than in exchanges between non-friends. Hartup (1964) found that the performance of nursery school children on a simple task was maintained better when such rewards were dispensed by disliked individuals than when delivered by a best friend. Reverse results, however, were obtained for elementary school children who were studied using a somewhat different paradigm (Patterson and Anderson, 1964).

Social responsiveness is greater between 7- and 8-year-old friends than between strangers in interactive humour situations (Foot, Chapman and Smith, 1977; Smith et al., 1977). When children watched 'Tom and Jerry' cartoons or listened to humorous recordings, both the duration and frequency of laughing, smiling, looking and talking were greater between friends (i.e. mutual sociometric choices) than between strangers (i.e. children from different classrooms who did not know each other). In addition, response matching, a measure of behavioural concordance between the two children, was greater between friends than between non-friends (Foot, Smith and Chapman, 1977). Intimacy interactions are thus maximized by friendships among elementary school children in a manner similar to the relation between familiarity and social interaction among toddlers (Lewis et al., 1975). These studies, of course, show only that friendship enhances intimacy in pleasant situations. The relation between friendship and the intimacy of social interaction in unpleasant situations has not been explored in research with children.

Do friends communicate with each other in ways that are different from communication with non-friends? No one knows. Gottman and Parkhurst (1977) have launched an extensive study of communicative sequences in the conversations of friends ranging in age between two and nine years. Preliminary analyses show that 'collective monologues', which are common in conversations between non-friends (Garvey and Hogan, 1973) are not common between friends. Overt corrections of miscommunications are also more common in the conversations of the younger friends than in the verbal exchanges of older friends. Whether this means that young friends are more emphatic in their communications than older friends is unlikely: older friends may assume (rightly) that their friends share their frame of reference, thus believing that overt clarifications are less necessary in their conversations than in the exchanges of younger children. Additional information will be forthcoming. Meanwhile, this investigation addresses some extremely important issues – the extent to which patterns of social influence, modes of communication and attributional processes occurring between friends differ from the interaction occurring between non-friends. Additional studies of children's behaviour with their friends, as contrasted with non-friends, would clarify the processes of friendship formation, the role of social attraction as a contextual variable in social behaviour, and the significance of friendships in the development of social competence.

Conclusion

Social competence derives from children's interactions with other children. Both social skills and emotional effectance are acquired within these contexts. As Harry Stack Sullivan wrote:

All of you who have children are sure that your children love you; when you say that, you are expressing a pleasant illusion. But if you will look very closely at one of your children when he finally finds a chum – somewhere between eight-and-a-half and ten – you will discover something very different in the relationship – namely, that your child begins to develop a real sensitivity to what matters to another person. And this is not in the sense of 'what should I do to contribute to the happiness or to support the prestige and feeling of worthwhileness of my chum.' So far as I have ever been able to discover, nothing remotely like this appears before ... The developmental epoch of preadolescence is marked by the coming of the integrating tendencies which, when they are completely developed, we call love, or, to say it another way, by the manifestation of the need for interpersonal intimacy. . . .

(Sullivan, 1953, pp. 245–6).

Current theoretical and empirical work in child–child relations is diverse. Peer interactions in early childhood are understood to be antecedents of adolescent associations; the child's awareness of the social world becomes more differentiated with age; social attraction rests on complex processes; and friendships derive from unique determinants. A vast increase in research on peer relations has occurred recently – witness the number of new citations in this essay. The current social psychology of childhood is thus changeworthy as well as diverse.

Notes

1 Preparation of this manuscript was assisted by funds from Grant No. 5–P01–05027, National Institute of Child Health and Human Development (USA).
2 Used with the permission of the letter-writer as well as the recipient (Professor Shirley G. Moore).

References

Allen, V. L. (ed.) (1976) *Children as Tutors*. New York: Academic Press.
Allen, V. L. and Feldman, R. S. (1976) Studies on the role of tutor. In V. L. Allen (ed.) *Children as Tutors*. New York: Academic Press.
Asher, S. R. (1973) The Influence of Race and Sex on Children's Sociometric Choices across the School Year. Unpublished manuscript, University of Illinois.
Asher, S. R., Gottman, J. M. and Oden, S. L. (1977) Children's friendships in school settings. In E. M. Hetherington and R. D. Parke (eds.) *Contemporary Readings in Child Psychology*. New York: McGraw-Hill.
Austin, M. C. and Thompson, G. G. (1948) Children's friendships: a study of the bases on which children select and reject their best friends. *Journal of Educational Psychology 39* (2): 101–16.
Barker, R. G. and Wright, H. F. (1955) *Midwest and its Children*. New York: Harper and Row.
Barnes, K. E. (1971) Preschool play norms: a replication. *Developmental Psychology 5* (1): 99–103.
Baumrind, D. (1967) Child care practices anteceding three patterns of preschool behavior. *Genetic Psychology Monographs 75* (1): 43–88.
Baumrind, D. (1971) Current patterns of parental authority. *Developmental Psychology Monograph 4* (1): Part 2.
Becker, J. M. T. (1977) A learning analysis of the development of peer-oriented behavior in nine-month-old infants. *Developmental Psychology 13* (5): 481–491.
Bigelow, B. J. (1977) Children's friendship expectations: A cognitive-developmental study. *Child Development 48* (1): 246–53.

164 Issues in childhood social development

Bigelow, B. J. and La Gaipa, J. J. (1975) Children's written descriptions of friendship: a multidimensional analysis. *Developmental Psychology 11* (6): 857–8.

Blurton Jones, N. (1972) Categories of child–child interaction. In N. Blurton Jones (ed.) *Ethological Studies of Child Behaviour*. Cambridge: Cambridge University Press.

Bridges, K. M. B. (1933) A study of social development in early infancy. *Child Development 4* (1): 36–49.

Brittain, C. V. (1963) Adolescent choices and parent–peer cross-pressures. *American Sociological Review 28* (3): 385–91.

Bronson, W. C. (1966) Central orientations: a study of behaviour organization from childhood to adolescence. *Child Development 37* (1): 125–55.

Bronson, W. C. (1975) Developments in behavior with age mates during the second year of life. In M. Lewis and L. A. Rosenblum (eds) *Friendship and Peer Relations*. New York: Wiley.

Byrne, D. and Griffitt, W. B. (1966) A developmental investigation of the law of attraction. *Journal of Personality and Social Psychology 4* (6): 699–702.

Cabral, G., Volpe, J., Youniss, J. and Gellert, B. (1977) Resolving a Problem in Friendship and Other Relationships. Unpublished manuscript, Catholic University of America.

Cantor, G. N. (1972) Effects of familiarization on children's ratings of pictures of whites and blacks. *Child Development 43* (4): 1219–29.

Challman, R. C. (1932) Factors influencing friendships among preschool children. *Child Development 3* (2): 146–58.

Charlesworth, R. and Hartup, W. W. (1967) Positive social reinforcement in the nursery school peer group. *Child Development 38* (4): 993–1002.

Cohen, D. J. (1962) Justin and his peers: an experimental analysis of a child's social world. *Child Development 33* (3): 697–717.

Combs, M. L. and Slaby, D. A. (1977) Social skills training with children. In B. Lahey and A. Kazdin (eds) *Advances in Clinical Child Psychology, Vol. 1*. New York: Plenum Press, in press.

Cowen, E. L., Pederson, A., Babijian, H., Izzo, L. D. and Trost, M. A. (1973) Long-term follow-up of early detected vulnerable children. *Journal of Consulting and Clinical Psychology 41* (3): 438–46.

Criswell, J. H. (1939) A sociometric study of race cleavage in the classroom. *Archives of Psychology 235*: 1–82.

Davitz, J. R. (1955) Social perception and sociometric choice in children. *Journal of Abnormal and Social Psychology 50* (2): 173–6.

Dawe, H. C. (1934) Analysis of two hundred quarrels of preschool children. *Child Development 5* (1): 139–57.

Eckerman, C. O. (in press) The human infant in social interaction. In R. B. Cairns (ed.) *Social Interaction: Methods, Analysis and Illustrations*. Hillsdale, NJ: Erlbaum.

Eckerman, C. O., Whatley, J. L. and Kutz, S. L. (1975) The growth of social play with peers during the second year of life. *Developmental Psychology 11* (1): 42–9.

Edelman, M. S. and Omark, D. R. (1973) Dominance hierarchies in young children. *Social Science Information 12* (1): 103–10.

Eder, D. and Hallinan, M. T. (1977) Sex Differences in Children's Friendships. Unpublished manuscript, Stanford University.

Fagot, B. I. and Patterson, G. R. (1969) An *in vivo* analysis of reinforcing contingencies for sex-role behaviors in the preschool child. *Developmental Psychology 1* (5): 563–8.

Ferguson, N. (1965) Peers as Social Agents. Unpublished M.A. thesis. University of Minnesota.

Foot, H. C., Chapman, A. J. and Smith, J. R. (1977) Friendship and social responsiveness in boys and girls. *Journal of Personality and Social Psychology 35* (6): 401–11.

Foot, H. C., Smith, J. R. and Chapman, A. J. (1977) Individual differences in children's social responsiveness in humour situations. In A. J. Chapman and H. C. Foot (eds) *It's a Funny Thing, Humour.* Oxford: Pergamon Press.

Freud, A. and Dann, S. (1951) An experiment in group upbringing. In R. Eisler et al. (eds) *The Psychoanalytic Study of the Child, Vol. 6.* New York: International Universities Press.

Furfey, P. H. (1927) Some factors influencing the selection of boys' 'chums'. *Journal of Applied Psychology 11* (1): 47–51.

Furman, W. (1977) Friendship selections and individual peer interactions. A new approach to sociometric research. Paper presented at biennial meetings of the Society for Research in Child Development, New Orleans, La.

Furman, W., Rahe, D. F. and Hartup, W. W. (1978) Rehabilitation of low-interactive preschool children through mixed-age and same-age socialization. Unpublished manuscript, University of Minnesota.

Garvey, C. and Hogan, R. (1973) Social speech and social interaction: egocentrism revisited. *Child Development 44* (3): 562–8.

Gottman, J., Gonso, J. and Rasmussen, B. (1975) Social interaction, social competence, and friendship in children. *Child Development 45* (3): 709–18.

Gottman, J. M. and Parkhurst, J. T. (1977) Developing may not always be improving: a developmental study of children's best friendships. Paper presented at the biennial meeting of the Society for Research in Child Development, New Orleans, La.

Graziano, W., French, D., Brownell, C. A. and Hartup, W. W. (1976) Peer interaction in same- and mixed-age triads in relation to chronological age and incentive condition. *Child Development 47* (3): 707–14.

Haller, A. O. and Butterworth, C. E. (1960) Peer influences on levels of occupational and educational aspirations. *Social Forces 38* (4): 289–95.

Harlow, H. F. (1969) Age-mate or peer affectional system. In D. S. Lehrman, R. A. Hinde and E. Shaw (eds) *Advances in the Study of Behavior, Vol. 2.* New York: Academic Press.

Harris, P. J. (1977) The development and stabilization of social interaction in a clinical peer-group. Paper presented at biennial meetings of the Society for Research in Child Development, New Orleans, La.

Hartup, W. W. (1964) Friendship status and the effectiveness of peers as reinforcing agents. *Journal of Experimental Child Psychology 1* (2): 154–62.

Hartup, W. W. (1970) Peer interaction and social organization. In P. H. Mussen (ed.) *Carmichael's Manual of Child Psychology, Vol. 2.* New York: Wiley.

166   Issues in childhood social development

Hartup, W. W. (1974) Aggression in childhood: developmental perspectives. *American Psychologist 29* (5): 336–41.
Hartup, W. W. (1975) The origins of friendships. In M. Lewis and L. A. Rosenblum (eds) *Friendship and Peer Relations.* New York: Wiley.
Hartup, W. W. (1976) Peer interaction and the behavioral development of the individual child. In E. Schopler and R. J. Reichler (eds) *Psychopathology and Child Development.* New York: Plenum.
Hartup, W. W., Glazer, J. A. and Charlesworth, R. (1967) Peer reinforcement and sociometric status. *Child Development 38* (4): 1017–24.
Hartup, W. W. and Lougee, M. D. (1975) Peers as models. *School Psychology Digest 4* (1): 11–26.
Heathers, G. (1955) Emotional dependence and independence in nursery school play. *Journal of Genetic Psychology 87* (1): 37–57.
Hess, B. (1972) Friendship. In M. W. Riley, M. Johnson and A. Foner (eds) *Aging and Society, Vol. 3.* New York: Russell Sage Foundation.
Horowitz, F. D. (1962) Incentive value of social stimuli for preschool children. *Child Development 33* (1): 111–16.
Horrocks, J. E. and Thompson, G. G. (1946) A study of the friendship fluctuations of rural boys and girls. *Journal of Genetic Psychology 69* (2): 189–98.
Ipsa, J. (1977) Familiar and unfamiliar peers as 'havens of security' for Soviet nursery children. Paper presented at the biennial meeting of the Society for Research in Child Development, New Orleans, La.
Izard, C. E. (1960) Personality similarity and friendship. *Journal of Abnormal and Social Psychology 61* (1): 47–51.
Kail, R. V. (1977) Familiarity and attraction to pictures of children's faces. *Developmental Psychology 13* (3): 289–90.
Keasey, C. B. (1971) Social participation as a factor in the moral development of preadolescents. *Developmental Psychology 5* (2): 216–20.
Kinsey, A. C., Pomeroy, W. B. and Martin, C. E. (1948) *Sexual Behavior in the Human Male.* Philadelphia: W. B. Saunders.
Kobasigawa, A. (1968) Inhibitory and disinhibitory effects of models on sex-inappropriate behavior in children. *Psychologia 11* (1–2): 86–96.
Koch, H. L. (1935) The modification of unsocialness in preschool children. *Psychological Bulletin 32* (9): 700–1.
Kohn, M. and Clausen, J. (1955) Social isolation and schizophrenia. *American Sociological Review 20* (3): 265–73.
Konner, M. (1975) Relations among infants and juveniles in comparative perspective. In M. Lewis and L. A. Rosenblum (eds) *Friendship and Peer Relations.* New York: Wiley.
Ladd, G. W. and Oden, S. L. (1977) The relationship between children's ideas about helpfulness and peer acceptance. Paper presented at the biennial meetings of the Society for Research in Child Development, New Orleans, La.
Lakin, M., Lakin, M. G. and Costanzo, P. R. (1977) Group Processes in Early Childhood: a dimension of human development. Unpublished manuscript, Duke University.
Langlois, J. H., Gottfried, N. W., Barnes, B. M. and Hendricks, D. E. (1978)

The effect of peer age on the social behavior of preschool children. *Journal of Genetic Psychology 132* (1): 11–20.

Lee, L. C. (1973) Social encounters of infants: the beginnings of popularity. Paper presented at the biennial meetings of the International Society for the Study of Behavioral Development, Ann Arbor, Michigan.

Lewis, M. and Rosenblum, L. A. (eds) (1975) *Friendship and Peer Relations*. New York: Wiley.

Lewis, M., Young, G., Brooks, J. and Michalson, L. (1975) The beginning of friendship. In M. Lewis and L. A. Rosenblum (eds) *Friendship and Peer Relations*. New York: Wiley.

Lieberman, A. F. (1976) The Social Competence of Preschool Children: its relation to quality of attachment and to amount of exposure to peers in different preschool settings. Unpublished doctoral dissertation, The Johns Hopkins University.

Livesley, W. J. and Bromley, D. B. (1973) *Person Perception in Childhood and Adolescence*. London: Wiley.

Lougee, M. D. (1978) Children's Imitation of Younger and Older Peers. Unpublished doctoral dissertation, University of Minnesota.

Lougee, M. D., Grueneich, R. and Hartup, W. W. (1977) Social interaction in same- and mixed-age dyads of preschool children. *Child Development*, in press.

Mannarino, A. P. (1976) Friendship patterns and altruistic behavior in preadolescent males. *Developmental Psychology 12* (6): 555–6.

Marshall, H. R. and McCandless, B. R. (1957a) Relationships between dependence on adults and social acceptance by peers. *Child Development 28* (4): 413–19.

Marshall, H. R. and McCandless, B. R. (1957b) A study of prediction of social behavior of preschool children. *Child Development 28* (2): 149–59.

Maudry, M. and Nekula, M. (1939) Social relations between children of the same age during the first two years of life. *Journal of Genetic Psychology 54* (1): 193–215.

McCandless, B. R. and Marshall, H. R. (1957) A picture sociometric technique for preschool children and its relation to teacher judgements of friendship. *Child Development 28* (2): 139–48.

McGrew, W. C. (1972) *An Ethological Study of Children's Behavior*. New York: Academic Press.

Merei, F. (1949) Group leadership and institutionalization. *Human Relations 2* (1): 23–39.

Money, J. and Ehrhardt, A. A. (1972) *Man and Woman, Boy and Girl*. Baltimore, Maryland: The Johns Hopkins University Press.

Moore, S. G. (1967) Correlates of peer acceptance in nursery school children. In W. W. Hartup and N. L. Smothergill (eds.) *The Young Child, Vol. 1*. Washington: National Association for the Education of Young Children.

Moreno, J. L. (1934) *Who Shall Survive?* Washington: Nervous and Mental Disease Publishing Company.

Mueller, E. and Lucas, T. (1975) A developmental analysis of peer interaction among toddlers. In M. Lewis and L. A. Rosenblum (eds) *Friendship and Peer Relations*. New York: Wiley.

Parten, M. B. (1932) Social participation among preschool children. *Journal of Abnormal and Social Psychology* 27 (3) : 243–69.

Patterson, G. R. and Anderson, D. (1964) Peers as social reinforcers. *Child Development* 35 (3) : 951–60.

Patterson, G. R., Littman, R. A. and Bricker, W. (1967) Assertive behavior in children: a step toward a theory of aggression. *Monographs of the Society for Research in Child Development* 32 (Whole No. 113).

Peevers, B. H. and Secord, P. F. (1973) Developmental changes in attribution of descriptive concepts to persons. *Journal of Personality and Social Psychology* 27 (1) : 120–8.

Peifer, M. R. (1971) The Effects of Varying Age-grade Status of Models on the Imitative Behavior of Six-year-old Boys. Unpublished doctoral dissertation, University of Delaware.

Piaget, J. (1932) *The Moral Judgment of the Child.* Glencoe, Ill.: The Free Press.

Roff, M. (1961) Childhood social interactions and young adult bad conduct. *Journal of Abnormal and Social Psychology* 63 (2) : 333–7.

Roff, M. (1963) Childhood social interaction and young adult psychosis. *Journal of Clinical Psychology* 19 (2) : 152–7.

Roff, M., Sells S. B. and Golden, M. M. (1972) *Social Adjustment and Personality Development in Children.* Minneapolis: University of Minnesota Press.

Rubin, K. H., Maioni, T. L. and Hornung, M. (1976) Free play behaviors in middle- and lower-class preschoolers: Parten and Piaget revisited. *Child Development* 47 (2) : 414–19.

Rubin, Z. (1973) *Liking and Loving: An Invitation to Social Psychology.* New York: Holt, Rinehart and Winston.

Rule, B. G. and Duker, P. (1973) Effects of intentions and consequences on children's evaluations of aggressors. *Journal of Personality and Social Psychology* 27 (2) : 184–9.

Scholtz, G. J. L. and Ellis, M. J. (1975) Repeated exposure to objects and peers in a play setting. *Journal of Experimental Child Psychology* 19 (3) : 448–55.

Selman, R. L. (1976) Toward a structural analysis of developing interpersonal relations concepts: research with normal and disturbed preadolescent boys. In A. D. Pick (ed.) *Minnesota Symposia on Child Psychology, Vol. 10.* Minneapolis, University of Minnesota Press.

Selman, R. L. and Jaquette, D. (1977) Stability and oscillation in interpersonal awareness: a clinical-developmental analysis. In C. B. Keasey (ed.) *The Nebraska Symposium on Motivation, Vol. 25.* Lincoln, Neb.: University of Nebraska Press, in press.

Shatz, M. and Gelman, R. (1973) The development of communication skills: modification in the speech of young children as a function of listener. *Monographs of the Society for Research in Child Development* 38 (Whole No. 152).

Sherif, M., Harvey, O. J., White, B. J., Hood, W. R. and Sherif, C. W. (1961) *Intergroup Conflict and Cooperation: The Robbers Cave Experiment.* Norman, Okla.: University of Oklahoma.

Shure, M. B. (1963) Psychological ecology of a nursery school. *Child Development* 34 (4) : 979–92.

Smith, A. J. (1960) A developmental study of group processes. *Journal of Genetic Psychology* 97 (1) : 29–39.

Smith, H. W. (1973) Some developmental interpersonal dynamics through childhood. *American Sociological Review 38* (5): 543–52.

Smith, J. R., Foot, H. C. and Chapman, A. J. (1977) Nonverbal communication among friends and strangers sharing humour. In A. J. Chapman and H. C. Foot (eds) *It's a Funny Thing, Humour.* Oxford: Pergamon Press.

Smith, P. K. and Connolly, K. (1972) Patterns of play and social interaction in pre-school children. In N. Blurton Jones (ed.) *Ethological Studies of Child Behaviour.* Cambridge: Cambridge University Press.

Strayer, F. F. (1977) Peer attachment and affiliative subgroupings. Paper presented at biennial meetings of the Society for Research in Child Development, New Orleans, La.

Strayer, F. F. and Strayer, J. (1976) An ethological analysis of social agonism and dominance relations among preschool children. *Child Development 47* (4): 980–9.

Sullivan, H. S. (1953) *The Interpersonal Theory of Psychiatry.* New York: W. W. Norton.

Suomi, S. J. and Harlow, H. F. (1972) Social rehabilitation of isolate-reared monkeys. *Developmental Psychology 6* (3): 487–96.

Supnick, J. (1964) Unpublished senior honors thesis, Clark University (cited by Livesley, W. J. and Bromley, D. B. 1973).

Thelen, M. H. and Kirkland, K. D. (1976) On status and being imitated: effects on reciprocal imitation and attraction. *Journal of Personality and Social Psychology 33* (6): 691–7.

Thompson, G. G. and Horrocks, J. E. (1947) A study of the friendship fluctuations of urban boys and girls. *Journal of Genetic Psychology 70* (1): 53–63.

Thorpe, J. G. (1955) A study of some factors in friendship formation. *Sociometry 18* (3): 207–14.

Vandell, D. L. (1977) The Development and Characteristics of Early Peer Social Interaction. Unpublished manuscript, University of Texas at Dallas.

Vandell, D. L. and Mueller, E. C. (1977) The effects of group size on toddlers' social interactions with peers. Paper presented at biennial meetings of the Society for Research in Child Development, New Orleans, La.

Vincze, M. (1971) The social contacts of infants and young children reared together. *Early Child Development and Care 1* (1): 99–109.

Wahler, R. G. (1967) Child–child interactions in five field settings: some experimental analyses. *Journal of Experimental Child Psychology 5* (2): 278–93.

Waldrop, M. F. and Halverson, C. F. (1975) Intensive and extensive peer behavior: longitudinal and cross-sectional analyses. *Child Development 46* (1): 19–26.

Walters, J., Pearce, D. and Dahms, L. (1957) Affectional and aggressive behavior of preschool children. *Child Development 28* (1): 15–26.

Wareing, S. (1977) Giving, cooperating and helping: the beginnings of reciprocal altruism. Paper presented at biennial meetings of the Society for Research in Child Development, New Orleans, La.

Wenger, M. and Whiting, B. B. (1977) Child nurses in a changing society: the social interaction of children with their two year old younger siblings. In B. B. Whiting, J. M. W. Whiting and J. Herzog (eds) *Family Life in Ngecha: a Study of Rapid Social Change in a Kenya Community*, in preparation.

Whiting, B. B. and Whiting, J. W. M. (1975) *Children of Six Cultures: A Psychocultural Analysis.* Cambridge, Mass.: Harvard University Press.

Winder, C. L. and Rau, L. (1962) Parental attitudes associated with social deviance in preadolescent boys. *Journal of Abnormal and Social Psychology 64*: 418–24.

6 Sex-role differentiation in social development

Corinne Hutt

Introduction

In the process of becoming a boy or girl, man or woman, an individual is constrained in certain ways, primed in others, and biased to accept, reject or modify the manifold impresses of society. The biases, predispositions and proclivities of an individual influence his interactions with his social environment, both as actor and re-actor; the individual is also affected by the demands and pressures of the society and culture in which he develops. But this chain of interacting events has a natural beginning, namely at conception. During foetal development, male and female organisms are differentially affected and by the time sexual differentiation is complete males and females are organized and biased in distinctive modes. As Whalen (1968) argues: 'Experience always "works upon" a biological substrate and modifies that substrate; the biological substrate always sets the limits for the effects of experience.'

In this chapter several processes relevant to the differentiation of sex-roles are considered: first, the biological origins of sex differentiation; next the characteristic aptitudes and propensities of girls and boys – how these may arise and what implications they have for later development; finally, the manner in which boys and girls construe masculinity and feminity, and in so doing how they develop their gender identities and fashion their sex-roles. Here, gender identity is taken to mean the internalization of and identification with a male or female gender; it relates to the feeling an individual has of being a girl or boy, woman or man. Sex-role, on the other hand, refers to the manner in which the feminity or masculinity is portrayed and to the behaviours which are considered to be appropriate to one sex or other.

In most cases, sex-role and gender identity are congruent with each other, a girl differentiating a female sex-role while having a feminine gender identity. But there are cases in which the two progressions are in discord: transvestites, for instance, have gender identities which accord with their biological sex but prefer to adopt the sex-role of the opposite sex, as when men dress in 'drag' and display the mannerisms characteristic of women. Transsexuals, on the other hand, have a gender identity contrary to their biological sex, and have difficulty playing out the biologically appropriate sex-role; often these individuals seek to have the physical denotations of their sex changed by surgical and hormonal means.

In general, though, an individual adopts a sex-role compatible with his or her gender identity, the particular attributes of the sex-role being dependent upon the social environment in which he or she grows up.

The biology of sex differentiation

In mammals the active process of sexual differentiation is masculine, that is, female differentiation occurs only when and if male differentiation fails to take place. Furthermore, there are several sets of characteristics, occurring in a regular sequence, which serve to distinguish one sex from the other (See Figure 6.1).

First, sex is determined by the constituent chromosomes of the sex cells: XX for a female and XY for a male. The sex chromosomes are referred to as the genetic sex. The presence of the Y chromosome induces the medulla of the embryonic bipotential gonad to differentiate into a testis. In the absence of a Y chromosome the cortex of the embryonic gonad will differentiate into an ovary. Ovaries and testes therefore constitute the gonadal sex of individuals.

Once formed, the testes secrete the androgenic hormone which organizes the differentiation of the male reproductive tract from the primordial wolfian ducts. It is thought that the testes also secrete a hormone which inhibits growth of the mullerian ducts and causes their involution (Federman, 1967). In the absence of these testicular hormones, the mullerian ducts develop and differentiate into the female genital tract. After the eighth week of embryonic life the external genitalia differentiate, in similar manner, according to a male or female pattern. Thus, according to the gonadal hormones secreted, we may talk of the hormonal sex of an individual. Finally, when vascular transportation is adequate, the testicular hormone acts upon the brain, in particular the hypothalamus, to organize it according to a male pattern, i.e. to produce the gonadotrophic hormones at and after puberty – the male hypothalamus doing this in an acyclic manner while the female hypothalamus conforms to a monthly cycle. Gonadal hormones thus have two functions – an organizational or inductive one in foetal life, and an activational one at puberty.

At every stage of sexual differentiation, then, nature has provided that, if male differentiation does not occur, female differentiation will inevitably follow. These stages are illustrated in Figure 6.1. In fact, female differentiation of the reproductive tract and the external genitalia are largely independent of the presence of the ovaries; it is the male testicular substance which is the active organizer of 'maleness' (Money and Ehrhardt, 1972). We may therefore even speak of genital sex with reference to the external genitalia and brain sex according to whether there is a cyclic or acyclic release of gonadotrophic hormones.

Anomalies in sex differentiation

Frequently, errors and mistakes may be more informative and instructive than correct responses and this is particularly true of the process of sexual differentiation. Here, nature's mistakes concern one or other of the stages of sexual differentiation so that ultimately there is incongruity between two or more aspects of the individual's sex. There are many such clinically recognized syndromes (Federman, 1967; Hutt, 1972a; Money and Ehrhardt, 1972) but only three will be briefly discussed here.

In *Turner's syndrome* one sex chromosome is missing so that the karyotype is XO. The gonads are only primitive streaks, and are not differentiated into ovaries. Thus there is no gonadal hormone. Nevertheless, the individual differentiates as a female and when born has unmistakably female genitalia. There is no difficulty about sex assignment, and although there may be associated problems like mental subnormality, psychosexual immaturity and amenorrhea, individuals with Turner's syndrome differentiate an unequivocal feminine gender

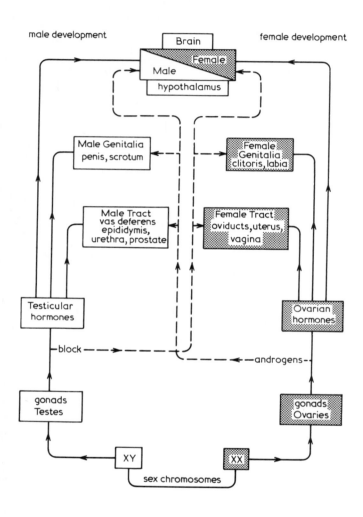

Fig. 6.1   Diagrammatic sketch of the process of sexual differentiation in male and female. The sequence of events is read from bottom to top. By and large, presence or absence of testicular hormones in a genetic female and male, pushes differentiation in the opposite direction (from Hutt 1972a)

and adopt female sex-roles (Money and Ehrhardt, 1968; Ehrhardt et al., 1970; Money and Ehrhardt, 1972). At puberty, these girls often need oestrogen therapy to help them develop secondary sex characteristics.

In the cases of the *adrenogenital syndrome* (AGS) the foetus is exposed to a surfeit of androgenic hormones due to a genetic defect of the functioning of the adrenal glands. While in the male foetus such a surfeit of androgen may not result in undue difficulties, there are problems with female foetuses due to masculinization, particularly of the external genitalia. The degree of masculinization of course depends on the amount of androgen to which the foetus is exposed, and if it is great it is probable that a genetic female with female reproductive tract and gonads may nevertheless be assigned a boy. Such an individual would continue to be under the virilizing influence of the excess androgen being produced. AGS females who were also postnatally androgenized in this manner were found to be typically 'tomboyish', interested in physical and athletic pursuits but uninterested in having or caring for children (Ehrhardt et al., 1968; Money and Ehrhardt, 1972). Many of them also reported bisexual imagery and experience, though none of them professed to be dissatisfied with her assigned sex. Many of these foetally androgenized females, however, were prevented from further postnatal masculinization by cortisone therapy. Even so, these girls (who were only foetally androgenized) in later childhood were more tomboyish than controls, expended greater physical energy in their pastimes and showed greater preference for playing with boys (Money and Ehrhardt, 1972; Ehrhardt and Baker, 1974). These girls also showed a preference for practical, functional clothes and hardly ever played with dolls. The older girls showed a lack of interest in infants, in caretaking or other nurturant activity, and most of them were intent on pursuing a career. 20 per cent of these girls would have preferred to be boys, 33 per cent were ambivalent and only 47 per cent were content with their female role, but none requested a sex reassignment (Money and Ehrhardt, 1972).

More recently, Money and Dalery (1976) have given an informative account of seven AGS females, three of whom were reared as boys and four as girls. There was apparently no ambiguity about the sex of the three patients reared as boys and their true genetic sex was only discovered later, when surgical correction and hormonal therapy were carried out. These three were unexceptional as boys, had unambiguous masculine gender identities and unreservedly adopted male sex-roles.

On the other hand 'the four girls did not follow exactly the stereotypic pattern. They played with dolls only rarely. They preferred traditional boys' toys such as cars, trucks, guns and blocks. They liked to ride bikes or motorbikes' (p. 365).

All seven patients showed a conspicuous lack of interest in infant caretaking, neither the boys nor the girls readily helped their mothers with the housework. In common with other AGS females, the girls in this sample expended a great deal of energy in tomboyish behaviours, and they showed a preference for playing with boys rather than with girls and were more competitive with boys.

The *testicular feminizing syndrome* occurs in genetic males whose testes secrete the normal quantities of androgen, but due to a biochemical defect the target organs are insensitive to androgen and the testes generally are undescended. The appearance of these individuals at birth is female even though the vagina may be ill-formed. Individuals with this syndrome nevertheless differentiate as females, have feminine bodies and at puberty develop female secondary characteristics. These phenotypic females have characteristically feminine interests and attitudes and most (90 per cent) are fully content with their feminine role (Money and Ehrhardt, 1972).

These anomalous syndromes of sexual differentiation clearly implicate the androgenic hormones as the critical factor in the development of maleness or femaleness, and subsequently of masculinity and feminity. As Money and Ehrhardt (1972) succinctly put it:

> In the absence of androgen, the genetic female differentiates genitally as a female. In the absence of oestrogen, the genetic female differentiates as a female. In the absence of gonads and their hormones in entirety, the foetus develops as a female, regardless of genetic sex.
>
> (p. 105)

In other words, without the influence of the testicular hormone, sex and gender differentiation appear to accord to a female pattern. These gender anomalies reveal the significance of early exposure to androgen in affecting not simply sexual differentiation, but also subsequent patterns of behaviour and interests. In other words, exposure to androgens during the sensitive period confers a masculine 'flavour' upon behaviour, whilst in the absence of androgen behaviour is essentially feminine in character. This is the conclusion at which several authors have arrived and which has recently been reiterated by Reinisch (1974).

The psychology of sex-role differentiation

Many theories of sex-role differentiation have been advanced, but only those which have implications for the pyschological processes of socialization generally will be discussed here. In this section, a brief overview will be given of theories representing social learning, cognitive-developmental, and psycho-sexual differentiation viewpoints.

Social learning theory

Kagan (1964) distinguishes between a sex-role standard and sex-role identity. The former is a 'learned association between selected attributes, behaviours and attitudes, on the one hand, and the concepts of male and female on the other' (p. 138). Thus, sex-role standard is defined both by overt attributes like physique and behaviour and by covert attributes like feelings, motivation, etc. Kagan assumes this standard to be acquired by three processes: (i) identification with models; (ii) expectation of affection and acceptance on possession of the attributes; (iii) expectation that possession of such attributes will prevent social rejection. Once acquired, this standard acts as a censor against which subsequent behaviours and attitudes are evaluated.

Sex-role identity on the other hand is 'the degree to which an individual regards himself as masculine or feminine' (Kagan, 1964, p. 144). This is what we have previously termed gender identity, and the term which will continue to be used. Central to the acquisition of such an identity is the process of identification with a model. 'An identification is a belief that some of the attributes of a model . . . belong to the self' (Kagan, 1964, p. 146). Kagan argues that for strong identification three conditions must be met: (i) the model must be perceived as nurturant; (ii) the model must be perceived as being in command of desired goals and task competence in desired areas; (iii) at the outset, the child must perceive objective bases of similarity in attributes between the model and him or herself. Identification with a father who is not very strongly sex-typed weakens the gender identity of a boy because of the negative reinforcement he receives from his peers and retards the acquisition of further sex-typed responses. The boy who is identified with a strongly sex-typed father, on the other hand, is facilitated in acquiring further sex-typed behaviours. It is far from clear, however, why the model's strength of sex-typing should principally affect the child's gender identity as opposed to his sex-role behaviours. Poor identification with the same-sex parent may present difficulties for acquiring sex-typed behaviours though gender identity too may be affected. Kagan's main emphasis, however, is on the motive to match behaviour to a standard, the desire to comply with social expectations of sex-roles. Nevertheless, much of the argument concerning the acquisition of gender identity and sex-role behaviours seems *ad hoc* – there are no prescriptive rules or principles according to which one or other is achieved nor is their relationship and mutual influence explicated.

Mischel (1966) on the other hand regards the development of sex-typed behaviours to be the results of social learning. Sex-typed behaviours are defined as those that 'typically elicit different rewards for one sex than for the other' (p. 56). Sex-typing, according to Mischel is the process whereby the individual acquires sex-typed behaviours – by discriminating them initially, by generalizing from them, and by performing and practising them. Mischel also notes that it was pointed out by Bandura and Walters (1963) that what is termed 'imitation' in experimental and social psychology is termed 'identification' in personality and psychodynamic theories, both these constructs being forms of observational learning. Mischel's view is simply that children's behaviours are determined, not by their gender roles but by their social-learning histories.

Such learning of course is considerably facilitated by the sex-role stereotypes which prevail in the society. 'Stereotypes involve expectations about the dispositions and typical behaviours supposedly displayed by members of a category' (Mischel, 1970, p. 6). As Mischel goes on to argue, broad categories, classes and stereotypes are ways of organizing or 'chunking' the deluge of information we are called upon to process. This is an efficient and economical way of enabling the limited capacity of our memories to deal with the variety of input presented to them. By their very nature, therefore, stereotypes are generalized and oversimplified; they refer to central tendencies and disregard the overlap. Mischel argues that theories which hypothesize the existence of such broadly and generally formulated attribute-stereotypes are difficult to disconfirm. While accepting these limitations of stereotypes, it may be pointed out that the central premise of social-learning theory, which assigns, *post hoc*, the acquisition of sex-typical behaviours to processes such as modelling and imitation, is difficult to disconfirm.

The importance of distinguishing between the acquisition of sex-typed behaviours and the performance of these is also emphasized by Mischel (1970). Many more sex-typed behaviours are acquired than are necessarily performed: while reinforcement may be essential for selection of responses in performance, the acquisition of such responses appears only to be facilitated by it. But whether reinforcement, in the conventional sense, is crucial even for performance is open to doubt: in looking at the sex-typing in the play interests of four-year-olds, Fling and Manosevitz (1972) found little correlation between measures of parental influence and their children's sex-typing scores. Moreover, according to social-learning theory, individuals become less dependent on external sources of reinforcement while relying more on self-monitoring and self-evaluation in relation to sex-role standards, applauding or reproving their own behaviour accordingly. Although the increasing self-regulation of behaviour is indisputable, it seems unlikely that sex-typical behaviours are quite so self-consciously performed.

In many ways the social-learning theorists' use of the construct of identification makes it little different from the processes of imitation, modelling or observation learning, and although reinforcement itself is given less emphasis, it does nevertheless play a part, particularly in cross-sex influence. Although social-learning theories regard the acquisition of sex-typed behaviours as a significant part of socialization and personality development, they do not see that different principles of learning or influence are necessary to account for other processes of socialization (Mischel, 1970). It could be argued, however, that the acquisition of sex-typed behaviours concerns special processes, insofar as there is an unambiguous dichotomy in the models and the behaviours that are attributed to sex stereotypes. Models are men or women, observers are boys or girls, behaviour is masculine or feminine, male or female, influences are from same-sex models or cross-sex models. Thus, it is not unreasonable to suppose that behaviours, attitudes and interests that pertain to the sex of the individual are rather differently acquired to those that concern, say, the development of morals.

Cognitive-developmental theory
The cognitive theory of sex-role differentiation gives a central role to the child's recognition of the biological or physical features which characterize his/her sex (Kohlberg, 1966). The child organizes its perceptions, its learning and its expectations around this physical conception of himself as a boy or herself as a girl:

... patterning of sex-role attitudes is essentially cognitive in that it is rooted in the child's concepts of physical things – the bodies of himself and of others – concepts which he relates in turn to a social order that makes functional use of sex categories in quite culturally universal ways.

(Kohlberg, 1966, p. 82)

The emphasis is on the child's active organization and structuring of his experiences around his sexual self-categorization. This cognitive process changes with age as do other cognitive processes. Cognitive theorists see this self-categorization or gender identity as the fundamental organizer of sex-role differentiation: it is relatively irreversible and immune to conventional reinforcements and influences. The essential process is well summed up by Kohlberg: 'I am a boy, therefore I want to do boy things, therefore the opportunity to do boy things (and to gain approval for doing them) is rewarding' (p. 89).

In tracing the genesis of this gender identity, Kohlberg demonstrates that the primitive gender constructs of the young child are very different from the complex ones of the adult. Nevertheless, the fulcrum for these constructs, at whatever developmental stage, is the self-categorization of male or female, a categorization which can be accurately made by the age of three years.

In reviewing theories of the development of sex-role identity, Emmerich (1973) makes a valuable distinction between competence in gender identification and performance of sex-role behaviours. Extending the model proposed by Flavell and Wohlwill (1969) (in which these authors distinguish between the structures, schema or mental operations embodied in the task, and the actual mechanisms required for processing the input and output) Emmerich uses this distinction to demonstrate the presence or absence of gender constancy as reflected in the experiments (employing Piagetian paradigms) which were used by Kohlberg in 1966; de Vries in 1969; and Shipman et al. in 1971. Emmerich concludes that 3½ to 5-year-old children have little gender constancy. Since these experiments are often quoted it may be instructive to consider what was required of children in this test. The children were presented with a picture of a child of one sex or the other, appropriately labelled; the examiner then made successive changes either visually or verbally – changes which were characteristic of the opposite sex. If the child maintained the original sex identification of the stimulus, despite the transformations, he revealed constancy of gender identity – if he changed his judgement early, he was assumed to lack such constancy. Although systematic age-changes have been demonstrated – accompanying other developmental cognitive changes – it might be argued that this conclusion was fallacious: that the child who changed his judgements early had a stronger (if more rigid) gender identity, thereby making him less tolerant of the transformations. The fact that a categorical label was affixed to the stimulus at the outset seems irrelevant since some of the transformations would contravene the 'rules' of that appellation. Moreover, the parallel with the conservation experiments is spurious since in these experiments tangible materials are presented to the child, whilst in the gender experiments it is pictorial representations that are produced. It seems that tolerance of ambiguity might reveal more about the personality traits of the individual than of the stability of gender identity.

Psycho-sexual differentiation
Contrasting with the psychological theories discussed hitherto is one which focuses primarily on the clinical anomalies described in the previous section.

The original formulations of psychosexual neutrality at birth put forward by Money et al. (1955a, b; 1957) regarded the differentiation of gender identity and sex-role to be the result of a process akin to imprinting: during the first two or three years of its life, the child acknowledges, presumably, its sex of assignment and, through a process of identification and attachment to the like-sex parent, acquires sex-typical behaviours, attitudes and interests in accordance with his/her gender identity. Such a formulation would suggest that such processes would be considerably weaker in the sons of absent fathers, who would therefore differentiate a weaker gender identity and sex-role than their female siblings. And indeed there is evidence that boys who have a strong identification with their mothers show less strongly masculine behaviours (Biller, 1971), as well as experiencing considerable gender confusion (Stoller, 1968; Green, 1969).

More recently, however, Money has conceded that differentiation of gender identity is not exclusively a matter of sex-of-assignment and postnatal environmental influences: 'it is premature to attribute all aspects of gender-identity to the post-natal period of gender-identity differentiation' (Money and Ehrhardt, 1972, p. 18).

Nevertheless, the empiricist emphasis is very evident in the formulations of these authors. They see the process of gender differentiation as analogous to that of bilingual differentiation in a child who possesses two native languages. Just as the child in a bilingual environment is exposed to different vocabularies, different syntaxes, idioms etc., so children are also exposed to two sets of behaviour – male and female: one set is imitated or identified with, and the other is reciprocated in a complementary manner. The two gender schemas are respectively coded as positive and negative – the former 'cleared' for daily use, the latter a 'template of what not to do and say, and also of what to expect from members of the other sex' (p. 165).

This somewhat contrived analogy is misleading in many respects. First, the bilingual child does not usually ascribe positive and negative valencies to the two languages. Second, both languages are learned in essentially the same manner whereas 'positive' and 'negative' gender behaviours must necessarily be learned in contrasting ways – if identification and imitation of same-sex behaviours results in the acquisition of the positive set, what process enables learning of the proscribed set? Third, whereas languages to a large extent are distinct in their structure, their constituents, and their organization, there are no such distinctions in gender behaviours since there are no gender-exclusive behaviours (except for those to do with reproduction); differences in sex-typical patterns of behaviour result almost entirely from the frequency with which a particular behaviour is performed. For example, boys can cry and girls can hit, but they learn that each behaviour is more or less sanctioned for their sex. Finally, this analogy does not explain how children come to discriminate and imitate the behaviour of same-sex adults and repudiate that of opposite-sex adults.

In support of their case, that sex-assignment by the age of two years is the critical factor in the development of stable gender identity, Money and Ehrhardt describe the case-histories of three matched pairs of hermaphrodites. The members of each pair had the same diagnosis but were discordant for gender identity. These cases are indeed persuasive of the obligatory force of sex assignment upon gender identification. But Stoller (1967) provides as many cases of individuals who were dissatisfied with their gender, even though this was concordant with their biological sex. Many of these cases, however, were hypogonadal males who wished to be reassigned to the female sex. Stoller sees these imperative urges to adopt the gender of the opposite sex as illustrative of a 'biological force'. Certainly, the decision to adopt the opposite gender against social opposition and stigma does require a considerably strong motivation and one which might quite justifiably be termed a 'force'. The salutary point about Stoller's cases, is that they argue against psychosexual neutrality at birth just as strongly as Money's cases argue for it.

If Stoller's cases reveal a biological force, cases of transsexuals demonstrate the significance of early experience in establishing gender identity. Many male transsexuals have a dominant female parent and a physically absent or emotionally indifferent father, and they tend to undergo 'role transformation from an extremely ambivalent, confused gender role during childhood and primary school years, to one involving homosexuality in post adolescence to that of drag queen (experimental cross-dressing) to that of self-declared, permanently cross-dressed transsexual' (Levine et al., 1975, p. 175).

Of these several theories only the cognitive-developmental takes cognizance of the individual's biological sex; most emphasis is generally given to the social, experiential influences that operate during development. Yet the sex of the individual is an integral part of his or her self-construct; it also predisposes the individual to act in certain ways rather than others, thereby eliciting certain responses from its social environment rather than others. It is the constraints which the individual's sex places upon its experience that deserve more consideration than these theories allow. This aspect will be elaborated further in the final section.

Boys and girls: nature and nurture

As we have seen in an earlier section the active process of sexual differentiation is masculine. Inherent in this process are three characteristics which have pervasive effects upon the male's development into adulthood. These characteristics are (1) vulnerability; (2) phenotypic variety; (3) retarded development. Thus, males, in general, are more susceptible to a variety of stressful and noxious agents and tend to be overrepresented in many categories of physical and psychological illness or debility. In addition, the greater expression of phenotypic variety in males means that in many measurable attributes they will be represented at the extremes more frequently than females. Thus, with respect to stature, there will be more male giants, but also more male dwarfs; with respect to intelligence, more male geniuses as well as more male defectives. This tendency to express a wider range of 'scores' may be seen sometimes even in highly selected groups (Heim, 1970, Hutt, 1974). Third, because of the male's maturational retardation, a number of sex differences appear in early development but may disappear later on. For example, girls reach their milestones ahead of boys – they sit, walk and talk earlier than boys and for a while may have greater proficiency in these skills, though the boys would have caught up by the age of five years. A theory which implicates the Y-chromosome in extracting more information from the genetic blueprint has been proposed by Ounsted and Taylor (1972). This theory, briefly, states that the Y-chromosome, though carrying no genetic information itself, nevertheless elicits more information from the genome; this increased genetic 'readout' (manifest as greater phenotypic variety) is made possible by the slower development of the male. If more genetic information is expressed in the male, it follows that more disadvantageous as well as more beneficial traits will be manifest – hence the predominance of males at the extremes of a distribution.

From birth, males are better equipped physiologically for a physically active life (see Hutt, 1972b). Boys have a higher basal metabolic rate, a greater vital capacity, greater muscle development, a greater capacity for carrying oxygen in the blood (as haemoglobin levels increase) and are more efficient at neutralizing the by-products of exercise and work. Many of these features are a result of the facilitatory action of the male hormone.

It comes as little surprise then to find that the activity levels of boys at birth and during childhood are greater than in girls (Korner, 1969; Goggin, 1975). Neither is it surprising that pre-school boys engage in physical activities more often than girls (Clark et al., 1969; Brindley et al., 1973) and that the preferred leisure activity of young boys is some sort of physical pursuit (Hutt, 1974; 1978a). The fact that even indoors, boys engage in physical leisure activity suggests that, even in unfavourable conditions, parents permit such activity in boys (Hutt, 1978a). Thus, the greater tolerance of adults towards boys' physical and athletic activities, towards their restlessness, towards related characteristics like untidiness and messiness even, may reflect an acknowledgement of inherent biological characteristics. This sequence of interaction serves as a particularly apposite example of the dependency of nature and nurture.

Similarly, parents of first-born infants rated girls as softer, more fine-featured and smaller than boys. Fathers in particular described their sons as firmer, stronger and more alert than did the mothers (Rubin et al., 1974). In these perceptions are reflected both generalizations about actual differences as well as parental expectations, stemming perhaps from sex stereotypes. The Rubin et al. study also revealed that mothers rated sons cuddlier than daughters and fathers rated daughters cuddlier than sons. It may be for this reason of course that for the first few months of life boys receive more proximal behaviour (i.e. touching, holding, rocking, kissing) from their mothers than do girls (Lewis, 1972). Moss (1967) too showed that in the first few weeks of life boys tended to be picked up more and cuddled, but that this in part was due to the fact that they tended to be more irritable. By six months of age, however, girls receive more proximal behaviour than boys and thereafter girls have more physical, vocal and visual contact with their mothers (Goldberg and Lewis, 1969; Messer and Lewis, 1972). In an exploratory or stressful situation girls show more dependency upon the mother and in turn mothers are more protective toward their daughters and show less haste in encouraging independence or autonomy in them than they do in their sons (Baumrind and Black, 1967; Hoffman, 1972). Thus we see that in the socializing process, components of nature and nurture are inextricably intertwined.

Similar admixtures may be seen in other developmental processes. For instance, females are superior in verbal skills; this may be because mothers more often talk to and imitate the babbles of their infant daughters than those of their sons (Moss, 1967). This maternal behaviour, however, may be due to the fact that female infants, having lower auditory thresholds and better auditory discrimination (see McGuinness, 1975a) are more responsive to their mother's speech. Moreover, this auditory sensitivity may play a significant part in developing the linguistic modality since even at a few months of age vocalizations are a good measure of attention in girls (Kagan, 1969) and are good predictors of subsequent intellectual development. Finally, girls not only have a higher Speech Quotient at eighteen months but this quotient is also a good predictor of the course of language development: 'linguistic development runs a steadier course from an earlier age in female infancy' (Moore, 1967). This proficiency in linguistic skills in turn is undoubtedly aided by the earlier and more complete lateralization of such functions in the left hemispheres of girls (see Hutt, 1978b).

Another example from social behaviour may be considered: even at pre-school age, boys tend to play in groups, in 'packs' or on their own, whereas girls form dyads or trios (Brindley et al., 1973; Hutt, 1972). Such proclivities, moreover, remain consistent throughout life, culminating in the rituals of the Freemasons, Rotarians and Rugger Clubs on the one hand, or the more selective and intimate coffee tête-à-têtes on the other. Both male-bonding and solitariness have their evolutionary origins in forms of hunting (see Tiger, 1969; Jonas and Jonas, 1975). It is perhaps as a result of these propensities then that we find that boys are more susceptible than girls to pressure from their peers (Hollander and Marcia, 1970).

A recent study of sex differences in parent–infant interaction (Weinraub and Frankel, 1978) showed that by eighteen months of age the impact of the same-sex parent was greater on infants than that of the opposite-sex parent. Parents talked to, sat on the floor with, and tended to play with the same-sexed rather than opposite-sexed infants; infants also were more distressed in the absence of same-sexed parents. The origins of this same-sex affinity are yet to be determined, but from eighteen months on it will affect many socializing and affective processes. Whereas such dependency is subsequently discouraged in boys, it is permitted in girls (Kagan and Moss, 1962; Sears et al., 1965). These adult attitudes may be influenced by the fact that caretaking in childhood is mainly done by the mother who feels more affinity with her daughter, and these attitudes in turn may enhance the affiliative needs (for praise, for support) and dependency in girls while encouraging autonomy in boys. Consequently, in stressful situations girls, more often than boys, withdraw or seek help from others (Crandall and Rabson, 1960), lack confidence and underestimate their abilities (Crandall et al., 1962; Hamm and Hoving, 1969). With their greater confidence, independence and physical activity boys explore their environment, thereby increasing their confidence (Hoffman, 1972) while girls tend to be more frequently inhibited and fearful in an exploratory situation (Hutt, 1970; Hutt and Bhavnani, 1972). It seems hardly surprising, then, that girls tend to avoid difficult situations which are considered 'challenging' by boys (Moriarty, 1961).

Differences between boys and girls are a fact of nature. Some of these, like physique, sensory and conceptual capabilities are innate and give a certain bias to the further development of perceptual-cognitive structures (see McGuinness, 1975a and b; 1976). What nurture makes of these differences should be our concern, since, in many cases, as we have seen, it serves to enhance them.

Later sources of socialization
During childhood, adults are influential socializing agents and parents

and teachers may often perpetuate traditional stereotypes in their treatment of girls and boys (Holter, 1970; Joffe, 1971). Boys are disciplined more often than girls (Becker, 1964), though Holter's evidence suggests that Scandinavian mothers may be less permissive in their treatment of girls. In later childhood, however, the influence of peers and institutional groups becomes increasingly important. Peers, for example, exert an important influence by reinforcing same-sex behaviours (Fagot and Patterson, 1969).

The origins of other forces however are more difficult to discern. For instance, boys are constrained to adopt appropriate sex-role behaviours earlier and more strongly than girls (Hartley, 1960); knowledge of male sterotypes also develops earlier (Best et al., 1978), and boys show a stronger preference than girls do for same-sex objects and clothes (Nadelman, 1974). The female sex-role, on the other hand, is less rigidly prescribed: girls may be tomboyish, wear trousers and do boyish things (Tavris and Offir, 1977).

Other powerful socializing agents are represented by the media. The sex-role expectations purveyed by the media are that boys and men are more highly valued than girls and women, that boys are active and achieving while girls are passive and emotional. As Weitzman et al. (1972) point out 'Children's books reflect cultural values and are an important instrument for persuading children to accept those values. They also contain role prescriptions which encourage the child to conform to acceptable standards of behaviour' (p. 1126).

At a time when legislation has had to be introduced to prevent discrimination against women, the sex-role portrayals in the media merit some consideration, since these must exert a formative influence upon attitudes. The sex stereotypes are often so exaggerated as to be distortions. For instance, Friedan (1963) found an idealization of the woman who is 'young and frivolous; fluffy and feminine, passive' in large-circulation American magazines, and the most desirable goal for such a woman was the pursuit of a man. Holter (1970) describes investigations by Liljestrom in Sweden and Skjonsberg in Norway of books for adolescents:

> Boys are presented as more aggressive, objective and emotionally neutral than girls . . . boys are active, initiating and ready to explore the world outside the family, whereas girls are passive . . . devoted to the family and inclined to stay at home . . . Besides being passive,

helpful and interested in people (the girl) can also be a competent and independent heroine – when no boys are present.

(pp. 205–6)

An American survey in 1972 by *Women on Words and Images* (described by Tavris and Offir, 1977) looked at 2,750 stories from 134 children's books from different publishers and found that the traits Americans value were mostly portrayed by men and boys: ingenuity, courage, perseverance, achievement, sportsmanship.

Boys make things. They rely on their wits to solve problems. They are curious, clever and adventurous. They achieve; they make money. Girls and women are incompetent and fearful. They ask other people to solve their problems for them . . . In story after story, girls are the onlookers, the cheerleaders . . . even accepting humiliation and ridicule. In 67 stories, one sex demeans the other – and 65 of these involve hostility of males against females.

(Tavris and Offir, p. 177)

The results of the survey by Weitzman et al. (1972) are even more germane, since these authors looked at sex-role portrayals in the very best of American children's literature – winners of the Caldicott Medal. They report:

It would be impossible to discuss the image of females in children's books without first noting that, in fact, women are simply invisible. We found that females were underrepresented in the titles, central roles, pictures, and stories of every sample of books we examined. Most children's books are about boys, men and male animals, and most deal exclusively with male adventures. Most pictures show men – singly or in groups. Even when women can be found in books, they often play insignificant roles, remaining both inconspicuous and nameless.

In the sample of winners over the previous five years there were 261 pictures of males compared with 23 of females; the ratio of titles featuring males to females was 8:3; only 2 of the 18 books were stories about girls and in nearly one-third of books there were no women at all. Boys were portrayed as active and adventuresome, girls as passive and immobile, most often found indoors, often performing service activities. The roles of the girls were defined primarily in relation to boys and men, a feature Virginia Woolf (1929) lamented in the portrayal of women in adult literature. The adult role models provided by these books were equally stereotyped: women worked *in* the home, men went *out* to work; no woman had an occupation and men always filled the exciting prestigious roles; where men led, women followed.

This highly exaggerated picture is repeated in the medium of television, and since the typical American teenager is likely to have spent more time watching TV than being at school (Tavris and Offir, 1977) the prospect for attitude formation is an alarming one. Sternglanz and Serbin (1974) looked at the programmes with high popularity ratings in an annual season but found that half these programmes had to be discarded because they did not portray females. Even with the programmes selected for the presence of a female, females were very much in a minority; thus, modelling opportunities for girls were considerably reduced. Males were portrayed as aggressive, constructive and helpful, females as deferential and passive. As the authors comment sardonically: 'female children are taught that almost the only way to be a successful human being if you are female is through the use of magic' (p. 714).

Since the sex-roles portrayed on TV are so highly stereotyped and distinct for the two sexes, Frueh and McGhee (1975) supposed that the amount of time children spent watching TV would be related to their strength of sex-role development, and indeed found this to be the case in both boys and girls. There are two interpretations of this finding: either children are modelling themselves on these fictional characters and hence incorporating more sex-typed attributes and behaviours into their sex-role standards, or that the more strongly sex-typed individuals find similarly biased programmes rewarding to watch. Both are equally plausible.

It is a curious irony that sex-roles should be so caricatured in the United States, a society which gave birth to the feminist movement. Quite legitimately the feminists complain that 'it's a man's world'. Although the media must necessarily reflect rather than create the values and attitudes of the society at which they are aimed, the results of the American surveys cause some concern as to the nature of the sex-roles portrayed to children. Whether the position in Britain is any more conciliatory is difficult to assess without similar surveys, but at least public pressure has successfully persuaded the begetters of the widely-used *Ladybird* books to revise the ultra-conventional image of Janet and John pursuing Mummy- and Daddy-type activities. British television too can claim to have as its hardy perennials programmes like

'Crossroads', 'Coronation Street', or 'General Hospital', which have women as their central characters. It may be argued, however, that these are programmes designed for the adult rather than the child market. If producers and publishers do reflect public opinion, it seems that children will be exposed to an unrealistic and unflattering image of women for some time to come.

Sex-roles or sex stereotypes?

Sex-roles constitute the sum of those interests, attitudes, behaviours and expectations which an individual, as a result of being man or woman, boy or girl, holds, enacts and fulfils.

Stereotypes are economical and convenient ways of categorizing and generalizing our knowledge. Stereotypes, therefore, embody our notions of what is typical, of what is characteristic of most of the members of any category. When categories are dichotomous, such as male and female, the stereotypes tend to be extreme, since traits are more readily regarded as sex-typical or not. What stereotypes ignore is the degree of overlap there is between the categories, but such an omission is inevitable in exclusive categorical generalizations. Moreover, the categories of male and female are more definitive than any other form of categorization of behaviour, traits or attitudes, since they are based on generally unambiguous physical characteristics.

Arising from these stereotypes are sex-role standards or expectations about the way members of each sex should behave. It is customary and fashionable to deplore these sex stereotypes and the consequent sex-role standards as a procrustean imposition of 'Society', thereby ascribing to an abstract social construct the properties of operators and manipulators. Society, however, consists of people, of agents, of institutions, of organizations, and the pressures that emanate from these sources and the manner in which they operate are by no means similar. Nothing is to be gained, in understanding or in argument, by the ascription of influences to an ephemeral and mythical agency. What is required is a close examination of how individuals – parents, teachers – institutions, the media, etc. convey their expectations and exert their influences. Furthermore, it is imperative to enquire as to the source of these expectations: why does 'society' expect males to be aggressive and females to be affiliative, males to be achieving and competitive and females to be dependent?

Such examinations, however, often reveal that the bases for some of these expectations lie in differences in aptitudes or behaviour between the sexes. For example, Stein and Smithells (1969) looked at sex-role standards about achievement in certain academic areas. Their subjects were 7-year-olds, 11-year-olds and 16- to 19-year-olds. Altogether, social, artistic and reading skills were considered most feminine (and least masculine) whereas athletic, spatial and mechanical and arithmetic skills were considered most masculine. It may be seen that, in general, the subject-areas which are rated feminine are the areas in which girls perform better and vice versa (see Hutt, 1972a; Buffery and Gray, 1972). Thus expectations, preferences and choices are to a large extent determined by differences in aptitude which in turn appear to have some biological basis.

Or consider again Haavio-Mannila's (1967) survey of sex-role expectations and performance in Finland which showed that women were expected to participate less in social activities outside the home than were men. In terms of their *actual* behaviour this difference was borne out, despite the fact that two-thirds of Finnish women work outside the home. Furthermore, women were more satisfied with their occupational positions, even though few of them occupied influential or prestigious ones – than with the division of household tasks. This example from a society which professes to hold egalitarian views of sex-role again illustrates that the stereotypes and expectations have some factual basis, however slight. Of course it could be argued that men or women behave in a particular way because they have been socialized to do so but this circular argument is both facile and sterile, and leaves unanswered the question of why socialization pressures are the way they are.

Sex-roles and sex stereotypes have their origins in the division of labour associated with reproductive roles. Only women menstruate, gestate and lactate. In primitive societies these three functions alone led to the differentiation of other associated activities as sex-typical behaviours. Broadly speaking women were concerned with those activities to do with the rearing of children and this function inevitably meant a focusing of attention on domestic functions, even if these sometimes entailed physically exacting activities like carrying heavy jars of water long distances to the home. Males, on the other hand, were traditionally concerned with the procurement of food and therefore predominantly with labours outside the house, and which eventually involved them in the decision-making processes associated with the apportionment of resources (Tiger, 1969). Friedl's analysis (1975) of the roles of men and women in the distribution of these resources still leaves the 'administrative' balance in favour of the males.

A number of aptitudes and characteristics were also associated with these traditional sex-roles and were clearly selected for in the process of evolution (Buffery and Gray, 1972; Hutt, 1972a, b and c). Many of the characteristics have a neural or hormonal basis, suggesting that in the struggle for survival they did confer a selective advantage (see Hutt, 1978a). Such characteristics form the bases of sex differences like the spatial superiority of males and linguistic superiority of females. Many of these characteristic differences also constitute the bases of sex-roles. The aggression, competitiveness and assertiveness of the male and the nurturant, affiliative propensities of the female have some hormonal basis (Hutt, 1972a).

Consideration of the outcomes in those societies which have espoused an ideological commitment to the abolition of the sexual differentiation of labour is particularly instructive, since in every case the disparity between the ideology and the practice is considerable. The exploitation of women in the Soviet Union is explicitly proscribed but Lenin's exhortations have an ironic ring in the context of a system which determines that one job for the man means two for the wife. The statistics provided by Tikhomirov et al. (1971) present a gloomy picture indeed of the working mother's life and leisure. Scott (1974) too finds that the picture is far from rosy for Russian women: they are under-represented in the decision-making machinery and over-represented in the more menial jobs. In the People's Republic of China similar distinctions prevail (Tavris and Offir, 1977):

> Some occupations are still regarded as 'women's work': almost all teachers in primary school, nurses, daycare attendants, and flight attendants are women. All visitors observe that fathers and grandfathers have a warm and tender relationship with their young relatives and spend much time with them, but there have been no efforts to get men to work professionally with children.
>
> (p. 280)

In Scandinavia, where protagonists of egalitarianism have been vociferous, no less than in many other countries, and irrespective of national policy or ideology, the traditional division of labour is maintained (Haavio-Mannila, 1975; Safilios-Rothschild, 1971).

It is perhaps in the Kibbutz that the strongest endeavours have been made to eliminate sex-roles and to achieve complete equality of the sexes. After the initial period of ideological fervour, however, there has been a gradual reversion to a more traditional pattern where men work in the production industries and women in the service industries (Tiger and Shepher, 1975). This tendency is even more marked in the generation which had received its socialization in the Kibbutz and therefore had been exposed to no pressures which emanated from the recognition of sex differences. Women eventually showed a clear preference for the conventional female roles, in particular for childcare, and insisted on undertaking these roles despite the objections of the men. Their participation in the Assembly and administrative machinery correspondingly decreased (Gerson, 1971).

Evidence of this kind provides some support for the view that there are biological bases for sex-roles – for the predilections women have for close interpersonal relationships, for communication, for the education and care of the young, as well as for the assertive, competitive, largely impersonal needs of men. Such an inductive statement is often misconstrued as prescriptive and thus taken to imply determinism (see Archer, 1976). Such an interpretation, however, mistakes the nature of causes and places unnecessary restrictions on the manner of explanation. No rational scientist could be a determinist, of whatever sort, since this would imply a belief in an immutable sequence of events. The position adopted here is one that allows for the influence of biological factors in predisposing an individual to think and act in certain ways rather than others. Statements about 'causes' therefore become translated into statements about 'probabilities' and, in this particular case, hormonal exposure in early life is considered to set a certain bias in the individual's responses to his environment.

What is to be deplored, however, is the value-system which depreciates the attributes and work of women (Broverman et al., 1972) so that women underestimate their ability (Crandall et al., 1962; Crandall, 1968). Men as well as women have lower estimations of females than males (McKee and Sherriffs, 1959) while even able women are fearful of success (Horner, 1972), and what is attributed to skill in men is attributed to luck in women (Deaux and Emswiller, 1974). Such a value-system leads inexorably to a discriminating end.

An epigenetic view of sex-role differentiation

Sex is the ascription to an individual of maleness or femaleness on the basis of biological features such as gonads and hormones and commonly ascertained by the external genitalia. Gender, on the other hand, is the individual's psychological identification with one sex or the other. The individual's sex is an integral part of his or her personal identity from the earliest moments of awareness. A child is named, dressed, treated and spoken of as a girl or a boy. The use of the inappropriate pronoun in reference to itself is speedily and consistently corrected by adults. In fact, the concept of self is gender-differentiated. Thus, the first aspect of its identity that the child is aware of is its gender and thereby his/her similarity to the parent of the same sex as well as to peers of the same sex. So far, the process of gender identification is seen as essentially similar to that described by Kohlberg. Once gender identity is established, many processes may contribute to further sex-role development.

As Thompson (1975) argues, there are three processes in gender development: (i) learning to recognize there are two sexes, (ii) inclusion of the self under one category or other, and (iii) the use of a label to guide sex-role preferences. Thompson found that two-year-old children used simple, physical cues, e.g. cranial hair, and clothes, to distinguish the sexes; by the age of thirty months many children were aware of their own sex and those of others and were showing a preference for same-sex pictures; by the age of thirty-six months they were using gender labels to direct their preferences.

The predisposition of young children to imitate the behaviour of same-sex peers and to show preferences for the attributes and activities of their own sex appears to be particularly strong. This tendency need not necessarily be seen in terms of a cognitive assimilation and re-structuring of experience; it is more the result of an affective-conative drive to identify with the attributes and preferences of the same sex, thereby enabling the child to articulate more clearly an important part of its personal identity, vis-à-vis the opposite sex. Thus six-year-olds choose toys which they are told their own sex prefer (Liebert et al., 1971) and seven-year-olds are more attracted by and also perform better in a game when they are told it is a same-sex game (Montemayor, 1974). By the age of five years children already show a strong preference for same-sex clothes and objects (Nadelman, 1974).

Thus, the establishment of gender identity is strongly influenced by the gender assigned to the child. Where there is gender confusion it is as a result of parents' ambiguity about their own sex (as in cases of transvestism), or about the sex of the child. As Gershman (1967) points out 'The fact that the parents are clear in their belief that the infant is either male or female has permanent consequences for the child'. Where there is no equivocation on the part of parents or other adults about the child's sex, then definitive gender identification follows, as in Lev-Ran's series (1974) of sex anomalies, which demonstrates the potency of the gender appellation for the establishment of personal identity, even in severe cases of hermaphroditism. Any repeal of gender is tantamount to a violation of personal identity – for John to become Jane is not simply a matter of change of gender but a change of person involving a total reconstruction of social role. Thus, only the most recalcitrant problems of gender identity provoke a sex reassignment (Morris, 1974; Levine et al., 1975).

As Lewis (1977) argues, the infant manifests a concept of self during the last few months of the first year. This concept, however primitive, enables the infant to dichotomize social objects into those 'like me' and others, and subsequently to differentiate more finely amongst the category of 'like me'. Lewis regards three attributes of the self – age, familiarity and gender – as not simply being acquired very early in life but being the only ones necessary for the construction of a social matrix along which any social object can be located. Thus, gender is one of the earliest attributes of itself of which the child is aware.

Gender identity precedes the differentiation of sex-roles – the performance of sex-typical behaviours, and the adoption of sex-typical preferences (see also Biller, 1971). Sex-roles, moreover, are enacted with a characteristic masculine or feminine 'flavour' – a flavour which is imparted by the organizational influences of the gonadal hormones. A number of sex-role behaviours are also influenced by the natural aptitudes of boys and girls. The development of social and communicative preferences in girls has been neatly traced by McGuinness (1976): as mentioned earlier, greater auditory sensitivity in infancy makes girls more responsive to many properties of sound, among them intonations and inflections of speech; hence their early focus and dependence on the linguistic mode which is further facilitated by neural programming which determines earlier and more complete cerebral lateralization of language functions (see Hutt, 1978b, for review). The verbal proficiency of females continues to place emphasis on communicative skills, and thence social expertise, as well as to determine subsequent preferences. A similar argument could be made for the exploratory and mechanical aptitudes of boys, their interest in the impersonal rather than the personal, their preference for the physical and mathematical sciences – all being influenced by their visuo-spatial abilities, an influence once again enhanced by cerebral asymmetry. Sensory thresholds and perceptual skills determine attentional styles (Silverman, 1970) and thence influence the further processing of information. Preferences and propensities therefore are dependent on aptitude, and for many boys and men, for many girls and women, these will be of the kind already described.

Learning too may be easier for one sex than for the other, at least for certain materials. For example, performance on a memory task differed in girls and boys, depending on whether the material was presented auditorily or visually (May and Hutt, 1974). For reasons such as these, different educational procedures for certain types of learning have been advocated by Lynn (1972), Hutt (1972a), Coltheart et al. (1975) and McGuinness (1976). In a study more relevant to socialization and sex-role development, Flerx et al. (1976) found that sex stereotypes were evident in children by the age of three years; in an attempt to get children to develop more egalitarian attitudes, they employed an intervention programme whereby male and female models were presented whose activities contradicted conventional stereotypes. Although this egalitarian treatment reduced some stereotyped beliefs, it was less effective with boys, who also had more stereotyped beliefs to start with. Thus environmental influences do not operate on similar entities, nor in similar ways.

The manner in which nature and nurture interact is one that concerns all developmental psychologists, yet models of development are rare. Two models which are particularly applicable to the development of sex differences have been discussed by Archer and Lloyd (1975). Taking issue with what they term an 'additive' model of genotype–environment interaction, they put forward an alternative 'interactive' model: this latter model however does little other than represent the term 'interaction' as a series of boxes and arrows – no parameters are specified, no processes are outlined, and it allows no distinctive predictions to be made.

Nevertheless, the implication of such a 'model' is that the interaction involves complex processes, unspecified though they be, which are more than facilitatory or inhibitory. But the distinction between 'additive' and 'interactive' is more a semantic than a substantive one – the epigenetic view is precisely that the basic processes of nature–nurture interaction are those of facilitation and inhibition, of accentuation or attenuation. Environmental influences in the first instance can only modulate behaviour, activity, interests and propensities that are already extant. This is conceded by Archer and Lloyd in their description of an 'interactive interaction':

... the initial tendency for boys to cry more than girls may interact with the mother's response to the crying in a way which amplifies and extends the original sex difference ...

(p. 175)

It is the essence of the argument outlined here that sex-role differentiation presupposes the establishment of gender identity; gender identity itself is the result of social factors which are most often in accord with biological ones. Thereafter upon the bases of natural aptitudes, skills and proclivities, and motivated by the affective-conative desire to acquire a stable identity, sex-roles are developed through the processes of imitation, modelling, social learning and cognitive reorganization.

References

Archer, J. (1976) Biological explanations of psychological sex differences. In B. Lloyd and J. Archer (eds) *Exploring Sex Differences*. New York: Academic Press.

Archer, J. and Lloyd, B. (1975) Sex differences: biological and social interaction. In R. Lewin (ed.) *Child Alive*. San Francisco: Anchor Press.

Bandura, A. and Walters, R. W. (1963) *Social Learning and Personality Development*. New York: Holt, Rinehart and Winston.

Baumrind, D. and Black, A. E. (1967) Socialization practices associated with dimensions of competence in pre-school boys and girls. *Child Development 48*: 187–94.

Becker, W. C. (1964) Consequences of different kinds of parental discipline. In M. L. Hoffman and L. W. Hoffman (eds) *Review of Child Development, Vol. 1*. New York: Russell Sage Foundation.

Best, D. L., Williams, J. E., Cloud, J. M., Davis, S. W., Roberston, L. S., Edwards, J. R., Giles, H. and Fowles, J. (1977 in press). Development of sex-trait stereotypes among young children in the United States, England and Ireland. *Child Development, 48*: 1375–84.

Biller, H. B. (1971) *Father, Child and Sex Role*. Lexington, Mass.: D. C. Heath.

Block, J. H. (1976) Debatable conclusions about sex differences. *Contemporary Psychology 21*: 517–22.

Brindley, C., Clarke, P., Hutt, C., Robinson, I. and Wethli, E. (1973) Sex differences in the activities and social interactions of nursery school children. In R. P. Michael and J. H. Crook (eds) *Comparative Ecology and Behavior of Primates*. New York: Academic Press.

198 Issues in childhood social development

Broverman, I. K., Vogel, S. R., Broverman, D., Clarkson, F. E. and Rosenkrantz, P. S. (1972). Sex-role stereotypes: a current appraisal. *Journal of Social Issues 28*: 59–79.
Buffery, A. W. H. and Gray, J. A. (1972) Sex differences in the development of perceptual and linguistic skills. In C. Ounsted and D. C. Taylor (eds) *Gender Differences – Their Ontogeny and Significance*. London: Churchill.
Clark, A. H., Wyon, S. M. and Richards, M. P. (1969) Free-play in nursery school children. *Journal of Child Psychology, Psychiatry 10*: 205–16.
Coltheart, M., Hull, E. and Slater, D. (1975) Sex differences in imagery and reading. *Nature 253*: 438–40.
Crandall, V. C. (1968) Sex differences in expectancy of intellectual and academic reinforcement. In C. P. Smith (ed.) *Achievement – Related Motives in Children*. New York: Russell Sage Foundation.
Crandall, V. J., Katkovsky, W. and Preston, A. (1962) Motivational and ability determinants of young children's intellectual achievement behaviors. *Child Development 33*: 643–61.
Crandall, V. J. and Rabson, A. (1960) Children's repetition choices in an intellectual achievement situation following success and failure. *Journal of Genetic Psychology 97*: 161–8.
Deaux, K. and Emswiller, T. (1974) Explanation of successful performance on sex-linked tasks: what is skill for the male is luck for the female. *Journal of Personality and Social Psychology 29*: 80–5.
De Vries, R. (1969) Constancy of generic identity in the years three to six. *Monographs of the Society for Research in Child Development 34* (Whole No. 3).
Ehrhardt, A. A. and Baker, S. W. (1974) Fetal androgens, human central nervous system differentiation and behavior sex differences. In R. C. Freedman, R. H. Richart and R. L. Vande Wiele (eds) *Sex Differences in Behavior*. New York: Wiley.
Ehrhardt, A. A., Evers, K. and Money, J. (1968). Influence of androgen and some aspects of sexually dimorphic behavior in women with the late-treated androgenital syndrome. *Johns Hopkins Medical Journal 123*: 115–22.
Ehrhardt, A. A., Greenberg, N. and Money, J. (1970) Female gender identity and absence of fetal hormones: Turner's Syndrome. *Johns Hopkins Medical Journal 126*: 237–48.
Emmerich, W. (1973) Socialization and sex-role development. In P. B. Baltes and K. W. Schaie (eds) *Life-span Developmental Psychology*. New York: Academic Press.
Fagot, B. I. and Patterson, G. R. (1969) An *in vivo* analysis of reinforcing contingencies for sex-role behaviors in the preschool child. *Developmental Psychology 1*: 563–8.
Federman, M. D. (1967) *Abnormal Sexual Development*. Philadelphia: W. B. Saunders Co.
Flavell, J. H. and Wohlwill, J. F. (1969) Formal and functional aspects of cognitive development. In D. Elkind and J. H. Flavell (eds) *Studies in Cognitive Development: Essays in Honour of Jean Piaget*. Oxford: Oxford University Press.
Flerx, V. C., Fidler, D. S. and Rogers, R. W. (1976) Sex role stereotypes: developmental aspects and early intervention. *Child Development 47*: 998–1007.

Fling, S. and Manosevitz, M. (1972) Sex typing in nursery school children's play interests. *Developmental Psychology* 7: 146–52.

Friedan, B. (1963) *The Feminine Mystique.* New York: W. W. Norton.

Friedl, E. (1975) *Women and Men: an Anthropologist's View.* New York: Holt, Rinehart and Winston.

Frueh, T. and McGhee, P. E. (1975) Traditional sex-role development and amount of time spent watching television. *Developmental Psychology* 11: 109.

Gershman, H. (1967) The evolution of gender identity. *Bulletin New York Academy of Medicine* 43: 1000–18.

Gerson, M. (1971) Women in the Kibbutz. *American Journal of Orthopsychiatry* 41: 566–73.

Goggin, J. E. (1975) Sex differences in the activity level of preschool children as a possible precursor of hyperactivity. *Journal of Genetic Psychology* 127: 75–81.

Goldberg, S. and Lewis, M. (1969) Play behavior in the year-old infant: early sex differences. *Child Development* 40: 21–31.

Green, R. (1969) Childhood cross-gender identification. In R. Green and J. Money (eds) *Transsexualism and Sex Reassignment.* Baltimore: Johns Hopkins Press.

Haavio-Mannila, E. (1967) Sex differentiation in role expectations and performance. *Journal of Marriage and the Family* 29: 568–78.

Haavio-Mannila, E. (1971) Convergences between east and west: tradition and modernity in sex roles in Sweden, Finland and the Soviet Union. *Acta Sociologica* 14 (1–2): 114–25.

Haavio-Mannila, E. (1975) Convergences between east and west: tradition and modernity in sex roles in Sweden, Finland and the Soviet Union. In M. T. S. Mednick, S. S. Tangri and L. W. Hoffman (eds) *Women and Achievement: Social and Motivational Analyses.* New York: Halsted Press.

Hamm, N. K. and Hoving, K. L. (1969) Conformity of children in an ambiguous perceptual situation. *Child Development* 40: 21–31.

Hartley, R. E. (1960) Children's concepts of male and female roles. *Merrill-Palmer Quarterly* 6: 84–91.

Heim, A. H. (1970) *Intelligence and Personality.* Harmondsworth: Penguin Books.

Hoffman, L. W. (1972) Early childhood experiences and women's achievement motives. *Journal of Social Issues* 23: 129–55.

Hollander, E. P. and Marcia J. E. (1970) Parental determinants of peer-orientation and self-orientation among preadolescents. *Developmental Psychology* 2: 292–302.

Holter, H. (1970) *Sex Roles and Social Structure.* Oslo: Universitets forlaget.

Horner, M. S. (1972) Towards an understanding of achievement related conflicts in women. *Journal of Social Issues* 28 (2).

Hutt, C. (1970) Curiosity in young children. *Science Journal* 6: 68–72.

Hutt, C. (1972a) *Males and Females.* Harmondsworth: Penguin Books.

Hutt, C. (1972b) Neuroendocrinological, behavioural and intellectual aspects of sexual differentiation in human development. In C. Ounsted and D. C. Taylor (eds) *Gender Differences – Their Ontogeny and Significance.* London: Churchill.

Hutt, C. (1972c) Sexual dimorphism: its significance in human development.

In F. Monks, W. Hartup and J. de Wit (eds) *Determinants of Behavioral Development*. New York: Academic Press.

Hutt, C. (1974) Sex: what's the difference? *New Scientist 62* (898): 405–7, 16 May.

Hutt, C. (1978a) Biological bases of psychological sex differences. *American Journal of Diseases of Children 132*: 170–7.

Hutt, C. (1978b) Sex differences in cerebral asymmetry. *International Journal of Behavioural Development* (in press).

Hutt, C. and Bhavnani, R. (1972) Predictions from play. *Nature 237*: 171–2.

Joffe, C. (1971) Sex-role socialization and the nursery school: as the twig is bent. *Journal of Marriage and the Family 33*: 467–75.

Jonas, D. F. and Jonas, A. D. (1975) Gender differences in mental function: a clue to the origin of language. *Current Anthropology 16*: 626–30.

Kagan, J. (1964) Acquisition and significance of sex-typing and sex-role identity. In M. L. Hoffman and L. W. Hoffman (eds) *Review of Child Development Research, Vol. 1*. New York: Russell Sage Foundation.

Kagan, J. (1969) On the meaning of behavior: illustrations from the infant. *Child Development 40*: 1121–34.

Kagan, J. and Moss, H. (1962) *From Birth to Maturity*. New York: Wiley.

Kohlberg, L. (1966) A cognitive-developmental analysis of children's sex-role concepts and attitudes. In E. E. Maccoby (ed.) *The Development of Sex Differences*. London: Tavistock.

Korner, A. F. (1969) Neonatal startles, smiles, erections and reflex sucks as 'related' to state, sex and individuality. *Child Development 40*: 1039–53.

Lev-Ran, A. (1974) Gender role differentiation in hermaphrodites. *Archives of Sexual Behavior 3*: 391–424.

Levine, E. M., Shaiova, C. H. and Mihailovic, M. (1975) Male to female: the role transformation of transsexuals. *Archives of Sexual Behavior 4*: 173–85.

Lewis, M. (1972) State as an infant–environment interaction: an analysis of mother–infant behavior as a function of sex. *Merrill-Palmer Quarterly 18*: 95–121.

Lewis, M. (1977) The social nexus: the child's entrance into the world. Paper to the International Society for Behavioural Development, Pavia.

Liebert, R., McCall, R. and Hanratty, M. (1971) Effects of sex-typed information on children's toy preferences. *Journal of Genetic Psychology 119*: 133–6.

Lynn, D. B. (1972) Determinants of intellectual growth in women. *The School Review 80*: 241–60.

May, R. B. and Hutt, C. (1974) Modality and sex differences in recall and recognition memory. *Child Development 45*: 228–31.

McGuinness, D. (1975a) Away from a unisex psychology: individual differences in visual sensory and perceptual processes. *Perception 6*: 22–32.

McGuinness, D. (1975b) The impact of innate perceptual differences between the sexes on the socializing process. *Educational Review 27*: 229–39.

McGuinness, D. (1976) Sex differences in the organization of perception and cognition. In B. Lloyd and J. Archer (eds) *Exploring Sex Differences*. New York: Academic Press.

McKee, J. P. and Sherriffs, A. C. (1959) Men's and women's beliefs, ideals, and self-concepts. *American Journal of Sociology 64*: 356–63.

Messer, S. and Lewis, M. (1972) Social class and sex differences in the attachment and play behavior of the year-old infant. *Merrill-Palmer Quarterly 18*: 295–306.

Mischel, W. (1970) Sex-typing and socialization. In P. Mussen (ed.) *Carmichael's Manual of Child Psychology, Vol. 2*. New York: Wiley.

Mischel, W. (1966) A social learning view of sex differences in behavior. In E. E. Maccoby (ed.) *The Development of Sex Differences*. Stanford, California: Stanford University Press.

Money, J. and Dalery, J. (1976) Iatrogenic homosexuality. *Journal of Homosexuality 1*: 357–71.

Money, J. and Ehrhardt, A. A. (1968) Prenatal hormonal exposure, possible effects on behaviour in man. In R. P. Michael (ed.) *Endocrinology and Human Behaviour*. Oxford: Oxford University Press.

Money, J. and Ehrhardt, A. A. (1972) *Man and Woman, Boy and Girl*. Baltimore: Johns Hopkins University Press.

Money, J., Hampson, J. G. and Hampson, J. L. (1955a) Hermaphroditism: recommendations concerning assignment of sex, change of sex, and psychologic management. *Bulletin Johns Hopkins Hospital 97*: 284–300.

Money, J., Hampson, J. G. and Hampson, J. L. (1955b) An examination of some basic sexual concepts: the evidence of human hermaphroditism. *Bulletin Johns Hopkins Hospital 97*: 301–9.

Money, J., Hampson, J. G. and Hampson, J. L. (1957) Imprinting and the establishment of gender role. *Archives of Neurology and Psychiatry 77*: 333–6.

Montemayor, R. (1974) Children's performance in a game and their attraction to it as a function of sex-typed labels. *Child Development 45*: 152–6.

Moore, T. (1967) Language and Intelligence: a longitudinal study of the first eight years. Part 1: Patterns of development in boys and girls. *Human Development 10*: 88–106.

Moriarty, A. (1961) Coping patterns of preschool children in response to Intelligence Test demands. *Genetic Psychology Monographs 64*: 3–127.

Morris, J. (1974) *Conundrum*. London: Faber.

Moss, H. (1967) Sex, age and state as determinants of mother–infant interaction. *Merrill-Palmer Quarterly 13*: 19–36.

Nadelman, L. (1974) Sex identity in American children: memory, knowledge and preference tests. *Developmental Psychology 10*: 413–17.

Ounsted, C. and Taylor, D. C. (1972) The Y-chromosome message: a point of view. In C. Ounsted and D. C. Taylor (eds) *Gender Differences – Their Ontogeny and Significance*. London: Churchill.

Reinisch, J. (1974) Fetal hormones, the brain and human sex differences. *Archives of Sexual Behavior 3*: 51–90.

Rubin, J. Z., Provenzano, F. J. and Luria, Z. (1974) The eye of the beholder: parents' views on sex of newborns. *American Journal of Orthopsychiatry 44*: 512–19.

Safilios-Rothschild, C. (1971) A cross-cultural examination of women's marital, educational and occupational options. *Acta Sociologica 14* (1–2): 96–113.

Scott, H. (1974) *Does Socialism Liberate Women? Experiences from Eastern Europe.* Boston: Beacon Press.

Sears, R. R., Rau, L. and Alpert, R. (1965) *Identification and Child Rearing.* Stanford, California: Stanford University Press.

Shipman, V. C., Barone, J., Beaton, A., Emmerich, W. and Ward, W. (1971) Disadvantaged children and their first school experiences: structure and development of cognitive competencies and styles prior to school entry. *Educational Testing Service*, Report No. 71–19.

Silverman, J. (1970) Attentional styles and the study of sex differences. In D. I. Mostofsky (ed.) *Attention: Contemporary Theory and Analysis.* New York: Appleton Century Crofts.

Stein, A. H. and Smithells, J. (1969) Age and sex differences in children's sex role standards about achievement. *Developmental Psychology 1* : 252–9.

Sternglanz, S. H. and Serbin, L. A. (1974) Sex-role stereotypes in children's television programmes. *Developmental Psychology 10* : 710–15.

Stoller, R. (1967) Gender identity and a biological force. *Psychoanalytic Forum 2*(4).

Stoller, R. (1968) *Sex and Gender.* New York: Science House.

Tavris, C. and Offir, C. (1977) *The Longest War: Sex Differences in Perspective.* New York: Harcourt Brace Jovanovich Inc.

Thompson, S. K. (1975) Gender labels and early sex-role development. *Child Development 46* : 339–47.

Tiger, L. (1969) *Men in Groups.* London: Nelson.

Tiger, L. and Shepher, J. (1975) *Women in the Kibbutz.* Harmondsworth: Penguin Books.

Tikhomirov, N., Gordon, L. and Klopov, E. (1971) A study of the way of life of the workers and questions of social planning. *The Working Class and the Contemporary World 1* : 99–112.

Weinraub, M. and Frankel, J. (1978 in press) Sex differences in parent–infant interaction during free play, departure and separation. *Child Development.*

Weitzman, L. J., Eifler, D., Hokada, E. and Ross, C. (1972) Sex role socialization in picture books for preschool children. *American Journal of Sociology 77* : 1125–50.

Whalen, R. E. (1968) Differentiation of the neural mechanisms which control gonadotropin secretion and sexual behavior. In M. Diamond (ed.) *Perspectives in Reproduction and Sexual Behaviour.* Bloomington: Indiana University Press.

Woolf, Virginia (1929) *A Room of One's Own.* London: Hogarth Press.

7 The nature of social development: a conceptual discussion of cognition

James Youniss

The purpose of this essay is to discuss and offer a conceptual solution for the dichotomy between 'socialization' and 'cognitive' approaches to the study of social development. Other polarized disjunctives – genetic vs environmental determination of moral character; psychoanalytic vs learning theory bases of personality – have with time been resolved. There is no reason to believe that socialization and cognition will not also be found compatible some day. The present essay is an attempt to facilitate their resolution. First, differences and similarities between these approaches are discussed and then a speculation is offered on how the two can be integrated.

With respect to differences, there can be no doubt that cognitive theories were designed to modify the formula which made children's behaviour the direct result of socialization influences. Historically, the idea that children's actions are output and other persons' actions were input ran into trouble when investigators could not find statistical correlations between the antecedent and the consequent. One response was to insert cognition as a mediating factor. This was an attempt to recircuit the input–output linkage through an intervening way station.

At first this seems like a bold stroke. The impact of outer forces is dampened by the child's own cognition, thus passing some control of social development to the child himself. But on closer inspection, the introduction of cognition raises some serious questions. If cognition is defined literally as a process of self-construction with its own developmental course, then the risk is run that the environment of social agents can have minimal impact on social development. If, on the other hand, cognition is only one of several factors which intervene in development, its introduction is but a timid step. That is, cognitive theory becomes just another version of the old input–output model with its intervention merely adding complexity to the traditional formula.

Our premise is that a different conceptualization is needed for the kind of cognition which services social development. An alternative approach is presented by way of a general framework. It is based on an interpretation of Piaget's writings and is designed to clarify two conceptual issues: What is the nature of social knowledge? And, What is the process by which knowledge is socialized? The former question may be answered by Piaget's treatment of knowledge as a relation. This suggests that *interpersonal relations* rather than the entities of 'self' and 'other' be made the basic unit of analysis. The second question may gain resolution when subject–subject interactions are made the intentional topic of social knowledge. This is to be distinguished from making knowledge a grasp of 'other persons' inner psychological workings'.

Socialization and cognition

The study of social development has always had two points of focus. On one side there is the child's behaviour and on the second side there is the behaviour of other persons. The task of the social scientist is to explain the relation between them. In classical socialization theory the two sides of behaviour are said to come to a one-to-one correspondence. This is effected through the effort of other persons, called socializing agents, who influence and shape the child's actions, thoughts and feelings. Correspondence can be achieved through direct means, such as imitation or reinforcement, or indirectly, as when parents act so as to create an internal state (e.g. 'dependency') which in turn controls the child's output.

In the 1960s cognitive theory entered the study of social development and caused a switch in the concept of correspondence. Instead of looking for identity, researchers sought behavioural similarity between others' and children's behaviour. Similarity was made due to the achievement of corresponding thought. Children came to behave like other persons because they came to understand and share the same underlying rationale for behaviour. Shared reasons were themselves a developmental achievement due to the child's own development of capacities, skills and cognitive processes which permitted understanding of others.

Differences between socialization and cognitive approaches can be illustrated in several particular formulations. One concerns the distinction between imitation and modelling (cf. Bandura, 1969). According to socialization theory, the child can acquire behaviour which first exists in another person by imitating the behaviour of the other person. The other's exhibition is sufficient for the child to pick up and incorporate the behaviour as his or her own. According to cognitive theory, the transmission process may not be so simple. The other's behaviour does not flow in pure form into the child because the child cognitively acts on it and transforms it in order to incorporate it.

Starting with another's behaviour, the child first attends to it selectively. Second, the child notices some but not other features. Third, the child codes or internally represents some features. Fourth, the child rearranges the features, for example, by integrating them with other features taken from previous modelling occasions. Fifth, when a subsequent occasion for acting comes up, the child remembers in some way what has happened in the past and generates a behaviour appropriate to the present moment. In total, all of these cognitive activities are interposed between the other person's behaviour, which is input, and the child's own behavioural output. The result is a relation of similarity between behaviour expressed by socializing agents and behaviour manifested by the child. Similarity is only in part due to the socializing agent. It is equally due to the child's cognitive activity which intervenes in the transmission process.

Cognitive development
The relation of correspondence, in contrast to behavioural identity, is based on a model of the child as a thinker. External events in the form of stimuli are not considered as mere objective things to which behaviour can be attached. The child assigns interpretations to events and thus we may speak of the child's understanding of events. There are two aspects of any objectively incoming behaviour. One is the behavioural event as it can be measured by an outside observer. The second is the event as the child knows it. The connection between them

is attributed to processes by which the child converts external reality into mental reality.

Within the cognitive approach there is a group of theories which addresses the conversion process from its developmental side. For any process the child might use to comprehend an event, there is a potential developmental course which would explain whether and how the child employs it. For example, in Bandura's (1969) account of modelling, verbal representation of another's behaviour would be possible only when a child was able to use language as a descriptive and representative device. Roughly one would expect differences between very young and older children who were exposed to a model's behaviour and told to remember it. They should encode it differently and therefore may act differently when asked later to exhibit the behaviour themselves.

Cognitive development can be seen in even more complex fashion when one turns to questions of how children understand psychological causes of behaviour. Several researchers have observed that young children tend to act 'egocentrically' when they are exposed to another's behaviour. Egocentric children assume that the actor has the same ideas about his behaviour as they themselves have, almost excluding the possibility that the other person might have acted for different reasons. This kind of effect has been obtained in tasks of communication (Chandler, 1973; Flavell et al., 1968) and social reasoning (Feffer, 1970; Selman and Byrne, 1974). Egocentrism has been treated as a capacity factor. From a developmental perspective, it is a capacity restriction which describes younger children's tendency to convert external events to mental categories of their own making.

As a developmental phenomenon egocentrism wanes in a natural course. According to some theorists, its decline is accompanied by acquisition of a cognitive skill called role-taking. In distinction from their egocentric forerunners, older children tend to look on events from two perspectives. The first is their own and the second is that which another person might have. Instead of imposing their own perspective on the other, these children recognize the possibility of a difference and make an effort to probe the other's perspective (Flavell, 1974) and arrive at a kind of mutual understanding (Selman and Byrne, 1974).

In this and other examples of the cognitive developmental approach (e.g. Hoffman, 1970; Kohlberg, 1969; Livesley and Bromley, 1973; Scarlett et al., 1971; Shantz, 1976) emphasis is placed on cognition as an *enabling* device which mediates social development. As capacities, skills and processes develop children become able to know more and different things about other persons. With each step toward maturity, children are more able to free themselves from private interpretations and come closer to understanding social reality as other persons understand it. The advanced role-taker, for instance, should be able to achieve a kind of mutuality of understanding with another even to the point of viewing his or her own perspective as the other person might be construing it (Miller et al., 1970). Getting out of oneself and into another is an essential developmental advance in the general task of understanding persons.

Thus, theories of socialization and cognition have children arrive at a similar point with respect to the social milieu but by different means. In the socialization approach children can interact with other persons because other persons have shaped or otherwise influenced their social behaviours. That is, older children's actions reach correspondence with actions of others through the latter's agency. In the cognitive approach, correspondence results from children's cognitive development. It enables them to reach a shared understanding with others which, in turn, allows interpersonal correspondence in action.

The problem

The shift in approach from socialization to cognition has been accomplished for a wide set of phenomena and cast in a variety of theoretical languages. For present purposes differences among cognitive theories are minimized in favour of inspection of commonalities. It is in the latter that we intend to show a series of unresolved issues which will be addressed subsequently from a different perspective on cognition.

There is a consensus among contemporary theorists that the relation between behaviour in others and behaviour in children is best understood when cognition is made the mediating factor. Even though each theorist addresses different aspects of cognition, one general programme seems to describe most of them. The programme starts with another person's behaviour. As the behaviour flows inward, the child's cognitive initiative takes over and converts it into some mental state. This state then allows movement in two directions. With respect to the initial behaviour, the cognitive state is the basis for assigning it meaning or interpretation. Secondly, the state is the basis for the child's own behaviour. The initial and end conditions are behavioural and refer to both persons, child and other. They are linked through the mediational activity of the child's cognition.

When it is asked how the other person affects the child, one has to look at the child's mediating activity. What the other does objectively may or may not square with the child's interpretation. The interpretation, in turn, depends on the child's cognitive developmental status. For example, a preverbal child may have difficulty converting a parent's verbal instruction into a behavioural output. A non-egocentric, role-taking child should be able to get behind another's verbal instruction to gauge subtleties like the other's motive for giving the instruction or for anticipating a reaction. In either case, cognition is the tool for assignment of an interpretation to the other's behaviour and the child's own behaviour is a result of this interpretation.

This version of a mediation theory has conceptual advantages and disadvantages. As to the former, it has the potential to connect input and output which are not directly related in one-to-one fashion. Similar mediators are motivation, self-image, dependency, and the like – all of which have been used in the study of social development to link input from others with the child's output when the two are not replicas of one another. For example, in the case of dependency the link is between contrasting behaviours. Parents act coercively and in controlling fashion on the child. The child, in distinction, acts dependently in order not to lose contact with the parent (cf. Weinraub et al., 1977, for further explanation).

But if cognition mediates social functioning, one still has to explain its development. Theorists seem to divide on this point. Some consider cognition to have its own course of development in the sense that it refers to the general ways children construct means for knowing things outside themselves. Treated this way, cognitive development is semi-natural (normative) in character and proceeds on the basis of the child's own initiative. Actual experiences with objects, persons and events are mere occasions for organizing the world. Changes in organization issue forth in a step-by-step natural sequence (cf. Hoffman, 1970; Kohlberg, 1969; Livesley and Bromley, 1973; Selman and Byrne, 1974).

discrediting of socialization. Hypothetically, other persons can do whatever they like to present socializing instances to children, but children will assimilate whatever others do to some current level of functioning. For instance, the egocentric child will effectively discount the other's presentation to make it accord with his or her own present cognitive interpretation. Egocentrism blocks off or at least distorts the socializing influence of others as long as it persists as a capacity restriction. It could last, for example, throughout the preschool period (e.g. Flavell et al., 1968; Livesley and Bromley, 1973).

The same kind of limitation on socialization holds also for advanced levels of cognitive development. In Kohlberg's (1969) theory, for example, subjects functioning at upper levels of moral development interpret behaviour of persons according to formal principles based on propositions about ideal, right action. The potential risk is that subjects so operating lose touch with the details of external reality. When they analyse events logically and convert them to principles, they remove themselves from time, place and cultural context (see Riegel, 1976; Simpson, 1974). The further risk is that logical interpretations pre-empt phenomenological content also (Blasi and Hoeffel, 1974). In summary, this approach to cognition tends to sever the subject as thinker from the socializing influences of others and may even sever the subject as thinker from the feeling, doubting, phenomenological self.

The second approach to cognition as a mediating factor is more eclectic in nature. Cognition ranges in meaning from 'mental age' (Hoffman, 1970) to performance on some Piagetian task (Shantz, 1976) to some actual skill like role-taking. Researchers then look to see whether cognitive performance correlates with a social performance. (Is conservation correlated with understanding an actor's intention? Does perspective-taking in a perceptual situation correlate with communication skills?)

In this approach, socialization is studied for its potential effects on cognitive development. For example, styles of parental discipline are categorized then looked at as having differential effects on the child's cognitive growth (e.g., Bradley and Caldwell, 1976). Or, amount and types of peer experience are studied with respect to the development of role-taking skills (Chandler, 1973). In this kind of eclectic model, cognition is located either as a mediator on its own or as an output variable or both (see reviews of this approach in Hoffman, 1970; and Shantz, 1976, pp. 70–7).

The problem with this approach may be located in its logic. Socialization, measured in standard terms of what others do to children, is the antecedent for cognitive development. But cognitive development is simultaneously an antecedent for determining how the child will interpret input. That is, the child's present level of cognitive functioning is the basis for interpreting the meaning of socializing events. At present there is no empirical way to separate the other's effect from the child's contribution to other's effect. One and the same factor, cognition, serves as a mediator, a product, and an antecedent to the child's development.

The associated problem

Having broken the direct link between the other's input and the child, cognitive theorists have had to deal with a related issue. Once the child converts input into a cognitive state, he or she must then act by producing some behaviour. This behaviour is exerted toward the other person and occasioned by that person's behaviour. However, since the occasion has been transformed, output is influenced as much by cognition as by the original behavioural event. The issue is then to understand how cognitive states mediate the flow toward output.

For purposes of laboratory study, most theories have taken a restrictive focus, concentrating on the path from another's input to the child's judgement. For example, theories of person perception have tried to estimate how the child judges that another person acted intentionally, by chance or because of some persistent trait (Flavell, 1974; Livesley and Bromley, 1973). The analysis ends with the judgement – although it is understood that the child will frame a reaction on the basis of the judgement. Moral judgements, as in Kohlberg's (1969) theory lead to the same point. The aim of the cognitive analysis is to explain why children understand actions as right or wrong. But no claim is made that a person's knowledge of morally correct behaviour will lead to that or to some other action. This problem has led investigators to the necessary task of writing programmes designed to account for output. They begin with cognition and attempt to carry the flow from it to the child's production of actions (e.g. Dienstbier et al., 1975).

An alternative approach to cognition

The framework which is now presented is based on an interpretation of Piaget's writings. A preliminary sketch to it appeared in Youniss (1975). Others have used Piaget as a starting point and arrived at quite different views about the cognitive side of social development. The present framework is an attempt to exploit Piaget's writings for their epistemological meaning. In order to clarify conceptual issues one has to confront questions about the nature of knowledge and the process by which knowledge is acquired and develops. This is what we mean by epistemology: What is the general form of social knowledge? How is it acquired and how does it develop?

The sources used for this interpretation include an early work by Piaget (1932), *The Moral Judgment of the Child*, and a group of more recent writings which present further clarification of Piaget's position. The former work has an interesting history in that many theorists refer to it regarding notions of 'egocentrism', 'intentionality', 'stages', and the like. But rarely do theorists carry through to the underlying definitions of these notions. At least one other commentator has pointed to the different meanings that can be drawn when notions like intention are made phenomena in themselves, as opposed to focusing upon the knowledge process from which these notions are derived (Keasey, 1977). It is appropriate, therefore, that the 1932 work be summarized before addressing the two basic questions and presenting a framework for integrating cognition with socialization.

Summary of Piaget (1932)

The following points have been extracted to represent Piaget's (1932) approach to social knowledge, its definition and its development. They stop short of dealing with morality which the book goes on to address in greater detail.

(1) Children are born into a network of social relations in which they hold several positions with respect to other persons and vice versa. The network effectively touches the child when he or she and others begin to interact with one another. The child's cognitive task is to discover a means for ordering these interactions. In seeking to know what is regular in this ever-changing array, children look to their own actions as a means for constructing order (e.g. pp. 395ff.).

(2) Once the child achieves the concept of the permanency of things and of persons outside him or herself, other persons begin to play a direct role in the construction of order. When children focus on their actions, they necessarily take account of the actions of other persons. The things that other persons do or say stand toward the child's actions as a form of feedback. When the child extracts regularity from actions, the process includes the entire interaction which was composed by two independent actors (e.g. pp. 71 ff.).

(3) Order is derived from interactions when the child (as well as other persons) constructs rule systems, or *relations*. In any relation, a

child defines him or herself as a contributor to interactions with regard to particular other persons who are also contributors. The rules pertain to effects that interactions will have on the participants and on their relation. For example, in a *unilateral authority* relation, children's acts of obedience keep them in a known relation with respect to parents. Acts of disobedience violate the terms of the relation and set the interactive rule system into motion. That is, the parent may have to admonish the child, the child may have to own up to the violation and offer apology, and then the parent may accept the apology. This interactive sequence is designed to repair the momentary breach and bring the relationship back to normal. At this point the persons are able to resume interacting according to their relational agreement (e.g. p. 228).

(4) The division of self and others according to relational rule systems is required if children are to order themselves within existing social networks. Mothers interact with their offspring differently than with the children next door; children interact differently with friends than with mere classmates or newcomers to the neighbourhood. Piaget illustrates the interactive base for these separate constructions through a hyperbolic contrast between unilateral authority relations and relations predicated on reciprocity between equals. In the former, the child looks to an adult, for example, to set forth interactive rules which the child then tries to understand and integrate with other known rules. In the latter, rules are co-operatively constructed by both persons with neither having the right to impose a rule arbitrarily on the other. The distinction among rules stems from the method by which they originate (e.g. pp. 106 ff.).

(5) Any relation can be observed to develop in the sense that one or both parties can reconstruct themselves with respect to the other. One source of change is continued functioning within the relation. As two persons interact over time they generate new interactive data which are integrated into prior rule systems. The process of extracting and then co-ordinating novel material may lead to the discovery of new relational forms. The second source is also a process of integration which pertains to co-ordination among the several relations a child knows. Piaget illustrates this process with the suggested integration between authority and equality relations during adolescence. The result seems to be that the former come to be reconstructed along the lines of the latter – e.g. adolescents begin acting and treating their parents somewhat as they act toward and treat peers (e.g. pp. 394 ff.).

(6) Throughout development, especially during its early years,

there is an advantage to considering self and others, not as independent entities, but as relativistic conceptions. A child's conception of self is best understood as a multiplicity of views, each of which pertains to a particular relation. The same relational determination pertains to conceptions of persons. Characteristics which are assigned to the self or others are derived from relational conceptions. For instance, in an authority relation marked by unilaterality the child may understand the self to be *obedient, dependent* and *respecting*. The authoritative other may be conceptualized as *law-giving, free to change rules* and *respected*. These are not adjectives gleaned from a public lexicon but are extracted properties which mark the reciprocal relationship between the parties (e.g. pp. 360–1).

(7) Conceptions of persons, including self and others, are open to change as relations themselves develop. Piaget suggests, for example, that construction of a stable concept of self as an individual is contingent on integration among relations which the self knows. Reflection on relations is also the source of concepts like the self as-it-might-be (ideal) and persons in general. Understanding of persons as individuals with independent existence is not the starting point of development but is a late developmental accomplishment (e.g. pp. 95–6).

Social knowledge
The kind of social knowledge which this framework addresses is interpersonal, relational and interactive. It is interpersonal because the self (the child who constructs) views itself in connection to other persons and vice versa (Piaget, 1932, p. 36; p. 360). This is true for even the very young child who thinks that he or she has ordered him/herself to adults but has not yet discovered the rules which bind them (p. 36). It is equally true for older children who concur as to procedures for acting as peers (p. 71). Piaget avoids the risk of having knowledge be 'of persons' rather than interpersonal. That would place persons as objective things outside the self which the self then had to grasp or come to know. Piaget makes the social, interpersonal element basic to knowledge (p. 88). This is in keeping with the general theory in which knowledge is consistently treated in subject–object or subject–subject terms (Piaget, 1970, p. 721).

In Piaget (1932) knowledge is defined as a relation between two actors. Spatial relations, for example, develop as the child interacts with things. When the child throws a rubber ball, it changes location; when the ball is retrieved, it comes back to its previous location; then it is put on a table, it rolls to the floor; when it is set in a box, the ball remains in place. The child constructs order between these two sources of action by placing them in a relation where the joint actions are known to have regular effects. As a result of this relation, the child also knows about rubber balls and other objects. But the study of development is not about the child's knowledge of rubber balls, trees, wood blocks, marbles, and so forth. It is about the general, ordered relations between the child's actions and the actions of objects or, in the present context, between the child's actions and the actions of others (cf. Piaget, 1970).

Synonyms for social relations include 'bond', 'contract', 'agreement', and 'sympathy'. Interpersonal relations are the topic of social thought. They are general forms for ordering real and possible actions and their effects derive from everyday exchanges between persons. Piaget (1932) takes relation, as the language depicting knowledge, for granted. He therefore addresses his discussion to ways persons form, distinguish, maintain, deviate from, re-establish and become conscious of their relations with one another.

The interactive nature of social knowledge is tied to the idea that relations serve as rule systems for interpersonal exchanges. Distinctions among relations are founded in the 'procedure' (p. 71) or 'method' by which interactive rules are formed. In non-democratic authority relations, rules are imposed by one person on another in a kind of 'coercion' (p. 86) and 'constraint' (p. 90). In relations of equality rules are co-operatively constructed (p. 71) through 'mutual consent' (p. 97).

Interactions are the bases of these methods. Imposition of rules, which leads to relations of unilateral authority, comes from instances like the following: the child sits down to eat, but the parent interrupts the moment by telling him to get up and wash his hands first. Or, the child is playing and the parent stops play by telling her to go to bed (p. 191). In authority bonds of this type there are thousands of 'categorical obligations' (p. 135) which adults lay out for children independently from coherence with their on-going words, actions, feelings or intentions. Relations of equality, by contrast, are derived from and account for interactions in which the subjects act co-operatively through an actual 'sympathy' (p. 196) and 'reciprocity' (pp. 231 and 294).

The socialization of knowledge
Social knowledge about interpersonal relations is constructed by both

persons who enter into interactions. For the sake of clarity we will focus on these constructions from the child's vantage point. In this case mother, father, siblings, neighbours or friends, represent the other persons who join into interaction. The question is, how do they contribute to the child's constructions? In so far as interpersonal relations refer to rules of interactions, the answer to this question has to be posed in terms of interactive processes.

Piaget (1932) considers the other person as an essential ingredient to social knowledge. For an action to be understood as a rule, it has to be 'frustrated' and the child must 'search' for regularity (p. 87). The child is concerned with constructing a general form for the actions 'which takes account of the particular object that is being handled' (p. 87). The child incorporates objects into already known forms of actions and adapts these forms to the object's actions (p. 87). The idea of a rule comes when the child finds a way to correlate these two sources of action – the subject's and the object's (pp. 87–8). The object makes itself knowable by acting in return to the subject's initiative. For instance, marbles reveal themselves to children by rolling away, falling into holes, bouncing off one another, and so forth, according to particular actions which the child performs.

In subject–subject interactions the other person stands toward the child in the following terms: the other is a critic, constrains, frustrates, disputes, exerts pressure, acts contrary to, contrasts with, or is otherwise a distinctive actor from the child. When the other person's turn comes up, he or she can contribute freely to the interaction. The child who is concerned with order has to take this contribution into account and discover a means to relate it to his or her own action. The idea of opposition is basic to the acquisition process. Without it, the child's constructions would be utterly egocentric and aimed toward 'subjective satisfaction' (p. 99). But if social knowledge is to be serviceable, as is knowledge concerning physical objects, the child has to situate him or herself so as to 'submit' to others; i.e. the social reality outside themselves (p. 107).

Piaget (1932) describes two types of subject–subject interactions in an exaggerated contrast. One is a method of *constraint*; the second is a method of *reciprocity*. Both lead to interactive rules but each implies a different outcome with regard to morality (e.g. p. 90; pp. 340–3). The method of interacting by constraint involves two actors, one of whom acts arbitrarily instead of in coherence with the other. Most of Piaget's (1932) examples refer to adults who pose actions to children which are based on external rather than intersubject reasons. That is, both the adult and the child bring rules to interactions but, when asserting their rules, adults frequently do not attempt to co-ordinate them with the rules children might have (e.g. pp. 138 and 191). Nevertheless, the child will make an effort toward co-ordination by incorporating the adult's rule but not necessarily integrating it with other rules (e.g. pp. 36 and 191).

The method of reciprocity is based on two persons interacting by presenting their rules tentatively toward one another (pp. 71 and 100). Reciprocity occurs when a child and another 'make allowance' for each other and submit their respective rules for mutual inspection (p. 92). This can be done by merely acting in reciprocal fashion, discussing differences, jointly analysing disputes, and so forth. There is to this method a literal co-operation (p. 95) which Piaget (1970, p. 721) suggests implies a co-construction of rules. That is, two subjects agree to decide together on the rules by which they will interact and therefore make the process of constructing knowledge a joint venture.

Piaget (1932) considers both methods as direct means for socializing children's knowledge (cf. pp. 89 and 92), and so indexes them (p. 407). In either method, the other person serves as a counterpoint to the child's thought by providing data which the child on his or her own would not. The nature of human interactions is such that when one person passes the initiative for acting onto the other, the other is relatively free to compose whatever he or she will. The task of constructing order across everyday interactive episodes could not even get off the ground if the child could ignore the other person's contributions. In the present model, the child is obligated to take account of the other and, in so far as the child lives within an established social network, the construction of social knowledge is by definition a process of socialization.

General implications

In this section our general framework is elaborated through discussion of two of its implications; first, the result of making interpersonal relations the units of analysis is considered and then the consequences of schematizing interactions as relational *functions* are discussed.

Defining and finding an adequate methodology to assess relations are problems with a long history in the social sciences. Most theorists agree that interpersonal relations exist, but there is no consensus on what a relation is, how it is formed, or how one goes about studying it. Our thesis is that relations can be understood as general forms of interactive rule systems which are constructed to order the self with respect to one or several other persons. Because of the dynamic nature of social activity, relations have to be more than mental statements of 'who I am' and 'who the other is'. They refer to an order that can be maintained as self and other continue to interact through a series of changing content and effects. Our view is best described as a *functional* approach because it emphasizes that persons build their interactions around the principle that they can maintain their relative positioning through the diversity of content which everyday interchanges produce.

Relations as general interactive forms

The idea that social development is mainly a matter of 'coming to know persons' (Flavell, 1974; Shantz, 1976) typifies traditional theories of cognition. Knowing a person means to grasp that person's inner thoughts, feelings or motives in some valid way. The person is depicted as an object which has independent existence. Cognition is the tool the subject uses to reach toward and grasp the object validly, mistakenly, or not at all. The act of grasping depends on the tools the subject uses and in this sense cognition is a mediator. Since tools develop (e.g. egocentrism wanes; role-taking improves) older subjects are more likely to achieve valid appraisals of persons than their less able, younger counterparts.

In the present framework persons are known not as objects *per se* but in terms of relations. Social knowledge is achieved by putting oneself into an orderly interactive relation with another. Interactive rule systems allow the self and the other to generate interactions whose effects can be anticipated for the relation itself. Neither subject can predict exactly how the other will act when his or her turn comes up. But both subjects know how to put actions in sequence in order to produce effects within their relation (e.g. maintain it; repair it when it goes awry). This is social, interpersonal knowledge. In addition, continued operation on their relation allows each subject to develop conceptions of one another as persons who are related through a particular bond.

The need to posit penetration to another's inner workings is an unnecessary encumbrance. Logically, one person can never know for sure the details of another's private self. Any self can reserve parts from the public and purposely deceive. And, of course, it is not clear that a self can come to grips with its own inner workings fully. On what grounds then can persons know one another adequately? In the present framework, one answer is that persons can know each other in terms of their relation and conceptualize one another accordingly. They look upon their interactions as affecting each other as persons in so far as the interactions produce effects on their relation.

Consider the case of parent and child in the relational aspect of unilateral authority. It seems risky to suggest that the child understands the parent's conception of authority in its full sense. The parent's idea of authority has a history of which the child could not be aware and is probably embedded in the adult's conceptions of the role of child-rearing in the context of societal values. Simultaneously parents are probably unable to debrief themselves and get into the child's mind. Nevertheless, both parent and child can conceptualize their relation and agree to interactive rules predicated on it and designed to keep it intact.

The nature of this agreement is made explicit in the general rules derived from continued interaction. Consider the following examples taken from everyday life: (1) The child greets his mother with a kiss as she is making breakfast in the kitchen. She smiles and says: 'Comb your hair.' (2) The child comes home from school and runs to her mother who is talking on the telephone. The mother says: 'Don't bother me. I'll talk to you later. Go play.' (3) The child is playing out of doors when his father goes to the front porch and says: 'Come in now. It's time to eat.' (4) As the child sits down at the dinner table his father says: 'Get the milk.' (5) A brother and sister are playing while eating. Their mother says: 'Don't hit your sister.' (6) The child is playing a game with her father. Her brother walks into the room. The father says: 'Come and join us.' (7) Later, when the brother and sister are playing, the mother says: 'It's time to go to bed now. Put your toys away. You have to get up early for school.'

From one point of view, each example contains a parental rule in the sense of a norm for particular actions. But this is misleading; these are not norms. Children know that they can approach their mother when they come home from school and that they can hit one another in play. The sense of rule to be drawn from these examples is the following: the parent has the right to stop and start action in the child. The parent has the privilege of interrupting whatever the child is doing and redirecting the child irrespective of the coherence between the child's ongoing and the requested activity. As members of the relation, children have the right to act according to the parent's stated wishes. When children order themselves as recipients with respect to parents' impositions, they are drawing a reasonable conclusion about the general form of their interactions.

The authority aspect of parent–child relations refers to rules about the *method* by which parents and children interact. The rules deal explicitly with the procedures of interaction and only incidentally with specific behaviours. The general forms which are abstracted from actual give-and-take and co-ordinated in systems, specify procedures for carrying on social business: who may initiate interaction; how it can be initiated; who has the right to interrupt ongoing activity; how one goes about changing the current flow; who has to react to another's request; and so forth. Each particular interactive episode has its own content and momentary purpose. Additionally, however, each is composed according to relational rules so that as content varies from moment to moment the persons remain ordered to one another in a known way.

Procedures are acquired through socializing interactions between persons. This fact allows children to construct general forms which already include the other person's *behavioural* consent. Thus, when functioning in a familiar relation both persons can generate activities according to a shared rule system. Further, it permits children to order themselves in relations with persons who are unfamiliar. Just a few interactions may be sufficient for the child and the other to reach consensus on the relation they are in and therefore on the rules they should follow in generating new exchanges.

These ideas may be used to help clarify conceptualization of parent–child relations, a standard topic in the social development literature. Much effort has been expended on finding ways to differentiate styles in which parents exert authority over children. Styles of authority in rearing are then looked at for their outcomes in children's social behaviour. For example, punitive and hostile practices should yield different outcomes than love withdrawal and induction techniques (Becker, 1964; Hoffman, 1970; Kohlberg, 1969). In general, these and other reviewers agree that styles of rearing are correlated with children's social behaviours, but only moderately. This has led some researchers to seek more refined classifications for coding parents' input and other researchers to scepticism about the model itself.

From the perspective of our framework, there are three major weaknesses in this line of thinking. First, there is more in common in parental styles than there are differences between them. As Gadlin (1976) has suggested, stylistic approaches do not hide the fact that they are all forms of exerting control over children. Authority may be administered gently, subtly or emphatically but styles do not hide from children the fact that they are being controlled. Second, if the outcomes of different styles are to be understood, then children's conceptions of authority have to be studied (Damon, 1977). That is more than a nod to asking children what parents do and why. It requires a study of children's conceptions of the authority aspect of relations along with the development of these conceptions. Authority in the interactive sense of the present framework is not an absolute, frozen in time. It develops as the parent–child relation remains open to change through continued feedback from further interactions and from other known relations, as the child attempts to integrate them.

The third weakness concerns the distinction between the generic parent–child bond and the relational aspect of authority. Parents and children, more than any other persons, save perhaps husband and wife, interact across the gamut of interpersonal possibilities, ranging from deep intimacy to extremes of alienation. It is unsatisfactorily restrictive to view this generic bond solely in its authoritative aspect. Children's conceptions of authority go beyond their parents to older siblings, teachers, neighbours and clerks in stores. Simultaneously, their full relation with parents is only partially covered by authority. If rearing practices are to be meaningfully connected to children's social behaviour, then these other aspects of parent–child relations will have to be studied. This work is already under way and is illustrated in studies of attachment and love (Ainsworth, 1969; Escalona, 1968). As Weinraub et al. (1977) compellingly argue, the parent–child generic bond fits within a broader network of social relations. A whole range of interpersonal conceptions are available in this bond apart from authority and control. It remains for researchers to identify them within the parent–child bond and to connect them with their comparable forms in other relations.

Relations and interactions

In traditional theories of socialization, interpersonal interactions were considered the primary experiential base from which social behaviours were learned. Generally, the focus of analysis was a two-act sequence. A child acted, then another person reacted. The aim was to discover how the reaction affected the child's action. For example, did the reaction increase the probability of the action? Did it affect an internal state (e.g. dependency) which in turn influenced the reoccurrence of the action? Subsequently, this model was changed when it was pointed out that interactive influence flowed in two directions (Bell, 1968). Hence, careful analyses were done to display effects children's actions had on others' reactions and vice versa (e.g. Waxler and Yarrow, 1975). At present, further schemes are being considered such as treating interactions as a 'dialogue' (e.g. Bakeman and Brown, 1977) and studying interactions as they affect the establishment of a relation (Bell and Ainsworth, 1972).

The present framework offers a conceptual clarification along the lines of Ainsworth and her colleagues. If an interpersonal relation is the topic of social thought, then interactions may be understood to be composed to service the relation. That is, interactions can be analysed according to general relational functions. The following functions are a tentative list. Interactions serve to: (a) establish a relation; (b) keep a relation going; (c) correct a relation when it goes awry; (d) intensify a relation; (e) terminate a relation; and (f) change a relation from one mode to another.

It is important to distinguish the literal content of action from general forms which have a relational function. For example, *hitting* as an act may serve as a greeting (function b) between young boys who are friends. The same act initiated by a boy to his father would likely lead to function (e); if, on the other hand, the father hit the boy it probably would fit function (b), as attempt at correction (c). There is a difference between trying to specify effects interactions have on persons in the sense of literal content and effects interactions have on relations. The former leads to statements about particular actions (e.g. aggression, altruism) and about goals or motives of individual actors (e.g. she intended to help; he accidentally hurt him). The latter approach emphasizes the general form as a function which has a specified place in the relation. For example, when one person acts to benefit a friend, the content is almost irrelevant and the motive is as much due to the terms of the friendship relation as it is due to the actor. Further, the effect, while it accrues to the recipient equally benefits the relation itself. It may, for instance, ensure that the recipient will reciprocate to the actor when an appropriate occasion arises.

For the past three years we have been studying relational functions (a) through (e) in child–child and child–adult relations. Rather than studying naturally occurring exchanges, we have asked children to generate descriptions of interactions. A brief review of some of our findings is now presented to illustrate the usefulness of this functional scheme.

We have now interviewed over 300 subjects with respect to function (b), keeping a relation going. Children from ages 6 to 13 years were asked to tell us stories in which a child their age did something *kind* for another child their age; an adult; a friend; etc. We assume that kindness (for other children 'being nice' or 'showing that you like them') serves as an overt *acknowledgement* by one person to another that he or she wants to keep their relation alive. Two general results are now singled out. First, children describe quite different interactions as acknowledgements for different relations. For example, younger children describe kindness between peers in terms of *being together* or *giving* food or material items. The same subjects say that *obedience* expresses kindness in children's initiatives to adults (see also, Lo Cicero, 1974). The idea that two children do the same thing or have the same thing, which marks almost all the stories of younger children, puts into behavioural terms the relational characteristic of equality. Obedience, in contrast, acknowledges the inequality between children and adults as well as the location of the directives for action – the child does what the parent would like him or her to do.

Second, there are developmental changes in the meaning of acknowledgement for both of these general relations. Kindness between peers is described by 13-year-old subjects in terms of one child helping another who is in need. It is expressed in a wide variety of particulars: *loaning* when the other has lost something; *sharing* food when the other has none; *teaching* when the other does not know something; *inviting* the other to join a group when he or she is on the outside; or *giving advice* when the other is in trouble. Reciprocation is implied or sometimes stated and it is apparent that peers are equals except for the momentary need which puts one of the peers in a deficit state. After the kind initiative, both peers reach a literal position of equality. For 13-year-old subjects, kindness toward adults is depicted mainly by children *doing chores* when an adult requests or needs help on some project. The subjects often spontaneously bring in the notion of the actor's *voluntary* initiative even when the act was requested by the adult. In general, these developmental changes for child–child and child–adult relations, which were first observed cross-sectionally, hold also longitudinally across a two-year age span (Locker, 1977).

In our further exploration of peer relations, we have looked at the functions of establishing, intensifying and terminating peer relations (Volpe and Youniss, 1976). Children between ages 7 and 13 years agree as to the interactions which bring about friendship, change a relation of mere friends into *best* friends, and end the relation. And, most recently, we have begun to study the function of repair. We first asked subjects to tell us about those things which friends do that upset their relations. Then we asked other subjects how they would go about becoming friends again once these breaches occurred. One of the results is interesting because it highlights a distinction between peer and child–adult relations. Young adolescents were asked to describe interactions which would repair a boyfriend–girlfriend relation and adolescent–parent relation after the parties had had a fight. Subjects were asked who would have to take the first initiative and then they described how the parties would act in turn through four steps. The majority of subjects ($N = 400$) said that either or both the boyfriend and girlfriend could act first but that the adolescent had to act first after a fight with his father. Looking only at the first two turns of repair, we observed that the majority of subjects said that the boyfriend would apologize and then that the girlfriend would apologize or vice versa. As with kindness, this result was a literal expression of equality in terms of reciprocal action. In distinction, in the second episode, most subjects said that the adolescent would first apologize and that then the father would accept the apology. Instead of both persons admitting sorrow for having harmed the relation, the father simply accepted his son's admission without having to reciprocate in kind.

We consider these data useful for opening up an avenue to a systematic analysis of interactions. From the interactants' viewpoint, exchanges of behaviour are dynamic and free-form compositions. Once a person has acted and passed the floor to the other, the first waits to be affected by the second's action and then exerts an additional effect when his turn comes again. There are numerous occasions for the interaction to become a string of unconnected acts which might take the parties in various directions. On the other hand, if the parties agree to their relation, then the function which their interaction is serving reduces the sequence to a thematic whole. This is true even when the persons do not start off with the same functional goal in mind. The shared relation should allow them to identify disparity and come to a consensus as to how the current status of their relation is best served.

From an outside observer's perspective, the general question concerns the basis of agreement on which the parties are ordering their exchanges. This is the issue which ethnomethodologists have emphasized (e.g. Douglas, 1970). It is also the issue which some developmental psychologists have now begun to address. Ainsworth and her colleagues, for example, have adopted an approach compatible with the present framework with regard to establishment of a bond between mother and infant. Bell and Ainsworth (1972) have looked at interactions which lead to attachment via communication patterns. Stayton et al. (1973) have observed the function of re-establishing the relation when it is temporarily interrupted. And Blehar et al. (1977) have looked at interactions which serve to maintain the already established relation.

Conclusions

Socialization theory dominated the study of social development for several decades. It was based on a general model of the child, behaviour and behaviour's determination closely fitting learning theories of that day. In the 1960s cognition re-entered psychology in general and soon began to play a role in the study of social development. In the main cognition was introduced into this study so that it would be compatible with the foregoing model. That is, it was treated as an intervening or mediating variable. However, the addition of cognition to the old model caused difficulties. These difficulties have persisted up to the present. They pertain to the distinction between the child's contribution and the contribution of other persons to social thought. Contemporary cognitive theories, putting emphasis on the child's thought, either exclude or make confusing the effects of socialization on development. Incidentally, they also put a wedge between the child's thought and his or her social action.

I have tried to show that social knowledge can be approached through a different epistemology based on an interpretation of Piaget's writings. This is not an epistemology built on notions like role-taking or egocentrism but a framework which regards social knowledge as conceptions of interpersonal relations. Knowledge as a relation gives conceptual clarity to socialization which is made an integral part of the knowledge process. It also provides a means to connect knowledge to action insofar as relations are understood as rule systems for interactions. Interactions are then viewed as functions which serve relations.

The details of the proposed model need to be filled out with empirical data. Clear lines of research seem to follow from it and already some research is being done which shows its feasibility. One need not, of course, follow this epistemology in order to study relations in terms of interactive rule systems. In light of current theories, the present epistemology may be too radical. It posits relation as the unit of analysis rather than the entities of self and other. It stresses the unseverable connection between knowledge and action. And it takes development for granted because the knowledge process which serves construction simultaneously serves to ensure that known relations will be reconstructed.

Perhaps by taking such an extreme view in comparison with contemporary theories of cognition I have provided an opportunity for conceptual reflection. According to our framework, social knowledge thrives on counterpoint between actors who are seeking co-ordination. If the present framework resists immediate assimilation to other cognitive models, it may then serve to evoke discussion concerning some issues which will have to be resolved if the study of social development is to move beyond the point to which socialization theory brought us thirty years ago.

References

Ainsworth, M. D. S. (1969) Object relations, dependency, and attachment. *Child Development 40* (4): 969–1025.

Bakeman, R. and Brown, J. V. (1977) Behavioral dialogues: an approach to the assessment of mother–infant interaction. *Child Development 48* (1): 195–203.

Bandura, A. (1969) Social-learning theory of identificatory processes. In David A. Goslin (ed.) *Handbook of Socialization Theory and Research*. Chicago: Rand McNally.

Becker, W. C. (1964) Consequences of different kinds of parental discipline. In Martin L. Hoffman and Lois Wladis Hoffman (eds) *Review of Child Development Research, Vol. 1*. New York: Russell Sage Foundation.

Bell, R. Q. (1968) A reinterpretation of the direction of effects in studies of socialization. *Psychological Review 75* (2): 81–95.

Bell, S. M. and Ainsworth, M. D. S. (1972) Infant crying and maternal responsiveness. *Child Development 43* (4): 1171–90.

Blasi, A. and Hoeffel, E. C. (1974) Adolescence and formal operations. *Human Development 16* (5): 344–63.

Blehar, M. C., Lieberman, A. F. and Ainsworth, M. D. S. (1977) Early face-to-face interaction and its relation to later infant–mother attachment. *Child Development 48* (1): 182–94.

Bradley, R. H. and Caldwell, B. M. (1976) Early home environment and changes in mental test performance in children from 6 to 36 months. *Developmental Psychology 12* (2): 93–7.

Chandler, M. J. (1973) Egocentrism and antisocial behavior. *Developmental Psychology 9* (3): 326–32.

Damon, W. (1977) *The Social World of the Child.* San Francisco: Jossey-Bass.

Dienstbier, R. A., Hillman, D., Lehnhoff, J., Hillman, J. and Valkenaar, M. C. (1975) An emotion-attribution approach to moral behavior. *Psychological Review 82* (4): 299–315.

Douglas, J. D. (1970) *Understanding Everyday Life.* Chicago: Aldine.

Escalona, S. K. (1968) *The Roots of Individuality.* Chicago: Aldine.

Feffer, M. (1970) Developmental analysis of interpersonal behavior. *Psychological Review 77* (2): 197–214.

Flavell, J. H. (1974) The development of inferences about others. In Theodore Mischel (ed.) *Understanding Other Persons.* New Jersey: Rowman and Littlefield.

Flavell, J. H., Botkin, P. T., Fry, C. L., Wright, J. W. and Jarvis, P. E. (1968) *The Development of Role-taking and Communication Skills in Children.* New York: Wiley.

Gadlin, H. (1976) Spare the rod: disguising control in American child-rearing. Paper presented at American Association for the Advancement of Science, Boston, Massachusetts.

Hoffman, M. L. (1970) Moral development. In P. H. Mussen (ed.) *Carmichael's Manual of Child Psychology, Vol. II.* New York: Wiley.

Keasey, C. B. (1977) Young children's attribution of intentionality to themselves and others. *Child Development 48* (1): 261–4.

Kohlberg, L. (1969) Stage and sequence: the cognitive-developmental approach to socialization. In David A. Goslin (ed.) *Handbook of Socialization Theory and Research.* Chicago: Rand McNally.

Livesley, W. J. and Bromley, D. B. (1973) *Person Perception in Childhood and Adolescence.* London: Wiley.

Lo Cicero, A. (1974) *The Development of Children's Concepts of Kindness.* Doctoral dissertation, The Catholic University of America.

Locker, R. (1977) *Children's Conceptions of Kindness.* Doctoral dissertation, The Catholic University of America.

Miller, P. H., Kessell, F. J. and Flavell, J. H. (1970) Thinking about people thinking about . . . : a study of social cognitive development. *Child Development 41* (3): 613–23.

Piaget, J. (1932) *The Moral Judgment of the Child.* London: Routledge and Kegan Paul.

Piaget, J. (1970) Piaget's theory. In Paul H. Mussen (ed.) *Carmichael's Manual of Child Psychology, Vol. I.* New York: Wiley.

Piaget, J. (1971) *Biology and knowledge.* Chicago: University of Chicago Press.

Riegel, K. (1976) The dialectics of human development. *American Psychologist 31* (10): 689–700.

Scarlett, H. H., Press, A. N. and Crockett, W. H. (1971) Children's descriptions of peers. *Child Development 42* (2): 439–54.

Selman, R. L. and Byrne, D. F. (1974) A structural-developmental analysis of levels of role taking in middle childhood. *Child Development 45* (3): 803–6.

Shantz, C. U. (1976) The development of social cognition. In E. M.

A conceptual discussion of cognition   227

Hetherington (ed.) *Review of Child Development Research, Vol. 5.* Chicago: University of Chicago Press.

Simpson, E. L. (1974) Moral development research. *Human Development 17* (2): 81–106.

Stayton, D. J., Ainsworth, M. D. S. and Main, M. B. (1973) Development of separation behavior. *Developmental Psychology 9* (2): 213–25.

Volpe, J. and Youniss, J. (1976) Interactions that establish and terminate friendships. Paper presented at the 84th Convention of the American Psychological Association, Washington, D.C.

Waxler, C. Z. and Yarrow, M. (1975) An observational study of maternal models. *Developmental Psychology 11* (4): 485–94.

Weinraub, M., Brooks, J. and Lewis, M. (1977) The social network. *Human Development 20* (1): 31–47.

Youniss, J. (1975) Another perspective on social cognition. In Anne Pick (ed.) *Minnesota Symposium on Child Psychology, Vol. 9.* Minneapolis: University of Minnesota Press.

8 Young children's understanding of society

Hans G. Furth

A developmental approach to socialization

The society into which children are born and in which they grow up is as much a continuous and living part of themselves as any other part of their psychology. It would be futile to look for a particular point in time when a child first responds to societal events, affectively or cognitively, as if before that time the child existed apart from or without a societal context. As soon as children between one and two years of age develop the first glimmer of the capacity to become aware of self and 'objects', they encounter necessarily and primarily persons (one of whom is the self) and not merely physical and natural events. This 'object' capacity has two consequences: first, children begin to produce, use and understand symbols (whether in the form of external play or gestures, the conventional speech of society, or the internal images of fantasy); second, the interactions of the child towards persons and things take on forms which eventually come to be called 'adult', 'mature', 'logical', 'reasonable'.

Laurie Lee was a three-year-old boy living in a Cotswold village when World War I ended. He had heard constant verbal references to the ongoing war, to adult males being away in, or coming home from, the war and he had occasionally encountered persons and events connected with the war. In *Cider with Rosie* (Lee, 1959, pp. 21–8) he recalled his thinking at the time: 'All my life was the war and the war was the world.' In other words, for him the war was the wider societal context within which he felt his personal life, the life of his family and the village, to be enveloped. When he heard and experienced the excitement occasioned by the end of the war, he reasoned: 'Now the war was over. So the end of the world has come. It made no other sense to me.' However, experience did not confirm his expectations. 'Peace was here; but I could tell no difference . . . it brought no angels or explanation; it had not altered the nature of my days or nights . . . So I soon forgot it and went back to my burrowing among the mysteries of indoors and out.' In this connection he turned to explore the life around the cottage, 'The yard and the village manifested themselves at first through magic and fear.' The boy was now well aware of the difference between the familiar village and the strange outside world, the same world which shortly before he identified with the war: '. . . the thumping of heart-beats which I heard in my head was . . . the marching of monsters coming in from outside. They were creatures of the "world" . . .'.

Whatever else we may want to say about the young child's mind, this anecdotal example illustrates that growth of societal understanding is best conceptualized as a continuous process of the child's constructing, exploring and testing out theories in connection with personal encounters and interests. Piaget has described this growth from childhood to adulthood by focusing on the logical and physical world. On the evidence of controlled observations he has elaborated a theoretical perspective on the development and nature of intelligence which provides a radical and all-encompassing framework for a psychological study of human development, even in areas beyond the logical-physical. What is radical is most forcefully implied by the concept of 'object' mentioned in the first paragraph. In a Piagetian perspective an object is primarily a construction on the part of the person rather than an outside thing that somehow becomes connected to the person. If one takes this constructivist position in a seriously consistent manner, one comes to regard what has been called the child's socialization not as the impact of a given societal system on the child's mind and behaviour, but as the child's construction of his or her social and societal world. This construction is merely one part of the ongoing process of general development toward mature understanding. Investigators naturally limit their study to particular parts, such as Piaget did with physical-logical understanding and others may do for interpersonal, moral, political, person or self-understanding. But these partial perspectives are all interconnected in the person of the growing child and failure to recognize this in theoretical formulations can only lead to an inadequate picture of the child's development and to insoluble intellectual dilemmas.

In the social sphere, problems of how a child becomes an adult member of society or comes to perceive self or other persons will take on different meanings depending upon whether one considers these 'objects' as given from the outside or as constructed from within the child. In the radical constructivist view advocated here, children construct social and societal reality fully as much as they construct logical-physical reality. The continuity of intelligence and bodies of knowledge across generations is commonly depicted as a transmission from parents to children; something similar is said in the case of conformity to society and its customs. A more apt image, in accord with Piaget, is that of a continuing construction: society, like knowledge, is an ongoing construction, a fact which can be obscured by our capacity to have a synchronic and static view of 'objects' instead of seeing them in their diachronic and historical becoming.

Underlying this discussion is the assumption that in all human products, including what we call knowledge and human society, one can conceptually separate form and content, such that form refers to the general coordinations, rules or framework, while content refers to the particular instances. What is constructed and develops from within the child is the form or the framework; what is provided from outside, if you like, is particular content. Form is what makes the content 'human', 'reasonable' or 'mature'. In relation to a known *object*, we can say that a particular instance has structure or meaning; in relation to the *subject*, we can say the person has a structural capacity or understanding. It is Piaget's contention that the study of the development of logical understanding contributes both to our knowledge of the child's psychology and the nature of logical knowledge. Similarly one can expect that an investigation of the development of societal understanding will lead to a more adequate conceptualization of the nature of society as well as of human psychology.

However, for a variety of reasons the study of children's understanding of the broader society in which they live, e.g., the adult world of work, business and institutions, has been singularly neglected. This remarkable omission is all the more regrettable in that it reflects the unhappy split between the 'real' world of work on the one hand and, on the other, the somewhat esoteric world of academic theories of socialization and the educational policies to which they give birth. Berger and Luckmann (1967) point to the need for a comprehensive theory of socialization which encompasses not only the child's capacity to understand the self and other persons as individuals (in addition to the physical world and sundry verbal knowledge), but also the wider social world with which the child is in ever increasing daily contact. In this perspective, understanding of self, persons and society represents three sides of the same thing, namely, the child's socialization (Mead, 1934). A mature sense of self is unthinkable without a proportionate development of understanding other persons and of the society which all share in common. The latter includes not only a knowledge of persons but also a knowledge of the physical objects and verbal traditions created by and intimately linked to society. To understand any one product of society necessarily involves some intellectual grasp of its relation to the broader social context. For example, one cannot understand a television set without at least a rudimentary knowledge of its invention, production and distribution by persons in different social roles and its use as one of the principal media and sources of entertainment in our society.

The Figure 8.1 illustrates the developmental progression of understanding in the physical and the social spheres. On the right side are the stages Piaget has studied, on the left side is the hypothesized differentiation of social components which comprise a person's socialization. One of the main advantages of a Piagetian perspective is the bridging of the gap between action and knowledge. This split can be shown to be partially a pseudo-problem created by an inadequate theory of knowledge. Consequently, the stages of the outline refer to a person's practice as well as to theory, to behaviour and knowledge. The theoretical reason for linking behaviour and knowledge is twofold: first, all behaviour is governed by some form of knowledge (know-how), otherwise it would not be the behaviour of a living person; second, as Piaget has demonstrated, the most theoretical knowledge derives developmentally from action knowledge and retains its nature of know-how.

Socialization is manifested either in practice or in knowledge, i.e., as social *behaviour* or social *awareness* (something the child *knows*). Under either aspect socialization is considered to be an internal process of construction. Although internal, it is a process that is responsive to the person's experience of the world; in fact, it is nothing other than the

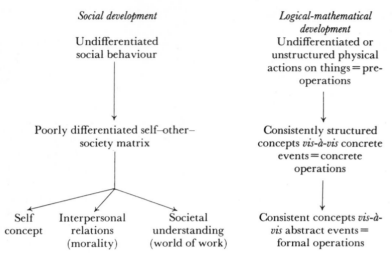

Fig. 8.1   Social development and Piagetian stages

gradual formation of the person who lives in a social world, from infant and child to adolescent and adult. How does the child come to make sense of the social world? Even a partial answer to this question would make a crucial contribution to general or specific issues that are being seriously investigated, such as moral and religious development and role taking. It would provide an integrating perspective for these part issues, none of which can be conceived in isolation from the society. The 'how' question is, however, premature until the 'what' question has been sufficiently clarified; that is, *what* knowledge or understanding do children and adolescents have of their society? It can be expected that a systematic probing of the child's social world would confirm the hypothesis that ego development, person perception and societal understanding are indeed three facets that have their common root in the child's undifferentiated self–person–society matrix. If that were the case, the *what* question would give a lead to the *how* question. As children's intelligence develops during the course of living and experiencing the world, they acquire not only logical know-how and understanding, but the basis for understanding the self, other persons and society in general. This developmental basis for 'social' intelligence is as real and as important for scholastic and occupational achievement as is general intelligence, of which it is a part.

Piagetian research and theory has been severely limited by an almost exclusive emphasis on strictly logical-mathematical thinking. If the theory is to be maximally useful, it is necessary to apply it to other areas. Such applications have been made in the field of role taking (Selman and Byrne, 1974) and interpersonal relations (Damon, 1977; Youniss 1975), in moral development (Kohlberg, 1966), in religious development (Goldman, 1964) and in art and music (Gardner, 1973). The exploratory study reported at some length in this chapter extends the developmental-cognitive approach to society and the world of work in a manner fully consonant with Piagetian theory. In a certain sense societal concepts have a greater degree of 'objectivity' than interpersonal concepts and therefore would seem to lend themselves to a stage-like analysis more readily than other more subjective concepts. However, Piagetian theory is employed here to provide a potentially useful philosophical perspective for the components and acquisition of knowledge rather than as a theory to be confirmed or rejected. Since no researcher is free from a philosophical perspective toward knowledge, it is considered an advantage that the present investigation explicitly adopts a clearly analysed developmental theory of knowledge.

With regard to developmental stages, Piaget is certainly the most explicit theoretician using the stage concept and relating his theory to societal understanding is a worthwhile attempt that could provide a firmer base to the developmental theory. Piaget's stage concept can easily be misinterpreted as a rigid, quasi-automatic succession of cognitive capacities with societal factors largely unavailing. Nothing could be further removed from the essence of Piaget's theory which aims precisely to explain that only through the experience of social living can a child's intelligence develop; in accord with the theory (not in spite of it, as often misunderstood) individual and social experiences, just as individual propensities transmitted by heredity, make a contribution particularly where specific content is concerned.

In Piaget's theory the thinking of a child develops on the basis of interaction with things and persons. However, societal institutions do not lend themselves to physical interaction and concrete representation as do physical things. The origin of a child's understanding of society must therefore be traced to the same source from which the concept of self and of other persons derives: the child's experienced interrelations between self and others. These 'others' can be adults or peers. It is clear that society is inherently an adult thing and, in contrast to peer relations, is of little interest to the young child. Piaget's theory strongly supports the thesis that equality based peer relations rather than the unilateral relating of adults to children, are the primary media through which the growing child comes to construct increasingly adequate patterns of relating. Concepts of self and of persons are products of further reflection and integration of this relating.

Piaget has employed the frequently misunderstood term 'egocentric' to describe the general attitude or mode in which young children construct and use concepts before these concepts acquire the logical and functionally 'real' character of the adult world. Essentially, children play at things and playing can well be called their favourite strategy of intellectual adjustment. They may be excited and curious about experiences connected with the speed, movement and sound of a car. Not being able to interact with the real car, they play at car and do that with the same or more interest than in the original event because now, thanks to their knowledge and symbol capacity, they are originators and not merely observers of the experiences. Many years later, when as adolescents they have constructed those criteria by which our society differentiates reality and play, their interest in cars will no longer be satisfied by play alone.

In the area of social development the child's interests in and first steps toward conceptualization are no doubt limited to personal relating. One could be tempted to assume that personal social understanding is far ahead of children's societal understanding. However, as suggested earlier, young children's concept of self and other persons is actually quite primitive and undifferentiated. Available research (Livesley and Bromley 1973) supports the opinion that it is primarily during the age range of five to twelve years that children come to understand these concepts in a gradually more mature fashion.

Regarding societal institutions one can assume a similar development as in social–personal understanding with this one major difference: whereas social–personal relating is going on all the time in a 'real' fashion during most of the child's waking life, encounter with 'society' is much more indirect. It is implicit, e.g. in the way parents, themselves influenced by society, treat their child; it is indirectly observed through symbols, ceremonies, customs, in adult life and conversation, and through a few occasional contacts with occupations, such as doctor or postman. Only with school is there a massive encounter with a societal role, namely, that of being a pupil. As a consequence and in line with Piaget's approach, one would expect that adult society is at first apparent to children primarily in an 'egocentric', that is, playful mode.

Only about age six, when they are experiencing the beginnings of internally controlled thinking (Piaget's concrete operations such as number, classifying, ordering), would they slowly come to apply such operations to personal and societal interrelations. One might even consider the child's almost total ignorance of society as one of the reasons for the relatively late understanding of what a person is. After all, every person in our society is not merely someone who relates on a personal level but also someone who functions within the society.

In fact, an understanding and differentiation of these two components, the personal and the societal, within the one social person is probably a critical prerequisite towards maturity of social development. A second prerequisite and one that lends itself more readily to observation and assessment, is the understanding of money and how it functions in society. The relation between money and societal roles becomes apparent when one notes the historical evidence: throughout the modern era the money economy has been a major instrument through which the sphere of the personal has been removed from societal relations. The latter are now mainly contractual and objectively valued in money terms.

One might therefore expect that around age six the typical playful images and elaborations of young children will slowly recede as they come to understand the function of money and of societal roles in their most immediate context. Eventually children will make inferences beyond the observed context based on partially adequate theories. They will finally come to eliminate 'childish' contradictions altogether through functionally adequate theories of how money works and what a societal – in contrast to a personal – role implies. One could, if one so wanted, call this the stage of concrete operations, in that children understand society as pictured in concrete instances. Once this stage of societal understanding is reached, children can then begin to make sense of society as a whole and think of it in terms of an organized multitude of interrelations. One could expect that after this time the concepts of government and general needs of a community will be further elaborated. To understand society as a whole is probably related to what Piaget calls formal operations. Strictly speaking, societal institutions are not concrete entities but vast systems of personal and societal interrelations that can only be adequately grasped in an abstract sense.

In support of this point scholars studying political thinking in children have explained the emergence of mature conceptions around age sixteen as founded on formal thinking (Adelson, 1971; Greenstein, 1965). Unfortunately, formal operations are perhaps the one stage of Piaget's theory that has been least clarified and is open to a wide range of interpretations. For this reason alone it may be wise to neglect the concrete–formal distinction altogether when dealing with the social area. Another problem of formal operations is related to motivation and opportunity. The development of cognitive capacities does not automatically lead to their use in all possible content areas. This is especially true with regard to formal operations in general (Piaget, 1972), and the content area of societal institutions in particular.

Previous studies

The following review of the literature pertaining to societal understanding in children of primary school age is divided into three sections dealing with money, roles and community respectively.

Money

Strauss (1952) investigated the 'development of monetary meaning' in 66 children, age $4\frac{1}{2}$ to 11, in Bloomington, Indiana. He categorized the children in nine stages of understanding and reported median age, range and number of children for each category.

Stage I (median age 5·4) involved merely recognition that money is associated with buying. The children held that more coins buy more things and that there is an exchange of money between customer and shopkeeper for no functional reason other than custom. Stage II to IV (median age 6·3 to 6·5) still does not include a proper grasp of the mathematics of money value. In Stage II children inferred that the shopkeeper pays for the goods, but without relating the shopkeeper's to the customer's money. They thought that the shopkeeper used the money for personal wants and that the exact amount, neither less or more, has to be paid for buying something. In Stage III they realized that change was not always given, but only if one pays 'enough'; they mentioned the motive of getting rich on the part of the shopkeeper who is considered the owner of the shop. In Stage IV they connected paying for goods with the notion that goods cost money or that the shopkeeper has to earn money; moreover, they knew that change is less than what you pay.

In Stage V (median age 7·10) children began to grasp the numerical value of money and described impersonal aspects of the customer–shop relations. Customer's payment was thought to go directly to the owner. These advances in thinking were continued and firmly established in Stage VI (median age 8·7), particularly regarding the impersonal nature of the shop and the reason why one cannot buy money. The customer's payment was now considered to be for the goods, not for the owner. In Stage VII (median age 8·9) children expressed the notion that one sells for more than one buys, but no reasons were given. Absent ownership was recognized and the need to distribute earnings between shopkeeper and helpers in some fair proportions. Finally, the big advance of Stage VIII (median 9·9) was an explanation of profit and in the last Stage IX (median 11·2) children understood that cheating to the detriment of the common good was possible. They still had difficulties with the need for and the existence of several middle men between maker and shop.

Table 8·1   Five substages of monetary understanding in Strauss, 1952

Stages	N	Range	Median	
I	7	4·8-5·11	5·4	Value = size
II–IV	19	5·9-7·2	6·5	Value differs from size
V	6	6·0-8·9	7·10	Numerical value and change understood
VI, VII	22	6·8-10·6	8·9	Shop uses customer's money to buy goods
VIII, IX	17	8·4-11·6	10·7	Profit and owner understood

By collapsing range-overlapping and logically related stages one can present Strauss's findings in five substages with the distribution of children and predominant characteristics as indicated in Table 8·1. It can be noted that even in this table there is large overlap of ages across substages, such that the increase in the lower range is less dramatic than the substantial increase in the median and the upper range. This means, for instance – if one can set aside questions of sampling – that a precocious youngster can develop from Stage I to VII in two years whereas a slower child may take more than twice that time.

Danzinger (1958) interviewed 41 Australian children, age 5 to 8 years, on their understanding of economic concepts such as rich and poor; of buying and selling, money; employer and employee. He summarized his results by suggesting two stages for the concept of money: I categorical, when children think of money exchange as a ritual or a moral custom, and II reciprocal, when they understand that the customer's pay is used to buy goods for the shop. Similarly, concerning the concept of the 'boss' there was Stage I, pre-categorical, when the boss is perceived as having no economic function at all or merely as a special person who 'wants' to pay the workers and Stage II, relational, when the boss is seen as owner in an economic sense. However, Danzinger points out that this stage does not include understanding of profit. He reports that five to seven-year-old children were invariably in the lower categories, so that a comparison between them and eight-year-old children yielded the most conspicuous contrast. Linking these findings with the Strauss study one could assume that Danzinger's two stages correspond to Stages I to V and Stage VI and VII, respectively. Danzinger classified a majority of eight-year-old children and no children below age 8 in the second stage, a result which appears generally in agreement with the American study of Strauss.

Societal roles

Past research on children's understanding of societal roles has been quite sparse and some early work has not been followed up. The main interest of Hartley et al. (1948) was children's spontaneous group identifications and their understanding of ethnic terms and multiple group membership. They interviewed 86 children in New York City, aged $3\frac{1}{2}$ to $10\frac{1}{2}$. They found that to the question: What are you? or What is your father? the youngest children replied principally by name whereas from age five upwards ethnic descriptions (e.g., Jewish, Italian) were predominant. When asked 'When daddy goes to work, what is he?' the vast majority of children, including the youngest, switched to designate the occupation. While multiple membership did not seem to cause problems, criteria and compatibility of roles were quite poorly understood, as illustrated by the reply of a child (5·1) 'I'm Jewish when I am awake, when I sleep I'm American' or another child's (4·8): Is your daddy Jewish? 'No he's a soldier.' Logical inconsistencies were observed right up to the oldest children studied and were similar to those encountered by the present author in a study reported below. In two subsequent papers, Hartley et al. proposed a developmental sequence in dual role perception, but their data on role permanence failed to support this hypothesis. This difficulty of identifying relatively clear developmental stages in societal role perception contrasts with stages in the understanding of money. Perhaps the concept of 'societal role' is not sufficiently critical or more likely not sufficiently analysed yet to be singled out in a developmental description of society.

Children's awareness of social class differences was probed in a study of 179 Scottish children, age six to nine, by Jahoda (1959). A pictorial social perception test yielded a performance and a verbal score, the latter based on children's verbal explanations. The expected age differences were reflected by the percentages of zero scores in six- and nine-year-old children: 21 per cent and 2 per cent for performance, 51 per cent and 7 per cent for verbal scores; in other words, nearly 80 per cent of the six-year-old children showed some measure of understanding the societal concept of class. Differences in test scores between working and middle-class children were largely accounted for by differences in measured intelligence. However, attitudes and feelings seemed to be determined by the children's particular social environment. Jahoda concluded that an incipient class concept was not dependent on verbal expressions and originated with gradual awareness of occupational status.

Subsequent studies by Jahoda and Crammond (1972) and Jahoda and Harrison (1975) confirmed the early grasp of certain societal concepts, even to the extent that they understand such 'adult' experiences as 'alcoholic', provided these societal roles have affective meaning within the children's own experience. The strong affective component in role perception is probably an additional component that obscures the concept of societal role.

In the area of personal relations, Livesley and Bromley (1973) documented the poverty of psychological descriptors in children below age thirteen. Children below age seven limited their descriptions of persons to superficial situational (extra-personal) characteristics, while above age eight they referred to personal characteristics. It was only around 12–13 years that organizing and qualifying statements appeared to an appreciable extent. Only the older children showed understanding of 'how the person's behaviour and inner personal states can be related to historical and biological factors' (p. 221).

An investigation by DeFleur and DeFleur (1967) on occupational role knowledge and television as its probable source sampled three sets of six occupations each. Set I included personal contact occupations, such as teacher, shopowner, mailman; Set II were television contact occupations, such as lawyer, waiter, reporter; Set III were general culture occupations with which generally children have neither personal nor television contact, such as printer, accountant, engineer. In a small American Midwestern town 237 children, aged 6–13 years, were asked questions about the activity, work hierarchy, place, instruments and preparation for each occupation. The results can be summarized as follows: children's knowledge test scores for Set I (personal contact occupations) rose from 39 per cent at age 6 to 73 per cent at age 12–13; for Set III the score was substantially lower at all ages; for the television contact occupations of Set II the mean score was between I and III such that at ages 6 and 7 it was close to Set III and then rose steeply to be close to Set I from age 8 onward. Occupational status consistency and similarity with adult rankings started from a near-zero level at age 6 and rose slowly with age: for the television contact occupations, however, the score rose rapidly to age 8 and subsequently remained higher than ratings for Sets I and III. Children from the lower class scored consistently lower than middle-class children; no sex differences were observed for Sets I and II, but boys were better on the general culture occupations of Set III. Further, the authors observed that the children's comments on the television contact occupation showed a 'stereotyped consistency', typical of the television source from which the knowledge derived. This observation is confirmed by the superiority of status rankings for Set II in so far as occupational prestige is a foremost example of stereotyped consistency. In conclusion, television certainly appears to provide children with some occupational knowledge; however, this knowledge frequently takes the form of superficial and misleading information about the labour force of their society. The authors warn about the potential personal and social problems occasioned by a distorted belief concerning particular societal institutions.

Country, community and government

Jahoda (1962, 1963a, 1964) studied children's understanding of concepts related to their country of residence; he tested 144 children in Glasgow and grouped them into three groups 6 and 7, 8 and 9, 10 and 11. Concerning national symbols he observed a relatively rapid rise with age in proportion to children who could name such symbols as the flag or the national anthem. In contrast to this largely affectively toned information, children's grasp of nationality (what it means to be Scottish and British) or of geographical concepts was quite deficient. Thus the percentage of children who confused a town with a street or a country was 41 per cent at the youngest age group and still 16 per cent at the oldest. An adequate grasp of nationality was shown by only 7, 27 and 66 per cent in each of the three age groups. Quite similar proportions obtained on adequate spatial representations (7, 25 and 57 per cent) and use of geographical terms (7, 41 and 70 per cent). The author concluded that logical understanding about country and nationality develops quite slowly during the primary school years whereas an intuitive grasp of national symbols and societal customs can occur at a much earlier age.

Estvan and Estvan (1959) interviewed 88 children of two age levels, 6–7, and 11–12, in an urban and a rural area of Wisconsin. They presented pictures of various life situations and social functions and coded the children's descriptions of these pictures on recognition and context on the one hand and attitudes and values on the other hand. Among the conclusions pertinent to this review was the relative lack of children's references to the town or village as a community, which made the authors wonder whether children, as they go about their societal activities, realize that they are participating as members of some community (p. 26). Similarly, children had very little to say about governmental functions, only 14 per cent mentioned them, even though nearly all recognized the State capitol building (p. 191). A picture of a factory elicited quite poor responses and was associated with negative affect, even from urban children whose fathers worked in a factory (p. 69). The authors concluded that the younger children were generally more sensitive to the interpersonal element than to the physical or temporal context in a societal situation (p. 257) and, understandably, that they were more interested in the children rather than in adults when both were shown in a picture such as the schoolroom (p. 208). Comments going beyond the immediate spatial or temporal context were quite infrequent even for the older children. Concerning children's concepts of time and history, Jahoda (1963b), summarizing past research, proposed a developmental progression of 'realized' (=understood) time. The sense of a historical context is not generally shown in children below age twelve.

Scholars who have studied children's political socialization have generally focused on attitudes rather than comprehension (Greenstein, 1965). An exception to this is Connell (1971) who interviewed 119 children aged 5–19 in Sydney shortly after an election which had been widely publicized and had engaged the interest and emotions of the adult population. Connell took issue with the view of political socialization as a system by which children are processed by agencies of socialization. He argued in favour of an historical process of construction on the part of the child. The children he interviewed were 'not *simply* reproducing adult ideas' and their thinking at different stages was 'much more than moments in the accumulation of a stock of adult ideas' (p. 235). He proposed four stages in political understanding: (1) intuition (below age 7), (2) primitive realism (age 7+), (3) construction of political order (age 10+), (4) ideological (age 15+). The first stage showed undifferentiated confusion of political and non-political material and imaginative elaborations of isolated facts. The second stage was characterized by the beginning awareness of the political and governmental realm in the form of an indistinct task pool. Children at this stage described the government in personal terms, as doing a few isolated tasks, and governmental persons were looked upon as 'special' and 'important'. Only at stage (3) was there an elaboration and division of the task pool and awareness of the multiple relations among the political actors. Political power was no longer seen as primarily personal, but as founded on hierarchically ordered institutions. Connell (p. 42) observed that children's grasp of this impersonal role structure preceded specific knowledge of details which are filled in unsystematically at a later age. While the idea of hierarchy appears at the beginning of this stage, the understanding of issue-conflict is a later product. Connell (p. 51) links Piaget's formal operations to the fourth stage with its conceptions of political argument, societies and policies as wholes.

Connell's constructivist approach to political socialization was also emphasized by Adelson (1971) who interviewed children on the purpose and limits of the law. The children were between 12 and 16 years. He found the younger children of his sample singularly immature. They centered the purpose of law in personalized, concrete instances, not on society as a whole; their range of time perspective was quite narrow (the sense of future developed earlier than the sense of the past) and they seemed to be unaware of inner complications in personality or motivation. The author concluded that the adolescent's immaturity 'stems not from an ignorance of facts but from an incomplete apprehension of the common conventions of the system' (p. 1029). Like Connell he attributed the older adolescents' grasp of these conventions to the elaboration of formal thinking about the world of political actions.

A study of children's societal thinking[1]

The constructivist approach outlined in the introduction provided the theoretical context for a study directed by the present author during 1974–75. The investigation was undertaken to explore children's thinking on a variety of societal issues and had a two-fold aim: to provide a systematic description of young children's understanding of the grown-up world and to explore the relationships between such understanding and the child's developing intelligence.

Procedure

The children interviewed in this study came principally from three primary schools within one area in southern England. A small village, a small town and a larger town were represented. The interviewer individually contacted as many children in these schools as proved practical without disturbing the school routine. A total of 98 boys and 97 girls were interviewed; their distribution from age 5 to 11 is shown in Table 8·2 (see p. 254).

A free interview technique was used to elicit children's comments on societal institutions. Particular guide lines were as follows: (1) The discussion was restricted as far as possible to persons, events and situations within the child's personal experience, (such as school, shop, electricity) and avoided direct questions on things concerning which the child could only have a hearsay acquaintance (e.g., politics). (2) However, the children were encouraged to go beyond mere description or factual knowledge and talk about underlying reasons and interpretations. In this sense the message to the child was clearly one of being given an opportunity to present his spontaneous personal thinking rather than being given a test of what he knew or remembered. (3) The contents of the interview included among other things the shop and its transactions, the nature of paid work, the difference between personal and societal roles, what a community (town, village) is and what it needs and how institutions and roles come about. (4) The direction of the interview varied according to the child's responses so that not all children commented on identical points. This has both advantages and disadvantages; but in an initial exploration the advantages of spontaneous openness to individual directions and predilection outweighed the disadvantage of lacking complete statistical data. An apparent idiosyncratic remark of one child concerning a particular societal custom may be set aside as a curious anecdote, but if such remarks are heard again quite independently even once or twice and fit into an overall tendency of children's societal thinking, such remarks become psychologically, if not statistically, highly significant. To illustrate, one child contrasted the initial freedom to choose a particular job from the obligation to stay on the job, 'once they have chosen they are not allowed to quit'. Only one other child quite independently and spontaneously made a similar remark and buttressed it with similar reasons. Yet the 'pseudo-conservation' of roles is clearly self-orginated and hence gives a valuable clue to children's thinking about society and occupation. One must assume that even in the best of cases children articulate only a small portion of what is going on in their mind and imagination.

The length of the interview depended on the child's cooperation and the school timetable. Generally, most interviews occupied between 15 and 25 minutes and only a handful of children were extremely reticent so that their records proved useless. All children's comments together with the interviewer's remarks were tape recorded and later transcribed verbatim. The records were analysed in terms of main content areas and then inspected for developmental characteristics.

Results
The results are presented in three broad sub-sections that correspond to the division of the literature survey under the heading 'Previous studies'. Sub-sections A and B focus on the two key concepts of money and societal roles, while sub-section C deals with children's images of government and community.

Money and the shop's business   For most of the youngest children, age five and six, a shop is a place where 'they sell food and you get money from them ... You pay him, you get things and he gives you some money back' (B33,5–10). In the children's mind the observed function of the shop is therefore two-fold, to get food and to get money. Why do they give you some money back? 'So that you get to buy food. You'd have to pay him though.' Another child (L01,6–0) reasoned explicitly: 'If people give money in and he doesn't give any money back, he wouldn't be able to buy food and then people would die.' Generally change is considered a major source of money. Money to save was said to come from the shop: 'He probably buys something, then the man gives some more (=different) money back and he gets a lot of money' (L43,6–8). Other children suggested that the more you buy the more change you get: 'The shopkeeper has to pay ... Sometimes he gives you four p(ence) for the sweets back and sometimes he gives you more when you want some bigger things.' (H74,6–8). The children not only confused buying and selling but also included money among the things being sold: 'You give money to the shopkeeper and he sells it for more things' (H54,6–9). When asked how the goods get into the shop, they mentioned the factory, vans, at times the government, but they denied that the shopkeeper pays any money on that occasion. For these children the function of money is observed but not understood. Paying at the shop is a ritual, a social custom, that has no other purpose than its own ritualistic performance.

The next stage in the understanding of the shop's business is observed in most seven and eight-year-old children. By that age they understand numbers and grasp the function of change; it is no longer considered a source of money: ' ... because the till is for the other people, if they have not got the right money ... if you give less (!), you can't have any change' (H76,6–10). Money is mentioned as something a shopkeeper needs 'to give people their change'. To give the right amount of change is thought the main prerequisite skill for a shopkeeper. What happens to the money paid into the till is unclear to these children. Hence they take resource to playful images: it is given to poor or blind people, to some kind of charity, to the queen or the government. Even when they mention payment to the factory it is more a vague afterthought rather than something required. 'If it's ninety (pence) and you've given one pound, you get ten p(ence) back ... It keeps on going like this ... he buys some things, gets change, it goes on like that' (L25,6–11). When this boy was further prodded and the idea of the till filling up was presented, he continued, 'No, the shop's got to pay (the factory). The money what people ...'.

To recognize that the customer's paying for the goods generalizes to the shop is a veritable achievement of logical inference. Here is a girl (B24,7–11) who at first denied payment to the factory but then corrects herself: 'I think it's sort of like just me walking into a shop to buy something. I think they have to buy the stuff. Why, I know that one ... from the money that they get from the people who walk into the shop every day.' This inference beyond the immediately observed is characteristic at the next stage of understanding when the general function of payment is taken for granted and selling and buying is clearly related. Stage III of monetary understanding was observed in the majority of nine- to eleven-year-old children: 'Shop pays factory, (with) the money he gets from the men who come into the shop and buy things' (B55,9–0). While this interpretation is easily recognized and mentioned as a matter of course, there is the potential difficulty of simple arithemic. If the clothes shop's money 'goes towards buying other clothes and things' (H49,9–0), are these things for the shop or for himself? The uncertain answer of this boy was 'yes' to both. Not really understanding how there can be money for both, the boy regressed to playful guessing and suggested that the shopkeeper, including 'his parents and his family . . . get six pounds'. The problem of how the shopkeeper gets money for his own is difficult enough when children believe that all the money in the till goes for buying goods. To overcome this hurdle the children prefer to think of a shopkeeper who gets paid by somebody else for working: 'If it's not his shop, he's just working in it, he'll get paid . . . I suppose he still gets paid when it is his shop' (L41,11–8). But this girl did not understand how this is possible. Other children make a compromise by calling on the government or some extraneous source: 'He pays the factories from the stuff he sells for that . . . (How does he get money for his own needs?) His wife gets it. She earns it . . . she does a job of some kind . . . somewhere else' (B53,9–2).

This difficulty of surplus money is probably compounded by a kind of moral consideration. It may be all right to use shop money for the buying of goods, for paying salaries, for tax, but to pay oneself seems improper to the thinking children at this stage. To get money for themselves, shopowners 'would get it out like any other normal person would, when they're not actually in the shop, because you couldn't really take the money out of the till . . . like an ordinary family, like mine, where we get money out of the bank or anything, and out of the tin . . . just like any other family, but when they're in the shop they take money from the till to buy stores for the shop. Money for himself (is) in the bank. Out of his own – if they won some money they'd probably put it in the bank so that at a later time, if they are hard up and need some money, they can go to the bank and take it out when they like' (B19,11–2).

Only a few children (14 per cent of the 8 to 11-year-olds) showed systemic understanding of the principle of buying and selling so that they could comfortably include profit towards the shopowner's own expenses. 'They pay a certain amount to get goods off big firms and then they make . . . they have to pay a tiny bit more for everything they sell . . . so that way they don't get paid by the government. They get their own sort of wages from that tiny bit more they get every time'

(B13,10–10). 'You buy the things from Cash and Carry. You make a profit by putting them up one or two p(ence) . . . with the half p(enny) VAT (Value Added Tax) on them . . . The profit is his, he just acts normally with the money' (L58,11-0). These children may understand the basic principle of buying for less and selling for more but they would certainly be astonished if they realized that the actual mark-up is considerably more than a 'tiny bit'. Actually none of these children thought of the expenses of running the shop.

The conceptual difficulties associated with the monetary system were shown in many other areas besides the shop's business. As an example, when children were asked whether teachers get paid, many 5 to 7-year-old children thought like this boy (L01,6–0): 'They teach when they are in school and when they are not at school they earn money to buy things.' Other children connected personal money with work and wages, an early association common even among the youngest children, but teaching was not considered work: 'Teachers don't get paid. (Who does?) Building houses, putting wall papers on. (Who pays?) The government, sometimes' (B34,6–0). 'She has money from her wages . . . for working . . . cleans up the house, other people's houses' (H73,6–8). The idea that dinner money or various kinds of school collections pay for the teachers' wages plus all the school things was common among 7 to 9-year-old children. Moreover, the amount of pay was related to the amount of work, as expressed by this boy (L44,7–8) who took pride in his insight: 'Because the one who does the most good things, gets the most money . . . something which I probably worked out.' Other children related the amount to benefits received: 'The worse ill you are, the more you pay him because the more glad you are to get better' (B01,7–0).

Societal roles.   Due to the numerical character of money transactions the description and classification of children's understanding of money and its use in the shop's business is relatively straightforward. It is more difficult in the area of societal roles even though the contrast between the least and most advanced thinking within the age range examined is just as strong and compelling. Questions like 'What kind of a person is a . . . (teacher, doctor)?' proved to be most revealing because they tapped both personal and societal understanding.

The youngest children answered by giving the name of a certain person or describing an activity that stood out for them: The headmaster is a 'strong kind of' person, 'able to smack people if they are naughty' (L61,5–11), 'who blows a whistle' (L60,7–3); a teacher is a person 'who can do sums like a hundred and millions' (H72,6–9). Others merely recorded their feeling toward the person: 'A policeman, they are very good, they don't let people go in the other people's houses' (L49,7–9). Even children in the upper age range of nine to eleven limited their comments to a few superficial qualities: 'An experienced person about robbers, same as the teacher, it (!) has to be an experienced person about robbers, what they do and how they can be so dangerous. You look in books, you learn a lot about robbers, you get a robber book, for instance, and you read it, you go over and over it again and it gets in your mind and you don't forget it and then when you're grown up, you still remember it and you want to be a policeman' (B54,9–10).

Compare all these 'childish' comments with those of a few children who responded to the same question from a different base of understanding. Significantly these children happen to be the same who had shown a systemic understanding of monetary functions. 'Teachers, they act differently . . . If they're going out, just normal town people, they're all happy. If they're going to school, grrr, all horrible, old loads of kids', 'Get on with your maths' (L58,11–0). These children spontaneously contrast the societal role and the personal life of a teacher. The next extract adds psychological insight into different personal ways of handling a societal problem. 'Some teachers have the same personality at home and at school . . . The teacher tries to put over politeness and does not want to put over any personal feelings and she doesn't really want to reveal her true personality because it might be embarrassing . . . but teachers who say what they really feel like, that gives the children much more of a punishment . . . they give them what they feel like giving them, not what they are meant to give them . . . If you're not very keen, you can bore your pupils . . . just got to be like any normal person, not like, 'cos most teachers seem very stuck up. Just say what you really think . . . and believe in what you are doing. I think it's more fun for the children if they're not quite told exactly what to do so they can use their imagination' (L07,10–8). In a word, these few children showed a developed sense of individual differences and personal understanding. They could describe how personal qualities and the societal demands of a role interact.

On the question of how someone becomes a teacher or a shopkeeper or something else, the youngest children referred almost exclusively to a personal decision. They talked about it the way they themselves would decide to do one thing rather than another. 'He just wanted to be one. He looked until he saw the shop he wanted' (B15,6–7). 'They ask people who were making houses if they get tired and then they start doing them' (B05,6–5). A builder gets up in the morning, 'he looks for a place to build something' (B38,6–11). There is also the notion of getting appropriate permission. She becomes a lollipop lady 'cos she wants to be. She has to ask if she wants a coat' (B29,5–10). Another child wondered, 'did he ask the queen whether he could be a shopkeeper?' (B33,5–10).

Somewhat older children introduced the government as a kind of supreme employment agency: 'He goes up to an important man who gives you jobs and he asks if he can be a shopkeeper and they give him some tests' (L16,8–4). Other children referred to their own career choice, like this girl who wants to become a doctor: 'If somebody wants to be a doctor, when they are at school, they sort of, when somebody falls over, rush to it and say, "I'll wash it up for you" and they enjoy doing that mostly and they are very intelligent at their work and pass tests for doctor' (L13,8–2).

In these examples the personal-voluntaristic origin of societal roles is quite obvious; in young children's images adults do what they want and because they want it; concomitantly they follow rules and get appropriate permission; apart from a few stereotypic exceptions the adults are invariably good, beneficial and happy. Without an adequate basis for understanding either personal or societal reality, the playful images are midway between serious opinion and pretend play. What can be more playful than this unexpected answer to the question, When a bus driver goes home, is he still a bus driver? 'Yes, they never give up. Once they choose they choose and have to do it until the end of their life. The bus, perhaps it's still all right and somebody else can choose it' (B46,6–4). Apparently this boy, like others, was impressed by two characteristics of the adult world, its stability and the career choice open to all persons. Both these points are then attached to rules and made concrete by the contrast between a permanent bus and the ageing bus driver. These playful images about persons in society, quite typical of younger children, were less prominent at the transitional stages and disappeared only in those few children who had advanced to a basic understanding of individual persons and societal roles.

Children's images of the community and government. The most direct way of discovering a person's understanding of society is probably to enquire about the community in which he lives. Accordingly the children in this study were asked questions like: 'What can you tell me about the town or village you live in? What makes it a town? What things, what persons are important?'

The children's comments on these issues were singularly children-centred, almost regardless of age. 'We need bosses to tell us what to do' (H59,5–5) said a five-year-old; 'a town needs houses, shops, parks, somewhere where children can play happily' (H01,9–8; L06,9–11) came from two nine-year-old children; a ten-year-old girl remarked: 'you need lots of people, mothers and fathers . . . to have some more children' (H34,10–3). Other children mentioned their father's occupation, 'A town needs bricks to make houses, dad is a building worker' (L80,6–10); some focused on the word 'important' and referred to authority figures like prime ministers, queens, policemen, the law.

In view of this poverty of understanding of community, it is not surprising that the children's ideas about the government were equally inadequate. The results largely confirmed what was found in various studies reported in 'Previous studies'. Between ages six and eight, when they mentioned the government, children referred to it as a special man, a rule giver or a job distributor. 'Because he's a precious man and God and Jesus and the mayor, they know where things are. The place where the Council is, these men have wigs on – I've seen them on television' (B47,7–0). 'The law, he's, this is all his world and he takes care of it . . . and he must sort things out . . . The person who wants the job goes to see the law' (L04,7–7). Here, just as in other areas, children have not yet reached a basic framework on which to construct a meaningful explanation: hence these playful images which reflect the children's active thinking. The notion of the government parcelling out all adult occupations is particularly striking. Since the first differentiation of the adult world is in terms of different occupations and government is an adult matter, this thought appears quite logical.

For somewhat older children, age nine to eleven, the function of government became more realistic. However, they are presented as isolated activities. 'The Council, they type . . . all kinds of messages, letters' (L35,9–10). Some children saw the Council as the primary source of money, 'a place where you have people who pay for things' (L32,10–6). One younger boy (H65,7–3) remarked that teachers get paid from the headmaster and he in turn gets money from the Council. 'I just guessed', he added, 'I only know that the Council owns towns, my mum taught me.' A few children expanded the notion of property owner and turned the Council into a business concern. The Council has money, 'they have to earn it. They go abroad, get money from bringing goods back and selling them' (B17,10–11). Twelve children, all ten- or eleven-years-old, clearly referred to governmental services and reciprocal payment in the form of taxation. However, only two of these children described the government's function in any differentiated manner.

Discussion
The adult world in the child's mind.   Seven characteristics can be listed as typical of how the grown-up world 'out there' may appear to a child around five to six years of age. This world is (1) undifferentiated, (2) personalized, (3) ordered according to known rules, (4) free of conflict, (5) with free access to money, (6) egotypical and (7) accepted and identified in its most superficial aspects. (1) 'Undifferentiated' means here the child's lack of awareness of individual differences in persons and institutional roles. Apart from a few familial persons, all other adults and all roles seem very much alike to this child. Without insight into specific differentiating functions the child is bound to be more impressed by two *common* features, namely unfamiliarity and being treated more or less similarly by all, rather than by the *differences* in adult society. (2) The personal–impersonal distinction of societal roles is absent from the child's thinking. While the first charactistic stresses the child's ignorance of what a person is, the second does the same regarding impersonal roles. 'Personalized' is used here in contrast to 'objective', but also as opposed to 'personal'. Children project personalized characteristics onto society because they fail to understand both personal and societal roles and are ignorant of the underlying difference in scale and perspective. Hence societal decisions are thought to emanate from the free will of a particular person: a person becomes somebody and occupies a role because of a simple act of will. The striking redundancy and frequency of the words 'to want' in children's comments confirm this. In contrast to children's experience of incessant constraint on their own will, adults probably are perceived as doing consistently what they want to do. (3) Concomitantly with the focus on free and voluntary decisions ('voluntarism') is an equal stress on rules which pervade societal life. Thus, a child may believe that an individual may become, say, a teacher by mere act of will but thereafter has to adhere rigorously to specific rules of the classroom which are themselves

laid down by some external agency. Free choice with no constraint is in a sense the polar opposite of a world of fixed rules where everything is ordered, if not pre-ordered. (4) Note that these two opposing tendencies do not lead to conflict in the child's mind. The conflict-free atmosphere gives a fairy-tale flavour to children's thinking about society where adults do both what they *want* and what they *must* do, and everybody is friendly and happy. (5) Since the use of money is only nebulously understood, access to money appears free and easy. (6) Ego-typical refers to the tendency of the child to generalize from a personal interaction across an entire range of situations. (7) Related to this tendency is the focus on the immediate external aspects of a role, such as the notion that a building or a uniform creates a particular role.

Each of these seven characteristics changes as the children's intelligence develops, and five years later most children are well on the way toward overcoming the misunderstandings and contradictions inherent in them. Their daily experiences and personal interactions expose them to the opportunity of new insights and their understanding becomes thereby detached from personal preoccupations and more 'reality'-oriented. Whether it is possible to subsume all or most of these descriptive characteristics under one or two main themes cannot be answered at this point. Two principal developments stand out, however, as proposed in the earlier review: the understanding of the use of money and the shop's business on the one hand, the understanding of personal and impersonal roles and their distinction on the other hand. The first was the clearest developmental pattern revealed in this investigation. An important point to be made, one referred to by earlier commentators like Marx or Simmel (1900), is that in our era money has become the most salient and versatile means underpinning the 'impersonal' society at large. In this sense money is the symbol for the impersonal role in the personal – impersonal distinction. The second development relates to differentiation of the personal side of this distinction. As children interact with others and begin to understand how persons, including the self, function and what it means to be a person, (Livesley and Bromley, 1973), they become able to understand the differences between personal-social relations, say of friends, and impersonal relations, such as prevail in a shop, or more subtly, between the personal and the impersonal components in a relation between pupil and teacher.

Four stages of societal understanding.   Using these two main themes as guides one can attempt to propose a developmental progression in societal understanding between the ages of six and eleven years. Four stages are here proposed, labelled I *playful*, II *functional*, III *part-systemic*, IV *systemic-concrete*, and are directly related to the two themes, money and social roles. Stage I is characterized by the playful attitude which Piaget called 'ego-centric'. There is undifferentiated personalized thinking, as shown by the seven characteristics listed above. Stage II is still largely playful but shows the first interpretations based on understanding of the immediately observed function, e.g., payment for goods, role-person differences. Stage III extends this to more distant relations as children become aware of and grapple with the problem of differences in scale between a personal and a societal perspective; this leads to a first differentiation within parts of the social and societal systems. Some part-systems are grasped and the personalized aspects recede; but there are still major logical inconsistencies which are most evident in the failure to understand personal profit or governmental money. Stage IV implies an overall, if rudimentary, understanding of how a society functions namely, in its government, community needs, economic system, and the consequence of personal and individual differences. Stage IV in no way involves an extensive and detailed understanding of society; it merely implies sufficient grasp of societal structures to avoid the major logical inconsistencies found in Stage III. Hence it is likely that a more mature stage, would follow Stage IV for those persons who apply their formal intelligence to society, its past history and its present functioning. Stage V could be called *systemic-analytic* to distinguish it from IV. Development in Stage V would be particularly focused in the areas of government, community, law and historical perspectives.

Table 8.2 provides an overview of the distribution of the 195 children in the present study in terms of these four stages of societal understanding. The main criterion was the child's comments on money and its function; where such comments were not available evaluations were based on: (a) the extent of playful images and functional interpretations; (b) functional inferences beyond the immediately observed event. While this implied some ambiguity, it was not difficult to reach a consensus among two judges. Moreover, an analysis based on only those 123 children who commented on money matters did not differ appreciably from the present table.

Table 8.2 Stages of societal thinking in 195 children, age 5 to 11, in percentages of age

Stages	Age and number of children						
	5 (16)	6 (34)	7 (25)	8 (29)	9 (46)	10 (34)	11 (11)
I	94	65	9				
II	6	32	72	76	28	15	
III		3	20	24	70	68	64
IV					2	18	36

One can consider children's societal thinking in Stage I as having the seven playful characteristics described above and the children in Stage IV as being free of these characteristics with an adequate understanding of some fundamental prerequisites to societal life. The transitional Stages II and III were observed in the societal thinking of most children between ages seven and ten. In Stage II there were first successful attempts to make functional sense of first-order societal interactions in which children participate. Stage III is of great psychological interest because here children make inferences beyond the observed events and construct theories about how societal events may function. These theories are partial and inadequate and lead to compromises and apparent conflict, as seen most clearly in connection with the issue of personal money for the shopowner. At the same time they demonstrate most clearly that understanding society is not primarily a matter of retaining particular knowledge or information, but a matter of constructing adequate theories.

Conclusion. In conclusion this study of societal understanding lends support to the developmental approach outlined in the first part. Four pieces of evidence mutually confirm one another. First, there were a number of observed cases of developmental experiences. Children in the course of talking about a societal issue spontaneously and without any suggestive remarks on the part of the interviewer gained a new insight, corrected previous playful statements and related previously unconnected bits of knowledge. Second, many children formulated theories that were clearly of their own making and could not have come to them from others. In Stage III these partial theories were frequently found to be mutually conflicting and at times experienced as such by the children themselves. Here then are not only theories constructed by the children but cognitive conflict generated by these same theories rather than by any new external input. This is the very constellation that is central to Piaget's equilibration model. Third, it was possible to discover age-related and logically consistent character-istics in which children organized their thinking around two main societal concepts: the use of money and the personal-societal role components. Fourth, the resulting stage differences were in no way a cumulative increase of moving from knowing less to knowing more, but related to the mode in which the children made sense of events. Between the playful images at Stage I and the logical consistency at Stage IV there is in the transitional Stages II and III the concern with first-order functional relations and with partial theories beyond the immediately observed events.

The principal objective of this essay has been to provide a systematic developmental account of young children's understanding of society. In addition, it has been demonstrated how societal understanding needs to be related to development in general. This mutual relation, if further confirmed and elucidated, could bring about a long overdue rapproche-ment between the study of the personal world, the traditional domain of psychology, and of the societal world, commonly regarded as belonging to sociology and anthropology. Piaget's theory of radical constructivism has a significant role to play in facilitating this rapprochement.

Note

1 The research reported here was supported in part by a grant from the Social Science Research Council of Great Britain. Janet Smith conducted the interviews and Mary Baur helped with the analysis. The code number of a specific child is followed by age in years and months.

References

Adelson, J. (1971) The political imagination of the young adolescent. *Daedalus* *100*: 1013–50.
Berger, P. L. and Luckmann, T. (1967) *The Social Construction of Reality*. London: Allen Lane.
Connell, R. W. (1971) *The Child's Construction of Politics*. Carlton, Victoria: Melbourne University Press.
Damon, W. (1977) *The Social World of the Child*. San Francisco: Jossey-Bass.

Danzinger, K. (1958) Children's earliest conceptions of economic relationships. *Journal of Social Psychology* 47: 231–40.

DeFleur, M. L. and DeFleur, L. B. (1967) The relative contribution of television as a learning source for children's occupational knowledge. *American Sociological Review* 32: 777–89

Estvan, F. J. and Estvan, E. W. (1959) *The Child's World: His Social Perception.* New York: Putnam.

Gardner, H. (1973) *The Arts and Human Development.* New York: Wiley.

Goldman, R. (1964) *Religious Thinking from Childhood to Adolescence.* New York: Seabury.

Greenstein, F. I. (1965) *Children and Politics.* New Haven: Yale University Press.

Hartley, E. L., Rosenbaum, M. and Schwartz, S. (1948) Children's use of ethnic frames of reference: an exploratory study of children's conceptualization of multiple ethnic group membership. *Journal of Psychology* 26: 367–86.

Hartley, E. L., Rosenbaum, M. and Schwartz, S. (1948) Children's perception of ethnic group membership. *Journal of Psychology* 26: 387–9

Hartley, E. L. and Krugman, D. C. (1948) Note on children's social role perception. *Journal of Psychology* 26: 399–405

Jahoda, G. (1959) Development of the perception of social difference in children from 6 to 10. *British Journal of Psychology* 50: 159–75

Jahoda, G. (1962) Development of Scottish children's ideas and attitudes about other countries. *Journal of Social Psychology* 58: 91–108.

Jahoda, G. (1963a) The development of children's ideas about country and nationality. *British Journal of Educational Psychology* 33: 47–60, 143–53.

Jahoda, G. (1963b) Children's concepts of time and history. *Educational Review* 15: 87–104.

Jahoda, G. (1964) Children's concepts of nationality: a critical study of Piaget's stages. *Child Development* 35: 1081–92.

Jahoda, G. and Crammond, J. (1972) *Children and Alcohol.* London: H. M. S. O.

Jahoda, G. and Harrison, S. (1975) Belfast children: some effects of a conflict environment. *Irish Journal of Psychology* 3: 1–19.

Kohlberg, L. (1966) Moral education in the school. *School Review* 74: 1–30.

Lee, L. (1962) *Cider with Rosie.* Harmondsworth: Penguin.

Livesley, W. J. and Bromley, D. B. (1973) *Person Perception in Childhood and Adolescence.* London: Wiley.

Mead, G. H. (1934) *Mind, Self, and Society.* Chicago: University of Chicago Press.

Piaget, J. (1972) Intellectual evolution from adolescence to adulthood. *Human Development* 15: 1–12.

Selman, R. and Byrne, D. (1974) A structural analysis of levels of role-taking in middle childhood. *Child Development* 45: 803–7.

Simmel, G. (1900) *Philosophie des Geldes.* Leipzig: Duncker und Humblot.

Strauss, A. L. (1952) The development and transformation of monetary meanings in the child. *American Sociological Review* 17: 275–84.

Youniss, J. (1975) Another perspective on social cognition. *Minnesota Symposia on Child Development* 9: 173–93.

Name index

Figures in italics refer to bibliographical references

Subject index

adaptive function, 5, 8, 10, 15–24
adolescent rebellion, 23
Adolescents, 234; comprehension of law by, 242; friends among, 154, 159; peer relations among, 145, 147; political awareness of, 242; quarrels among, 223
adrenogenital syndrome, 175–7
age; recognition of, 87–8, 92
aggression; age-mates and, 132, 138; instincts in man, 2; mixed-age groups and, 143; sex difference and, 143
altruism, 19–20, 21, 22; friendship and, 157–8
androgen, 175–7
animal models, 31–2
animals, 37, 41, 83
appearance, 113
Attribution Theory, 107, 113–14
Australopithecus, 8, 9
authority, 219, 220

baby-battering, 16
baby-talk; of adults, 56

Bali, 54
behaviour; modifiability of, 2, 3, 4
behavioural biology, 3–6, 15–17, 24; bias against, 2–3
Behavioural plasticity, 22–3
biopsychology, 3, 4, 41
bisexuality, 175
blind infants, 82
boss and workers; concept of, 238
brainsize, 8–10

care-giving, 12, 75, 91, 92
child-nurses, 132
China; sex-roles in, 192
chromosomes, 172; irregular, 173; Y, 184
class, 158, 239
club membership, 138–9
cognition, 203–25; compared with socialization, 204–7; shift from socialization, 207–10
cognitive development, 28, 205–7, 208–10
cognitive processes, 92–9